SB4 –

20 –

# PORTRAIT
## OF WAR

# PORTRAIT OF WAR

## THE U.S. ARMY'S FIRST COMBAT ARTISTS AND THE DOUGHBOYS' EXPERIENCE IN WWI

### PETER KRASS

BICENTENNIAL

1807

WILEY

2007

BICENTENNIAL

JOHN WILEY & SONS, INC.

This book is printed on acid-free paper. ♾

Copyright © 2007 by Peter Krass. All rights reserved

Published by John Wiley & Sons, Inc., Hoboken, New Jersey
Published simultaneously in Canada

Design and composition by Navta Associates, Inc.

Map credits: All maps are reproduced from *My Experiences in the World War* by John J. Pershing (New York: Frederick A. Stokes Company, 1931), except for "Situation American 2d Division: 6 June 1918 10:00 A.M." (page 94) and "Concentration for St.-Mihiel Operation" (page 198), which are reproduced from *United States Army in the World War 1917–1918*, volumes 4 and 8, respectively (Washington, D.C.: Center of Military History, United States Army, 1988).

Illustration credits: All photos are courtesy of the National Archives and Records Administration, College Park, Maryland, except the following: page 21, from *The American Front* by Ernest Peixotto, C. Scribner's Sons, 1919; page 261, courtesy of the Harding Family; page 248, Imperial War Museum London; pages 31 (bottom), 113, 180, 214, 229, 260, courtesy of the U.S. Army Center of Military History, Fort Lesley J. McNair, D.C.

For general information about our other products and services, please contact our Customer Care Department within the United States at (800) 762-2974, outside the United States at (317) 572-3993 or fax (317) 572-4002.

Wiley also publishes its books in a variety of electronic formats. Some content that appears in print may not be available in electronic books. For more information about Wiley products, visit our web site at www.wiley.com.

*Library of Congress Cataloging-in-Publication Data:*

Krass, Peter.
  Portrait of war : the U.S. Army's first combat artists and the doughboys' experience in
WWI / Peter Krass.
    p. cm.
  ISBN-13: 978-0-471-67023-0 (cloth : alk. paper)
  ISBN-10: 0-471-67023-5 (cloth : alk. paper)
  1. United States. Army. American Expeditionary Forces—Biography. 2. World War, 1914–1918—Europe, Western. 3. World War, 1914–1918—Art and the war. 4. War artists—United States—Biography.   I. Title.
  D570.K73 2007
  940.4'1273—dc22

                                                                                        2006010267

Printed in the United States of America

10  9  8  7  6  5  4  3  2  1

In memory of the men and women who made immeasurable sacrifices during World War I

*For Mom and Dad*

# CONTENTS

# PROLOGUE

ON A STEAMY SUMMER AFTERNOON IN FOUNTAINEBLEAU, France, an American walked resolutely across the main street to the gun shop and bought himself a pistol. While this was a small, simple action, it reflected the dire circumstance in which the European nations found themselves: on the eve of a great war.

That Saturday, August 1, 1914, Ernest Peixotto had left his home in the French village of Samois-sur-Seine for the nearby town of Fountainebleau, to gauge the people's mood and to obtain any updates on the rapidly disintegrating relations between France and Germany. That afternoon, answers to his queries were delivered in a most perfunctory way: "At 4:30 I happened to be in front of the Town Hall when a man came out," Peixotto reflected, "and, without any ceremony, tacked the order for General Mobilization upon the official bulletin board. Its appearance was received with a few cheers and some cries of 'Vive la France' but for the most part in silence."[1] It meant war, a war that would ravage the people's lives, as hundreds of thousands of soldiers were ripped from their families to report for duty. It was effective the very next day—no time to dally—for the kaiser's troops were already marching toward the border.

Across France town drummers paraded through the streets announcing the order, which was greeted by sad, anxious faces. Everyone felt the horror of the summons; there was impending tragedy signaled by the rolling drums, for they knew the war to end all wars had begun. To the general public, it was astounding how quickly tensions between the European nations had escalated: on June 28, Archduke Franz Ferdinand, heir to the Austro-Hungarian throne, was assassinated in Sarajevo. On July 28, an unforgiving Austria declared war on Serbia; in response, Russia immediately mobilized its army to come to Serbia's defense. Consequently, on August 1, Germany declared war on Russia, and, two days later, on France, which forced Britain to join the fray. Such was the way of treaties.

Although a prominent American artist, Peixotto had come to greatly appreciate his life in France and was determined to help protect the republic from any German onslaught, so immediately after the mobilization order was posted, he purchased the pistol. On his return to Samoissur-Seine, he volunteered for the local Communal Guard, the guard's duty to patrol the roads, the fields, and the riverbanks, on the watch for spies, deserters, and malefactors. Concerned only with the present German drive—a lightning attack launched through Luxembourg and Belgium—that would come within twenty-five miles of his home, Peixotto could not imagine that in four years he, too, would be in the trenches—as a captain in the American Expeditionary Force (AEF).

Peixotto would be one of eight U.S. soldiers who witnessed more of the American fighting experience during World War I than any other U.S. participant, military or civilian. Provided special passes by both the French and the American high commands, the AEF's "Eight," as they were called, were permitted to roam through the occupied zones, the battlefields, and the forward trenches. Their mission was a groundbreaking event in the annals of U.S. military history: they were the first artists recruited through official government channels, with the purpose of making a historical record of war.

Certainly, battlefield art itself dates from ancient civilizations, when kings demanded their conquests be glorified. And war has forever inspired magnificent pieces by the world's great artists: Michelangelo, Velázquez, Sargent, and Picasso, among so many others. Also, beginning in the mid-nineteenth century, during the Crimean War in Europe and the American Civil War in particular, dozens of artist-journalists hired by magazines and newspapers took to the battlefield to report events visually. Now, for the first time, the General Staff of the U.S. War Department wanted its own official artists in the heat of the action. Consequently, although they had no military training, these artist-soldiers joined the American Expeditionary Force, commissioned as captains—which was, they joked dryly, their free ticket to the greatest show. The artists entered the war determined to capture "the shock and loss and bitterness and blood of it" and earnestly considered themselves recorders of history. They not only made sketches and paintings but kept diaries, wrote letters, conducted interviews, and penned memoirs—all graphically detailing what they witnessed. Their poignant story is, at the same time, the story of the American soldier's experience in the Great War.

# 1

# The Journey into the Maelstrom

HIS MISSION BORDERED ON THE ABSURD. Yet, it was what he dreamed of doing. It was the most fantastic opportunity, although in pursuing it he would face his own mortality. As a captain in the American Expeditionary Force, Ernest Peixotto would be expected to thrust his way into the front lines. He would be expected to come under fire, but, due to his unique mission, no one expected him to engage the enemy.

Peixotto blinked against the morning's bitter rain, the soft pitter-patter beat drumming against steel and wool, flesh and wood. It was an exceedingly raw Thursday—March 14, 1918—and the temperature would reach only into the lower forties. He blinked with bewilderment against the surreal chaos around him. Looming ominously above were hulking gray ships half hidden in the mist, the massive troop transports that had been luxury ocean liners before the war now moored alongside the Hoboken, New Jersey, piers. On the mud-died water dimpled by raindrops, barges filled with barrack bags and bed rolls were unloaded. High overhead, long-armed cranes hoisted crates of equipment and supplies. Tons upon tons of the varied items would never be used, destined to be warehoused in France and then returned to be warehoused in the United States. This was just one element of war's numbing madness that Peixotto would witness.

Eyes shifting to beyond the piers, Peixotto gazed at the shadowy, jagged Manhattan skyline. While the city had been his home since just after the outbreak of hostilities in 1914, it now seemed so very distant and unreachable through the rain. Just a week ago he had been a mere citizen on that island, just one of many New Yorkers who lined Fifth Avenue—renamed Avenue of the Allies—to cheer the thousands of departing soldiers who marched so confidently. Any man in uniform received a kiss from the young ladies. All along the boulevard flags flew from the windows. And, in restaurants and theaters, bands played the national anthems of the allied countries. It was festive sending boys to war.

Peixotto knew that his wife, Mary, was somewhere in the city, in their East 66th Street apartment, perhaps. They had married in January 1897 and were inseparable. Both were students of art, both were artists, and both shared the same soul. Mary and Ernest had no children; they had only each other. Together they had traveled extensively across the United States and Europe, studied art in Paris, and lived part of every year in Europe since 1899, until the war. Illustrating how difficult the separation would be, before Ernest even boarded his assigned ship, Mary had penned a letter to him, a letter of longing.

Ernest Clifford Peixotto

After her husband left that morning, Mary sat at his desk for an hour, quietly meditating, and then she began to write. While she affirmed what a proud moment it was for her to write to him using his new title of captain in the army, she immediately became reflective: "You have been so splendid all these wonderful years of ours. What radiant and happy years. And you will be more splendid in these years to come." However effusive she was, she still had to convince herself of such a future. "Dear one—

you know all the things I am thinking of—they all are—you—you—you
. . ." Every few days she would write him a letter and—like millions of
other lovers, wives, and mothers—she would not know if those letters
reached him until long afterward.

Her pain was all the more poignant when that Thursday evening a
package arrived from Ernest's mother, who lived in San Francisco; it was
a pair of gray socks knitted by his aunt Georgie. Yes, he was still their little boy. Knowing what Ernest would face and desperate to keep her
faith, Mary prayed for him each morning and evening, and she spoke to
him, spoke to him in her own mind.[1] She also worried about his health,
which had been fragile at times. Peixotto was only five foot five inches
and 130 pounds—with a narrow face, high cheekbones, and piercing
eyes—not exactly the bruising soldier type. At forty-nine he was old for
the soldiering business. But he was not without courage; in fact, he had
applied to join a camouflage unit in the Engineering Corps, only to be
rejected because of his age, which had left him deeply discouraged.[2] He
said good-bye and good luck to younger fellow artists, including Homer
St. Gaudens, whose enlistments were accepted. St. Gaudens would suffer a head wound and another friend, Everett Herter, would be killed. As
for the fortunes of a disenchanted Peixotto, they would soon change for
the better.

You cannot make war without making propaganda. So, on April 14,
1917, a mere eight days after the United States declared war on the
Central Powers, President Woodrow Wilson issued an executive order
that created the Committee on Public Information, to package the war
for the American public's consumption. The word *committee* sounded
democratic, but its purpose was purely autocratic; it was a machine
driven by a man who assumed a great deal of power. Placed in charge of
the committee was the very earnest looking and devoutly patriotic
George Creel, an investigative journalist and the editor of the *Rocky
Mountain News*, who unabashedly declared his desire to create "a pas-
sionate belief in the justice of America's cause that would weld the
American people into one white hot mass instinct with fraternity, devo-
tion, courage and deathless determination."[3]

Subsequently, the committee created the Division of Pictorial Publicity, this subgroup to be in charge of generating posters and other artwork that supported the war effort, supported everything from selling

war bonds to recruiting volunteers. The artists who became involved quickly pointed out that the British and the French armed forces had recruited official artists to work in the war zone right alongside the soldiers, their stirring work used to aid their respective country's war efforts. Shouldn't the American Expeditionary Force do the same? What they failed to note was that the first hundred British artists sent into the combat zone had been forced to take up arms after their army had been routed at Ypres. Many of those artists would be killed, too. Not to be outdone by their European counterparts, the General Staff in Washington agreed that official artists should be appointed. While this appeared to be an enlightened decision, it would soon become apparent that art and war are not compliant companions.

Not until late 1917 did the plan coalesce, when the respected illustrator and painter Charles Dana Gibson, who had been placed in charge of the Division of Pictorial Publicity, was asked to recommend artists. Gibson just happened to be friends with Ernest Peixotto, and thus Peixotto, who had been turned away by the army, found himself one of eight artists recruited to go to France. Peixotto was commissioned as a captain in the Engineer Reserve Corps because its chief, Major General William M. Black, had championed the artists' cause. While his friend Gibson certainly showed him favor, Peixotto was a fine artist, painting landscapes and human-interest scenes that were reproduced in books and popular magazines, as well as being shown in salons and galleries. Also accomplished artists, the other seven made a living as book and magazine illustrators. Their deft skill as illustrators would come into play, as they would have to make quick sketches of their battlefield subjects and move on.

On February 21, 1918, the General Staff issued a press release explaining the selection of the artists who were part of a "plan for making a complete pictorial record of the American Army's participation in the war."[4] At the time that was exactly how the artists understood their mission: to make a "pictorial record of the war" for posterity. In letters the artists received before shipping out, their duty was reiterated: it was to prepare "oil paintings, portraits, sketches, etchings, etc., within the war zone for historical purposes."[5] There was no mention of sensationalism and propaganda. The men in Washington would soon change their purpose, however; the General Staff wanted to use the art to help fulfill Creel's vision of "deathless determination." This latter desire would quickly bring the artists into conflict with Washington.

Once Peixotto received news of his commission and passed his physical exam, events moved quickly: he had just two weeks to put his personal business in order. He arranged for $60 a month to be forwarded to his wife, Mary, beginning in March, the month he would ship out. In case tragedy struck, he prudently took out a $7,500 life insurance policy with the Treasury Department, Bureau of War Risk Insurance, as well as a permanent disability policy that would pay out $43.13 a month.[6] On March 5 he received his military Certificate of Identity, the document stating his age, eye and hair color, height, and weight. It also included his photo, a fingerprint of his right-hand index finger, and his signature. He then had to be vaccinated for typhoid and paratyphoid. The entire process was too efficient; it was like being pushed through a Ford assembly line at double-time.

Peixotto was ordered to report for duty on March 12 in Hoboken, at which time he was ordered to report to the officers' gangway, vessel number 33, pier 1, at 10 A.M. on March 14, at which time he would receive further orders. Yes, he had entered the bureaucratic maze of the American Expeditionary Force. And now here he stood, gazing across the pier jammed with supplies, stevedores, and soldiers. At the moment there were some fifteen thousand khaki-clad soldiers—a modest town's worth of human beings—lining the Hoboken piers, having been funneled from across the country to this port of embarkation. How many of these men would he see in the war zone? How many would come home in one piece? How many would not? Peixotto would lose good friends, both American and French, and it was this loss of a friend or a loved one that truly defined war's consequences.

Organized in tight columns, the troops were checked by their officers and then dispatched to the gangplanks extending from the dangerously seductive ships. More than 2 million American soldiers would eventually find themselves in France, so many of them young men who'd never left the state they were born in. Regardless of their varied backgrounds and past experiences—farmers, factory workers, fishermen, office clerks, college boys, from the Louisiana Bayou to the mountains of Montana, from the depths of Nevada's silver mines to the New York City skyscrapers—Peixotto was certain they were all about to embark on their greatest of adventures. He felt intense excitement, trepidation, and a sense of camaraderie among these strangers.

Any trepidation was certainly justified. For anyone with time to peruse the *New York Times* that morning, the front-page headlines blared: "Zeppelins Again Make an Attack on English Coast" and "German Troops Now Occupy Odessa." The British and French mood was particularly gloomy this spring because their Russian allies had capitulated to the Germans, signing a peace treaty on March 3, which meant that German divisions once occupied on the eastern front were free to strengthen their western front. Behind the capitulation was the Bolshevik Party, which had seized power in November 1917, and in July 1918 would execute the Russian royal family. In the face of this troubling development, the United States's attitude—either cocksure or foolish— was "So what? We're going to get enough men there to win." The Allies would win, of course, but not before total battle deaths surpassed 7 million.[7]

After hours of waiting, Peixotto climbed the officers' gangway to the *Pocahontas*, formerly the *Princess Irene* of the North German Lloyd fleet. The ship had been launched in June 1900, then seized by the United States once it entered the war, refitted as a transport, and assigned to the Cruiser Transport Force of the Atlantic fleet. Capable of holding three thousand men, the ship would complete eighteen round-trips to Europe by 1919.[8]

As an officer, Peixotto found himself assigned to a relatively spacious stateroom. After settling in, he met up with an acquaintance, Wallace Morgan, the one other artist assigned to the *Pocahontas*. Morgan was a New Yorker through and through; he had been born in the city and returned there to study at the National Academy of Design. At the turn of the century, Morgan quickly settled into the Bohemian scene of Greenwich Village and cavorted with friends at a small studio on West 23rd Street. They shared the studio with an eight-foot king snake, a bathtub full of eels, and more cats than could be counted. Young and prone to whims, Morgan and friends on occasion enjoyed a rousing visit to a local beer garden followed by skinny-dipping, which tended to outrage the neighbors.[9] Now, more than twenty years into his career, at age forty-five and with thick round glasses, Morgan was a man who had cultivated superior tastes and only drank Scotch. Like Peixotto, he was the antithesis of a lean doughboy thrilled to kill the kaiser. In spite of the dangers, these two artists would enjoy each other's company and travel many of the battlefields together, both sketching and watching out for each other while under fire.

The day wore on—the grayness and the rain were relentless—and not until late afternoon were the hawsers cast off and did the transport ship, which was easy prey for Germany's submarines, swing into the current of the North River, into the wind and the misty mournful air. As evening commuters on ferries cheered the convoy, Peixotto and Morgan watched the majestic Manhattan skyline, with its cozy steam-heated buildings, slide slowly past. It was all very supernatural to Peixotto. "It was cold and dark when we reached the outer bay," he wrote, "but I could feel other boats about us though they showed no lights. There were strange flashes every little while wigwagging and blinking like huge owl's eyes, while along the horizon, mysterious flares appeared from time to time, and beams from searchlights lit great circles on the low-lying clouds."[10] Everyone was tense, for there had been rumors of German submarines entering New York's harbor and rumors of a steel net sealing off the Narrows. Yet, safely they passed by the Statue of Liberty, through the Narrows, and into the wide-open Atlantic Ocean.

When Peixotto and Morgan went to the officers' mess for dinner that night, they discovered that among the two hundred officers aboard ship they were two of only five captains and there was only one officer who outranked them, a major who was in command. The two artists would quickly learn what it entailed to outrank almost three thousand young men. That first night Morgan was "dead tired and turned in with the chickens" at seven o'clock, as he explained in a letter home. However, at nine-thirty, the adjutant's orderly wakened him with an order that at seven forty-five the next morning he was to report as officer of the day. Yes, in the military's great wisdom, the inevitable had happened: on the first full disorienting day at sea, Wallace Morgan was to be OD.

Certain there had to be some mistake, Morgan dressed and, still half asleep, asked the commanding officer for an explanation. He received one all right: the ship was short of officers and both Morgan and Peixotto were expected to help out. Before dismissing Morgan, the CO

Wallace Morgan

kindly explained the job: for twenty-four hours his responsibilities would include posting forty sentries, ensuring that the few prisoners they had were under guard, and enforcing a myriad of regulations. It didn't matter that Morgan's only military training was this brief discussion. Not only did these artist-soldiers have no sense of military protocol, but their profession, by nature, was in direct conflict with military thinking: as artists they were accustomed to individual expression. A master of pen and brush, Morgan had had his own studio for almost ten years, his work in demand from the top magazines like *Collier's*, and he didn't see himself answering very well to salutes and commands. Regardless, as Peixotto wryly observed, "the very lives of all those on board" depended on the proper enforcement of regulations. They were "in the Army now" which meant obeying orders.[11]

Reveille was at 4:30 A.M.—an ungodly hour for Peixotto and Morgan—but at least they awoke to clear skies. After breakfast, Peixotto climbed to the promenade deck, which was reserved for the officers, and gazed in wonder at their convoy, which was accompanied by a big navy cruiser, the ships cutting through the endless ranks of waves. Two transports were camouflaged in the "dazzle system," painted in colored stripes to maximize light refraction and to blend in with the diamond sparkle of the ocean. Below Peixotto, gun crews were already at work, some polishing their six-inch guns while others practiced loading their shells. And the main deck was crowded with regulars, for the moment excited to be on the water, soon to be bored by the monotony of this endless desert of water.

Meanwhile, Morgan, along with two officers of the guard, went about his duty as OD. It included inspecting the posted sentries, this task alone made interesting as he negotiated the dark holds and the heaving decks, as the wind was blowing hard and the heavy seas were rolling the ship. While Morgan had always enjoyed the water and had his sea legs, the soldiers were clearly suffering. "Many of the men had never seen the ocean before," Morgan wrote to his sister Bess, "and were as much frightened as sick." It was an exceptionally long day, punctuated at midnight by a sentry from Virginia who started shouting for help, his shouts heard over the waves crashing like brass cymbals and flaring snare drums across the deck. Morgan came running, thinking the frightened man was deathly sick, only to discover that the poor boy thought the ship was about to sink—he was posted in a very exposed position where the water was breaking over the deck. After reassuring him all was well, Morgan left. Not long after, the Virginian again shouted for help. This time Morgan found him "shaking all over nearly out of his mind with fear." The fighting hadn't even started yet.[12]

Whatever humor Peixotto found in Morgan drawing OD on day one was extinguished on day two when Peixotto assumed the duty. And what special skills did he bring to the job? Well, when evaluating the artist prior to his commission, Major General Black, chief of engineers, had noted, "25 years professional work for leading magazines and books as well as current exhibitions of paintings." And at least he had "good appearance and address," according to Black.[13] At 8:15 A.M., Peixotto oversaw the mounting of the guard—135 men—to be relieved every two hours. Most of the guards' responsibilities were mundane: keeping soldiers off the railings and the passageways clear, not allowing tobacco use in the holds, and preventing anyone from meddling with the life belts. Two of the more important tasks were keeping the garbage chutes and the latrines clean. And then there was the top priority: the vigil search for enemy submarines.

At 10 A.M., Peixotto accompanied the CO, the ship's doctor, the chief police officer, and an officer of the guard for a complete inspection of the ship. Their final destination of the inspection was the holds aft—the bowels—where the "colored troops" were quartered, or rather stowed. These soldiers hoped for glory like any freedom-loving white soldier; however, with the regular army wholly segregated and bigoted, they would be given the most unpopular jobs in France. Helping to set the divisive tone, racial jokes were commonplace in the military's *Stars and Stripes* newspaper, which was simply giving its readers what they wanted. Many blacks would become marginalized members of the Service of Supply (SOS), which supported the combat divisions by handling mail and freight, shipping ammunition and rubber boots, building railroads, and raising encampments. Or worse, they would be assigned to the Quartermaster Corps Graves Registration Service, destined to gather the dead, organize the corpses, swing them into coffins, and bury them.[14]

There were two black combat divisions, the 92nd and 93rd, both of which would manage to spill blood with proficiency equal to that of their white counterparts.

As Peixotto later inspected some forty sentry posts, he kept an eye out for drinking and gambling, popular means of distraction during wartime. At night he made three more rounds into the poorly ventilated soldiers' quarters, which reeked of sour-smelling vomit. It was an eerie, foreshadowing experience: "Forward, in the fo'castle, I found the crew sleeping in hammocks suspended from the deck above, rolled like cocoons in their blankets. In the holds the soldiers' bunks, in double tiers, were placed as close together as possible, leaving just space enough between for a man to pass. From them, as I passed in the darkness, an arm, a leg, a foot, or a hand would protrude, inert, and in them I caught glimpses, in the ghostly blue light, of pale faces turned up, with eyes closed in a death-like sleep."[15] Their bunks were as snug as coffins—just another aspect of less-than-ideal living conditions.

Back on the deck, as the rain fell in torrents, Peixotto could barely distinguish the silhouettes of the submarine watches, who were tense and alert. Beyond them, the ocean water rolled in great billows. The high sea continued to take its toll on the boys, whose stomachs convulsed in protest. Peixotto listened to the sympathetic sailors who said in jest, "Don't worry; you won't be sick coming back; you'll be in a wooden kimono."[16] It was grim, morbid comfort. Their sense of security was hardly reinforced when not long into the journey, everyone was ordered to put on his life belt and to keep it on for the remainder of the trip. Through it all Peixotto played the part of soldier as best he could. "I admit the dismay I felt—an artist suddenly turned soldier," he wrote, "in a uniform scarcely three weeks old—at being thus suddenly thrown into a position of such responsibility, giving and carrying out orders, trying to conceal my real feelings, 'throwing out my chest' as I was advised to do, and striving to 'look the part' to the grizzled old sergeants."[17] Yes, that was his soldier training, "throw out the chest."

Peixotto and Morgan were not the only artists who would fumble through officer of the day duties. In a following convoy, George Harding was on the SS *Philadelphia*—a passenger liner with twin smokestacks built in 1899—part of a seven-ship convoy led by the cruiser *Montana*, which, on April 16, departed out of Hoboken.[18] A handsome man with a chiseled chin, the thirty-five-year-old Harding was ideally suited for the job of artist-soldier; he was filled with the adventurer's spirit: a half dozen years earlier he had made a two-year journey around the world that took him to Egypt, Arabia, India, Australia, China, and numerous exotic locales in between. He traveled by steamer, sailboat, stagecoach, and camel. Before that he had lived for a time in a lighthouse in Cape Race, Newfoundland. The lighthouse had suited him: as his fellow artists would discover, he was a loner who kept his thoughts to himself. Prior to his recruitment, Harding had been teaching art at the University of Pennsylvania, and his wife, Anita Cotheal Nisbett, and he, having recently purchased a house in Wynnewood, Pennsylvania, were eager to start a family. Yet, despite having settled down, he couldn't resist this escapade and would take great risks to capture the war as it was fought in the trenches, in the countryside, and in the towns.

Harding shared a stateroom with a Major Allen, who gave him all of five minutes of advice before the artist went on duty as OD their second day at sea, the artist jotting down his responsibilities on three-by-five-inch sheets of notepaper, which would become his war diary. Two hours into his stint as OD—at 4 P.M.—the sky was black, the rain was pelting down, and towering swells were tossing the ship. His face coated with sea salt, Harding had difficulty finding the covered hatches to get below for inspections, but with wry humor he wrote in his diary, "On first inspection I see more bare feet in rows of bunks in ten minutes than a chiropodist sees in a lifetime. My sergeant says to me: 'I don't mind the smell of the other fellow—its when I stink myself it gets me.' Had first gas training overseeing cleaning out of clogged toilets in stern of ship. The pitching finally clears them—into the ship." It was also disconcerting to Harding to discover that some of the guards were recent immigrants who spoke no English and many were illiterate. Completely overwhelmed, Harding suffered through his entire watch without a decent meal.[19]

George Matthews Harding

Aboard ship, dinner was served at five, and then afterward the officers would sit in a dark saloon listening to the Victrola—rousing tunes by Henry Burr, the Peerless Quartet, Shannon Four, and the Columbia Quartet: "We're All Going Calling on the Kaiser"; "I'll Come Back to You When It's All Over"; and "Over Yonder." Even during such relaxation there was tension. Absolute darkness was essential—all flashlights were to have been given to the adjutant—and there was no smoking on deck. There was only a faint glow from the portholes and the men's wristwatches and a few blue lightbulbs near the floor in the corridors. To further protect convoys from snooping German U-boats, nothing could be a thrown overboard—not a scrap of paper, not a cigarette butt—nothing the subs could use to track the transports. When it came to subs, the *Philadel-phia's* chief engineer, who, Harding noted, was just twenty-three years old with two young children at home, had already come under attack once.[20] As he did with the chief engineer, Harding made it a habit to jot down names of those who made an impression on him, their age, whether they had children, these observations making the war very personal for him. Another character he made note of aboard ship was a Captain Carter, who confided in the artist that he was engaged to be married, but he had just written to his fiancée to tell her "she is free."[21] The implication was all too clear: he didn't expect to return.

The fear of submarines came to the fore during the daily abandon-ship drills. These drills—summoned by the bugle—further exposed the artists as somewhat inept officers in charge of soldiers who had suffered boot camp. At his assigned lifeboat, Morgan found himself commanding sixteen regulars and four lieutenants, which boded well—surely the trained officers would know the order of action. As it turned out, all four lieutenants were doctors and as clueless as he. Over at collapsible boat number 13, Peixotto was relieved to find he had a regular army officer with him—a lieutenant—but then to his dismay he discovered the officer was an ornithologist—more fit for matters of the air than of the sea. To his further dismay, he realized that of the fifteen men under them, most were raw-boned soldiers from the Kentucky mountains who'd never seen the ocean. With their transport heaving in the seas, their lifeboat swung out over the water, then back, out and back like a carnival ride. Each time it smacked the ship's side, the men scrambled to grab the boat, missed, and tumbled into piles of legs and arms. This fine slapstick was far from amusing at the time.

When the *Pocahontas* entered the danger zone—off Ireland's coast—there was much talk of subs in subdued tones, and everyone jumped each time the ship rolled or a door slammed. It was easy to justify any paranoia. Just over a month ago—on February 5, 1918—a U-boat had torpedoed and sunk the transport ship *Tuscania*. It was hit while the men were at supper; of the some 2,500 men on board, 182 perished. And since October 1917, the enemy had torpedoed 2 U.S. destroyers with 65 killed, and 2 converted yachts, often used by the navy as decoys or transport ships, with 24 killed. In this same time frame, 14 other naval ships and 28 merchant ships had been sunk or damaged from a variety of causes: collision, fire, mines, or their seams simply splitting open, resulting in over 500 deaths.[22] Against this foreboding backdrop, Morgan felt moved to write his sister Bess, who doted on him, who organized his bohemian lifestyle, and who protected his interests.

Morgan wanted to tie up some loose ends, to put his personal matters in order for his own peace of mind, in case the worst should happen. Even his tailor's bill nagged at Morgan, who instructed his sister to pay it off over time. Most important, he wanted her to review the life insurance policy he'd taken out with Aetna. If Bess thought the premium was too much, she was to just drop it; after all, he also had a $10,000 government policy for her benefit. To alleviate any concerns on her part, he concluded his letter with: "I'm in tip top condition. Don't worry about me I'll take care."[23]

At the time her husband, Ernest, was entering the danger zone, Mary Peixotto sat under a tree in Central Park, dutifully writing to him. She updated him on her activities, which included war relief work and a trip to the theater to see *A Pair of Petticoats*. In a letter two days later—March 22—she expressed a strong desire to also come to France, to return to the home they still owned in Samois-sur-Seine and to work in the hospital there. This would put her in harm's way, too, but it didn't matter to Mary. She desperately wanted to be closer to her husband; she worried about him and warned him to take care of himself: "Don't over tax dear one. You know the emotion alone to be on French soil again is very great. And all of your nerves are ready to be played upon as are the strings of Casaderus and violi d'amour." To further comfort herself, she had begun to read the psalms of David at night before bed, from her husband's French-language copy of the Old Testament. And she continued to talk to Ernest, too: "The nights are wonderful—and we have the moon . . . I speak always into the night to you."[24]

Little did she know that a romantic moon was absolutely anathema to Peixotto and his shipmates. A moonlit night was "an excellent night for Fritz"—a good night for getting "a tin fish in you"—for U-boats could easily spot the transport's silver silhouette while the U-boats stayed hidden among the diamond shapes shimmering on the water's surface. On day nine at sea, Peixotto and Morgan's convoy was met by a dozen destroyers that were to escort them into port. The coloring of these warships caught Peixotto's eye; they were "brilliantly camouflaged like wasps, queerly striped with black and white, with spots between of yellow, gray-blue, and water-green"—the softened tone of Monet's paintings. "Like wasps too they darted about us," he wrote, "zigzagging across our bows, dropping astern, watchful, then, with a burst of speed, forging up ahead again."[25] Because the probability of an attack was high, that night no one was allowed to sleep in the lower holds; soldiers slept on decks, wrapped in blankets against the bitter headwind. It was a beautiful moonlit night.

Destroyers also met George Harding's convoy on day nine, five of the naval vessels converging on them from different directions. Everyone broke out in grins, assuming they had made it safely. "An hour later," Harding noted in his diary, "we pass half dozen bodies in life preservers and an upset life boat."[26] Why hadn't they climbed back into the lifeboat? Why hadn't they saved themselves? No doubt the moment they capsized in the high seas, the struggle to survive commenced. But the shock of the icy water triggered involuntary gasping and a sure swallowing of water that added to the panic—any man's blood pressure and heart rate would then skyrocket. With the frigid March water sucking the heat from their bodies, their core body temperature immediately began to drop and soon their ability to think clearly was impaired. After being in the water for a half hour, some of the men died—within a couple of hours they were all dead, victims of hypothermia. Harding wondered what catastrophe had caused them to take to the lifeboat in the first place.

A U-boat! Later that afternoon, lookouts on Harding's transport spotted one. "Sirens—gun fire—depth bombs on port side; eight were dropped by destroyers. The pile of water boils up like a full rigged ship under full sail," he wrote in his diary, and then added sarcastically, "The enlisted man who reported sick this morning was the first to reach deck after the alarm." The men were on edge, the tension palpable. Gun crews zeroed in on a whale, two black ducks, and even a floating box.[27] Not long after and without further incident, on April 26, they reached their destination: Liverpool, England, a port city on the island's west coast.

There Harding was outfitted with a handsome trench coat, a Sam Browne belt, rubber boots, and a sleeping bag—now he was feeling like a soldier. Then it was to Southampton, through beautiful countryside, with Harding taking note of the fields filled with dandelions and daisies and the hedgerows of hawthorn. The last leg of his journey to France took him across the channel. Aboard his transport were a number of Australians who had fought at Gallipoli, a failed attempt to open a passageway to the Black Sea. They kindly informed him that of the twenty-two thousand men in their 1st Division, only seven thousand remained. Nevertheless, with anticipation growing, in his diary Harding jotted, "A free ticket to the greatest fight in the world."[28]

On their final night, a moonlit night, Peixotto's convoy, which bypassed England, made a mad dash for the port of Saint-Nazaire, France, on the south coast of Brittany. As day broke over them, they passed by the rocky cliffs of Belle-Île-en-Mer, where the renowned stage actress Sarah Bernhardt kept a summerhouse. While one destroyer piloted the convoy up the channel to the port, an aeroplane appeared overhead to watch for submarines. Eager to go ashore, Peixotto searched the countryside with his binoculars and studied the houses with blue-slate roofs standing among the evergreens. From one house a girl waving a bright American flag came running across the lawn toward a white gate at water's edge.

Even though American soldiers had been arriving for months, the people of Saint-Nazaire, including the many streetwalkers, had not tired of greeting them. Peixotto took in the scene as an artist would, noting the subtle details and the emotions: "At one side of the lock a crowd of ragged urchins scrambled for the coppers that the soldiers threw them. At the other side a dense crowd stood silent, watching our packed decks. Women and children predominated, many of them in deep mourning." Standing out among the people: a French captain holding his daughter tenderly and a naval officer standing alongside his tired-looking wife on

*A Transport with Troops* by Dunn. A troop transport ship coming through the lock at Saint-Nazaire, the port city completely Americanized.

a balcony. There was little French atmosphere, however, as this port had been transformed into an Americanized city.[29]

It was six in the evening before the ship was tied to the dock, which meant one more long night aboard. At seven o'clock the next morning the troops marched down the gangplanks, their heavy heels drumming hollow against the wood, and formed up on the dock. By eight o'clock they had disappeared. The soldiers had marched away quietly, not know-ing to where they marched. Peixotto and Morgan—left to their own means until their orders arrived—strolled along the docks, through the weak, thin light of March. The huge mass of the vessels so impressed them that they took time to make drawings, the lines and geometry sketched with a heavy hand to capture the weight of the ships. They also rendered the rows of steel cranes, like great oak trees lining a boulevard, unloading American war material. There were the German prisoners put to work straining under the watchful eyes of bored guards, and the "Negroes" from "way down South" hefting equipment. And there were

*Ships Unloading American War Material* by Peixotto. While trapped in Saint-Nazaire, Peixotto captured the controlled chaos of unloading war material.

*Flirey* by Peixotto. Eager to push to the front, Peixotto would soon discover a different and destructive kind of chaos that left him unsettled, as was the case in the once picturesque village of Flirey.

the shrill whistles of trains, the rumble of trucks, and the spluttering of motorcycles as troops, weapons, and supplies were rushed to the front. As a contrast to this scenery, Peixotto studied the trees that were just beginning to bud; the daisies, tulips, and primroses blooming bright colors; the birds nesting and the cats prowling along the piers. And April, that cruelest month, was rapidly approaching.

The war remained distant for Peixotto, not yet real. For the British soldiers positioned in northwest France, however, the war couldn't have been more immediate. After the collapse of Russia, the German general Erich Ludendorff had determined, "Our general situation requires that we should strike at the earliest moment . . . before the Americans can throw strong forces into the scale. We must beat the British."[30] If the Brits could be rolled into the sea, the Germans could then turn on the French with their full fury. On March 21, the Germans opened their spring offensive along a fifty-mile front against the British Fifth Army and quickly penetrated almost forty miles in some sections. Ludendorff's plan appeared to be working brilliantly: over the next six weeks the British would suffer 280,000 casualties.[31] To stave off a complete collapse, units of the AEF would be ordered into the battle posthaste.

Certainly Peixotto and his fellow artists would not lack subject material upon their arrival at the front. They would witness all major American combat. They would witness man's inhumanity to man, which prompted Wallace Morgan to determine, "We have the duty of showing up fraud and pomposity and to get across human frailty."[32] In war there was plenty of fraud, pomposity, and frailty, as well as heroics. Using their heightened powers of observation, the artists would indeed not only record but also expose history as it unfolded. It was a historic time on many levels: it was the first world war; there were new weapons and tactics; and it was the first time the U.S. armed forces had ever deployed official artists. While they were pioneers, they were expendable like all soldiers, and, as educated men, they fully comprehended that odds were one or more of them would not return home. There were simply too many hazards in a war zone—particularly for men who wore soldier uniforms but were not soldiers.

# 2

# INTO THE
# TRENCHES

WITH THE GERMANS BATTERING THE BRITISH in northwest France and driving deep wedges into the Allied lines, Peixotto and Morgan were more eager than ever to travel into the forward zones occupied by U.S. troops; they were anxious to orient themselves before the doughboys engaged the enemy. However, it was two long days of meandering through Saint-Nazaire before they were finally ordered to Engineer Headquarters at Angers, in the heart of the Loire Valley, where they would encounter further delays, much to their displeasure.

As Peixotto walked across the courtyard between the AEF's barracks in Angers on a dull, gray day, he watched the soldiers drilling on a gas attack. Behaving very businesslike, groups of soldiers pretended to be waves of gas by running across the open space, while other groups worked frantically to put on their gas masks before being reached. The training was intense, condensed into three days, because one slipup, such as removing your mask for a bite of food, could result in death. It all would have been quite humorous—watching grown men flapping their arms as they ran around—except that gas warfare was deadly serious.

Poison gas had been introduced by the Germans in April 1915, during the Second Battle of Ypres. At first, the ignorant French defenders thought the strange yellow-green cloud was to mask an infantry attack, so they held the line. Then came "a pungent, nauseating smell that tickled the throat" and stung the eyes. Within seconds of inhaling what was chlorine gas, soldiers began choking and their respiratory systems were destroyed. As Harding later noted on visiting a field hospital, it was "awful to hear men drowning in their own blood." While there was no longer the element of surprise, the use of chlorine, phosgene, and mustard gas increased through 1918. Gas killed almost a hundred thousand human beings. Gas inflicted more than a million total casualties.[1] To be sure, Peixotto and his fellow artists would not venture into the trenches without a gas mask.

Leaving the bleak barracks, Peixotto explored the remains of Angers's feudal castle, where he encountered an older man and his daughter—refugees from the latest German onslaught. In spite of the hardships, the old man took a humorous outlook. "I thought it was time to take my daughter away," he explained to Peixotto, who spoke French fluently. "Whenever she heard an alert, she would go to her mirror to arrange her hair instead of descending to the cellar where she belonged." Glancing at her, Peixotto couldn't help but notice her "saucy eyes and uptilted nose," which lent a certain credence to the old man's story.[2]

There was no time to digest the glorious sights in the Loire Valley; on March 29, Peixotto and Morgan were ordered to proceed immediately to General Headquarters (GHQ) at Tours, not far to the east and still on the Loire River, yet another frustrating delay. The first train available was that night; however, the roads and trains were congested beyond hope with refugees as Parisians flocked southward to Touraine to escape the Germans' air raids and long-range guns. Just six days earlier, the Germans had unleashed their Paris Gun, also called Big Bertha. From seventy-five miles away—on the slopes of Mont de Joie in the German-held sector closest to Paris—the Germans were lobbing artillery shells into the heart of Paris. Peixotto spoke to several refugees who didn't care where they bedded down; they were simply relieved to have escaped the danger zone.[3]

When Peixotto and Morgan finally arrived at GHQ at Tours, they discovered it was for the Service of Supply and that their orders should have directed them to GHQ at Chaumont, located east southeast of Paris. Indeed, they were in the army now, controlled chaos at its best. They boarded another train, a night train, which pulled into Chaumont on April 1, April Fool's Day. It was also Easter Sunday. Built on a plateau, Chaumont was a gray old town, but its architecture was dignified, the houses sporting high-pitched, blue-slate roofs. The morning streets were filled with churchgoers returning home, most of them women in black, returning to empty houses. The AEF's headquarters was housed in a set of plain buildings, with whitewashed walls and red-tiled floors, the rooms starkly furnished. What stood out were the great maps carefully pasted together that covered the walls; they illustrated where the lines were drawn, where the trenches were dug, and where the men had died—and would die.[4]

Peixotto climbed a flight of stairs to find the office to which he was to report and was walking down a hallway "when, as I passed a door like all the others, my heart jumped as I read, printed upon it in black on a plain square of white paper: GENERAL PERSHING."[5] Clearly, Peixotto held General John J. "Black Jack" Pershing in high esteem compared to the bureaucracy beneath the general, which continued to confound the artists. Indeed, on reporting at GHQ, both Peixotto and Morgan were flabbergasted to learn that even though they were captains in the Engineer Reserve Corps, they were to report to the Press and Censorship Division—G.2.D.—of the Intelligence Branch. In addition, they were to submit their artwork to the Signal Corps—broadly charged with communications—which would then forward it to the General Staff in Washington, which would soon make its own demands on the artists. The artists were, Peixotto concluded, strange birds to classify. This awkward status was disconcerting because at times they would find themselves operating in a vacuum, their work hindered.

Soon after their arrival in Chaumont, Peixotto and Morgan met fellow artist J. André Smith, who had preceded them by almost two weeks. (The others, including George Harding, would arrive over the next month.) Smith had a hawkish face with hair combed straight back and a twinkle to his eye, and he was always quick with a sarcastic comment or wisecrack. He had been born in Hong Kong, where his father was a ship's captain. When the boy was just seven, his father died, prompting the family to move to Hamburg, Germany, and then, three years later, to Boston. Smith received a degree in architecture from Cornell but far preferred painting and etching. In 1911, he elected to pursue the artist's life. He modeled his work after Goya—allowing his mind to run wild with expression—and before long connoisseurs were buying his etchings for their private collections.

J. André Smith

When the United States joined the war, Smith, at age thirty-seven, volunteered. While attending officer training, he injured his leg on barbed wire; the wound never properly healed and eventually the leg was amputated. Despite the injury, he was commissioned a first lieutenant in the Engineer Reserve Corps and assigned to a camouflage unit, only to be selected as an official artist. As the sole artist with military training, he was appointed senior officer for the group, which would prove to be more of a punishment than a reward as he attended to the various bureaucratic headaches.

When Smith arrived in Chaumont in mid-March, there were no instructions or orders awaiting him; in fact, at that point, no one knew how or where to assign the artists or what orders to give them. Smith took it upon himself to write a letter to Major Kendall Banning—chief of the Pictorial Section, Historical Branch, General Staff, in Washington—outlining what he thought the nature of their work should be. It included creating a "distinct pictorial record of the war," as well as what was necessary in terms of supplies and studio space.[6] As a result, the artists were assigned to G.2.D. and placed under the care of Lieutenant Colonel Walter C. Sweeney. One of the first tasks Sweeney gave Morgan, Peixotto, and Smith was to find a suitable home base with studio space. After evaluating Paris and several other towns, they settled on Neufchâteau, situated about 186 miles east of Paris and an hour's ride north of Chaumont—that much closer to the front. At that time, Neufchâteau was the headquarters for the AEF's 1st Army Corps and would be for the Press and Censorship Division, under whose purview the artists now fell. They would not report there until the third week of April.

In the meantime, Sweeney had Morgan, Peixotto, and Smith submit a report that depicted optimal working conditions for them as artists. At the top of the list was the desire to be permitted as much freedom of movement as possible; after all, they were there to record the American experience, and that would require extensive travel. Sweeney granted the request. However, it didn't take a genius to know they wouldn't simply be allowed to wander the countryside without some kind of pass, so Peixotto, who had already learned to question the military's intelligence, met with Sweeney to find out if they would need an official document giving them the authority to travel and to make sketches. Sweeney replied that their captain's bars were sufficient. Not exactly reassured, Peixotto left the meeting with a plan:

> I was not quite convinced, however, so I went forth to make a sketch in Chaumont. I chose the house on the Main street in which General Pershing was living, and established myself in a point of vantage in a baker's shop across the street. I was making good progress with my sketch when a big Lieutenant of Marines with "M.P." on his arm, opened the door, saluted, and said "Captain, have you orders permitting you to sketch?" I admitted I had not. "I'm sorry" he said "but I must place you under arrest," and conducted me to the office of the Post Commandant who was luckily out. (I learned that one of the Lieutenant's men had spotted me but was afraid to tackle me himself.) Our own office was across the courtyard so my "Loot" took me over there and as we entered the Colonel looked up and said "How are you?" "I'm in trouble," said I. Then the Colonel saw the M.P., sized up the situation, and said to him "That's all right, I will vouch for this officer." And so it was agreed we would need written orders of some kind and these were given us.

GHQ provided the artists ID papers and passes in both English and French that would allow them to move freely throughout the occupied zone, which they proceeded to do. As Peixotto reflected, "We were privileged to see all the major combats of the American forces and our experiences became intensely vivid."[7] While it was still months before

*Neufchâteau* by Smith. The artists would eventually be billeted in Neufchâteau, which was conveniently located between the front and GHQ in Chaumont.

the AEF's first major engagement, Peixotto would soon get a flavor of the battlefield.

The General Staff in Washington wanted war drawings immediately— for their propaganda machine—so Sweeney ordered the three artists into the field and provided them with a motor car and driver. This order came before Morgan, Peixotto, and Smith had set up any kind of studio in Neufchâteau or procured any supplies beyond pencils, charcoal, crayons, and sketch pads, but the artists were game. On April 20, they departed for the Baccarat Sector, a region to the east not far from where the German, Swiss, and French borders intersect. There they would spend five days sketching and drawing elements of the 42nd Division, which had arrived in France in late 1917.[8] Currently, the doughboys held sectors along the eastern section of the western front that were relatively quiet areas, and had been for years; good places for green soldiers to become accustomed to trench life—until the day the artists departed for Baccarat.

154038

*A Field Encampment* by Smith. A typical encampment crowded with tents and soldiers provided plenty of opportunity for the spread of disease and lice.

On their drive, Peixotto, Morgan, and Smith passed through Nancy, just south of a little town called Seicheprey, situated on the southern flank of the German-held Saint-Mihiel salient. Here the 26th Division—the New Englanders—had just replaced the 1st Division—the Big Red—in a maneuver rife with so much confusion that it would require investigation. Observing the changeover, the Germans, whose wily spies would go so far as to learn the names of company cooks, were intent on testing the mettle of their new adversary. On the night of April 20—a perfect night for a full-scale raid as a dense fog blanketed the countryside—the Germans would unleash a vicious barrage on the Americans positioned in and around Seicheprey and then deploy squads of storm troopers. At 5 A.M. the next morning, a German raiding party of between 1,000 and 3,000 troopers would plunge into the town and make quick work of the Yankees, trapping 470 Connecticut boys whose escape routes were cut off. The enemy would take 136 prisoners and kill 80. Total casualties for the 26th would amount to over 600.[9] It would not be a pleasant baptism, even though the Germans would

*Our Cavalry* by Townsend. The cavalry juxtaposed with modern weapons provided an intriguing contrast.

subsequently retreat and the Americans would retake the town. While Peixotto would not witness the German attack against Seicheprey that night, before returning from this little jaunt he would find himself in German artillery sights.

Just hours before the Germans' artillery barrage opened on Seicheprey, Peixotto stood on a hill to the south overlooking Nancy and the villages beyond. From a distance, it was a beautiful scene; he described Nancy as "lying spread out beneath us, with its crowded red roofs, its towers, spires, and high church gables in the centre and, radiating from them, long streets, bordered with houses, reaching out like tentacles to vassal villages that lay about it."[10] From the hilltop the city looked intact, but upon closer inspection damage was evident. That's how war was: the farther away, the more inconsequential it appeared.

Now motoring down a road that ran parallel to the front, Peixotto and the others passed through small villages with snaking streets and alleyways bordered by workingmen's modest houses, the streets initially filled

*Camouflaging Light Tank Under Observation* by Townsend.

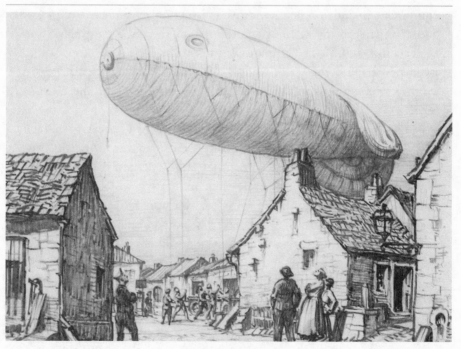

*An Observation Balloon* by Smith. The seemingly omniscient observation balloons were disconcerting.

with French soldiers in horizon-blue uniforms, but then with American khaki as the artists pushed eastward. Looking at the beauty of the surrounding wooded Vosges mountains, Peixotto understood why the Baccarat Sector was relatively quiet: it was on high ground, so any offensive by either side would be severely impeded by the terrain and result in high casualties. Here they encountered doughboys from the Rainbow Division—the 42nd—so nicknamed because it was comprised of National Guard units from twenty-six states and the District of Columbia, reportedly prompting Colonel Douglas MacArthur, who was instrumental in its formation, to say, "The Forty-second Division stretches like a rainbow from one end of America to the other."[11]

Contrary to the dramatic action the General Staff in Washington imagined, Peixotto, Morgan, and Smith discovered that for those doughboys along these quiet trenches, the days were mundane and regimented. Smith was so struck by the businesslike atmosphere, he would focus on incorporating the methodical nature of war into his pieces. At the makeshift bases, first call was at 5:30 A.M. and reveille ten minutes later; assembly at 5:45; mess at 6:00; first call for drill at 6:30; and assembly at 6:45. Drilling would continue throughout the day. Basic equipment included a helmet, arms as issued, a haversack, a mess kit, and a French gas mask.[12] For entertainment, there was card playing in the evening, and, if the Germans sent over a balloon with propaganda-laced newspapers, there was reading. And so the days passed slowly—drilling, guard duty, inspections, and more drilling—for the anxious boys.

When Peixotto, Morgan, and Smith finally reached Baccarat—a town taken by the Germans during their surprise onslaught in August 1914 but eventually retaken by the French—it was 6 P.M. and the streets were filled with soldiers lined up before the commissary, which consisted of horse-drawn wagons equipped with coal-burning stoves. Smith, who would sketch the "chow line" the next day, noted humorously, "Waiting around occupies about ninety per cent of a soldier's time; and it would seem that most of this time was spent in line or cue."[13] This was also true of going over top: hours of anguished waiting followed by minutes of absolute terror. Those soldiers not waiting for chow stood on street corners; they talked in groups or listened to a band playing in the hospital's courtyard. The music was uplifting—patriotic, foot-tapping tempos, John Philip Sousa marching tunes—in contrast to the rumble of heavy trucks and wagon trains, the groans of mules laden with supplies, and the rattle of ambulances over rough paving stones.

It was a strange scene as the horses, mules, and wagons all harkened the past, while the tanks and fearsome artillery guns looked to the future. War was at a crossroads, and it knew which way to go. The futuristic qualities were not lost on Smith, who likened the ubiquitous observation balloons to aliens from outer space. While the French called them "sausages," he felt that description was inadequate. "With its great gray body silently swaying between heaven and earth," he wrote, "its nose in the wind, and with its red, white and blue cockade looking all the world like a watchful eye, it impressed you as being, perhaps, some Martian monster, a cross between a gigantic elephant and a whale." The fact that the camouflage men even attempted to make the balloons inconspicuous Smith found laughable.[14]

On reporting in at 42nd HQ to state their mission and become oriented to the disposition of troops, the artists were assigned a billet for the night in a home that had been used briefly by a German general for his headquarters. Peixotto spoke with the owner, an elderly lady, her story the first of many tragedies he would hear. Before the war, the old woman explained, she had employed a number of girls to make embroideries, for which the area was known. When the Germans rolled in, they seized her entire stock, then valued at about 2,000 francs. And when the Germans left, the officers pillaged anything of value—jewelry, silver, furs—to give to their wives, their girlfriends, and their whores.

The next afternoon, Peixotto sketched the ruins along the River Meurthe; he made a drawing of troops and trucks entering town over a stone bridge, a spectacular cathedral with its spires and bell tower looming over them. In the hospital's courtyard, the band had again formed, only this time the music was not gay and inspirational, it was a funeral march. Next to the band was a motor truck with its canvas flaps rolled up high enough to expose a wooden coffin draped with an American flag. Peixotto suddenly realized that he was, for the first time, to witness the burial of an American soldier in French soil. As the procession passed by, he felt compelled to join it, to march with it, to acknowledge death and to participate in its consequences. The band was at the head, followed by a sixteen-member color guard, an army chaplain, and the truck with three pallbearers on each side. Behind the truck followed the dead soldier's platoon mates and their lieutenant. They were joined by three wailing women dressed in deep black; it did not matter that this doughboy was another woman's child.

They trudged up a muddy road bordered by a thin line of bare trees and then ascended a hill into an open field. Here the sky was heavy, a drizzle was falling, and sporadic cannon fire from the front punctuated the drumbeats. As they came over the rise, they were confronted with a military cemetery with gray crosses so tightly grouped they formed an impenetrable stockade fence. Tricolor cockades—the rosettes—on each cross gave life to the stick figures, the faceless specters greeting their newest comrade. It sent a shiver down Peixotto's spine. The next scene left an indelible mark on his memory. It was a scene that he would never forget, a scene that would haunt him:

> A grave-digger, with his sabots and corduroys stained with new red earth, stood by a fresh-dug grave in a corner reserved for Americans. The coffin was carried to the edge of the grave, the firing-squad took its position; the chaplain's droning voice intoned the

*The Morning Washup, Neufmaison* by Morgan. Displaying a sense of humor, Morgan drew striking similarities between horse and man during washup at the trough.

simple service, punctuated at intervals by the sound of distant guns; the three volleys rang out in stillness, then "taps." And then, from the little copse beyond, a second bugle, clear and strong, a perfect echo of the first, sounded "taps" again, like the voice of resurrection! How lonely, how desolate it seemed to be buried in this far corner of foreign land! How often thereafter was I to witness this same scene and hear the three volleys in the afternoon stillness![15]

Afterward, Peixotto learned that this young man had died in a hand-grenade accident.

After several days in the Baccarat Sector, Morgan, Peixotto, and Smith decided they had had enough of the tame stuff; they decided to push toward the front, toward the distant rumble of guns, to go as far into the trenches as they were permitted. As the rain continued to fall and fog enveloped the farmland, they headed for the Alsatian border, passing through village after village filled with American troops. In the open rolling countryside, the villages were primitive, with pungent manure piles in front of their houses, draining into open gutters. Yet, no matter how small or primitive the village, Peixotto noticed, there was always a church.

Most of the doughboys were billeted in barns, anywhere from twenty to fifty men per barn, spending the nights wrapped in their blankets on the straw. As the artists mingled with them and listened to their chatter, it became immediately clear to Smith that "rest billets were generally conceded as unrest billets" and the doughboys' "private opinion of billets would probably look crude in print. Describing the average one would impoverish his vast fund of profanity." But then again, Smith figured, 99 percent of a doughboy's conversation was "grumble talk, varying from the characteristic condemnation of the army life to some insignificant grievance between himself and his Bunkie. All this the doughboy fully enjoys."[16]

In the morning, the soldiers would gather around the troughs and the well pumps, to brush their teeth, shave in front of little mirrors or broken glass, and wash their arms and necks. These were small but meaningful gestures of domesticity. Considering their circumstances, Peixotto was impressed by their ruddy youthfulness, their good humor, their "scrapping"—even their teasing of an old woman who knew no English—and the confident way in which they sat with the local girls on the doorsteps. Unlike Peixotto, these boys had yet to see a funeral march.

The artists pushed north to Badonviller, the road approaching the village pitted by artillery shells and camouflaged by large screens of burlap and raffia. Looking at the camouflage, Smith felt a sense of comfort, of safety, and sincerely believed that it aided the soldiers. In an article he had written for *Architectural Record*, he observed that camouflage "increased efficiency of the men through the feeling of greater safety and the partial relief of mental anxiety. The long nervous strain, sometimes hours in a cold dawn, before the order comes to advance, may be somewhat relieved by the assurance of safety, or at least some degree of protection."[17] It was indeed purely psychological, because shells and bullets would slice right through the flimsy screens.[18]

Badonviller was on the front line—where the front line had been since 1914—so it was no surprise to discover it in ruins. And when elements of the 42nd Division had recently moved into town they

*Mars* by Smith. Artist André Smith's depiction of a desolate scene of no-man's-land.

received such a hot reception from German artillery that soldiers were still clearing debris from the streets. Sadly, the church steeple was blasted off, left looking like a broken ice-cream cone. The symbolism of this image—the shattered church—caught Peixotto's eye and he took time to sketch the ruin.

For lunch, the artists joined the division's officers at the officers' mess and listened to tales of recent trench raids. At this stage of their involvement, for the Americans, raids were just as much about training as they were about information gathering, their objective to reconnoiter the line or to capture a German to interrogate. The vast majority were conducted at night; the men would crouch, crawl, and scurry through small craters, abandoned trenches, and the brush sliced from the trees by artillery. Invariably, American patrols ran into German patrols and a modest gunfight ensued. If a prisoner could be brought back for interrogation—if he didn't die from wounds first—there was a series of standard questions to ask concerning the enemy's strength and intentions. The prisoner was grilled to ascertain what divisions and regiments were across the line; how the defensive positions were laid out; where machine-gun nests were positioned; how deep the trenches were; and about tanks and gas, road conditions, and how their rations were holding out. A report then had to be filed on the circumstances of capture and the information obtained.

After a lunch of stew and stories, a runner accompanied each artist into the trenches, into a netherworld. Peixotto took note of the duckwalks, the fire-steps, the sandbags, and the carefully braided revetments. Here were no cozy barns visited by milkmaids—here everyone was living in dugouts built into the sides of the trenches, which were infested with lice, rats, and bedbugs. On a positive note, after several days of no sleep, the doughboys found it easy to bed down with any of God's creatures. Beyond the trench line itself, across the swath of no-man's-land, there was nothing of substance to record except the absolute desolation.

In no-man's-land, the scenery had been reduced to a lunar landscape, the trees cut to bare posts—although some stood twenty feet or taller—the mud ubiquitous and the earth pockmarked with craters. No enemy soldiers were visible; they were hidden in trenches beyond eyesight. Yet, out there, on both sides were snipers in camouflaged suits with their camouflaged rifles, lying prone in patches of grass and scrub, positioned strategically to pick off any careless fool. Here the days passed slowly, too—as they did behind the lines—with only an occasional exchange of artillery and gas to enliven matters. So close to the enemy, there was no drilling except for lessons on dealing with barbed wire for when it came time to go over top. While the trenches were anticlimactic for the artists, this netherworld—a place where soldiers were trapped in their own purgatory, living like rats with the rats—was deeply unsettling. That night Morgan, Peixotto, and Smith retreated to the town of Baccarat, where they found a certain comfort in the officers' club.

The harsh scenery Peixotto had witnessed was in stark contrast to his last extensive tour through the French countryside. The year war broke out he had published an illustrated travel book, *Through the French Provinces*, his journeys having taken him up the Oise River to where soldiers now killed one another with impunity. Five years ago instead of a no-man's-land with smashed ruins and anxious doughboys, he had encountered "women at the *lavoirs*, clacking their Gallic tongues as fast as their wooden paddles; these pretty villas and châteaux set in formal gardens adorned with *corbeilles* of begonias and geraniums; these little smiling villages that now and then disclose their pink roofs and pointed belfries."[19] It would be difficult for him to reconcile such charming memories with war's harsh realities.

Near Reherry, where the 165th Infantry was positioned, the artists familiarized themselves with modern weapons of war as they inspected eight-inch howitzers hidden under camouflage netting in an apple orchard. They also visited with a lieutenant in charge of a battery of 75mm guns who was sodding over his dugout so it would be completely disguised. He provided a pleasant discourse on the guns, which he kept glittering clean among the mud. It was somewhat irksome for Peixotto that as the lieutenant spoke, he lovingly caressed the guns "like a father showing a favorite child" to them.[20] The 75s were French-built 75mm cannons mounted on a carriage with two wooden-spoke wheels. They were quick firing, able to unleash twenty to thirty rounds a minute; had a range of over seven thousand yards; and were relatively mobile, although six horses or mules were needed to pull each gun and its caisson.

On the move again, beyond Pexonne, the artists encountered another battery of 75s buried in dugouts emplaced in a hillside, again in an apple orchard, which they sketched in pencil and charcoal. It was sunny and the air was warm, but Smith was unsettled by the juxtaposition of guns and flowers: "Hardly ten feet from where I stood was a group of apple trees in full splendor of pink blossoms, and except for a gash of raw dirt and mud that marked the subterranean passage to a cave through whose narrow, horizontal window a gun pointed to the enemy, the grass about me was a mat of lusciousness. In a nearby field a man was ploughing. . . . Here was a picture of war that was not for a warrior but for a poet . . . a poet in a 'tin hat.'"[21] Smith had glimpsed the business side of war, and now the poetic side, but he was only beginning to grasp what they had to grapple with in depicting the upcoming mental and physical battles.

Meanwhile, Peixotto was so engrossed in his sketching that he failed to notice German artillery taking aim at their position. Yes, a German lookout must have spotted his captain's bars, for puffs of brown smoke spewing shrapnel kept coming closer. Finally, the lieutenant in charge of the battery poked his head out of the dugout and anxiously hollered, "Come in out of that, captain; that's a very unhealthy spot just now; they're trying to get our range."[22] In the future, the artists would be instructed to remove their captain's bars when venturing forward to avoid not only enemy artillery, but also snipers who relished picking off Allied officers.

After five days in this sector, the artists started back to Chaumont, passing through Lunéville, where they encountered a French infantry regiment on the march. Even though these men were clearly battle-weary and had lost hundreds of thousands of comrades, to the artists they still invoked a noble image. "How fine they looked," an enraptured Peixotto wrote, "these weather-beaten veterans in gray steel helmets, carrying their full marching equipment, and swinging along to the 'Sambre et Meuse,' with their guns held so high that, with the thin murderous bayonet that topped them, the narrow street fairly bristled with them, like the tall pikes of ancient men-at-arms."[23]

The night was spent in Nancy, which had impressed Peixotto from afar; however, once he was inside the city, the view wasn't quite as spectacular. Nancy had endured about 180 air raids to date, and of the 120,000 inhabitants only a third remained. Whole sections of the city had been rendered uninhabitable: building windows blown out, yawning holes in facades, and interior walls caved in. As they meandered through the avenues, Peixotto noted a particularly vivid scene: "One big group of buildings had just been bombed a night or two before and lay disemboweled like a poor picador's horse, with its entrails—timbers, stone, furniture, laths, and plaster—dragging in the street."[24]

On their return to Chaumont, the artists turned their sketches into more finished drawings, which they submitted to their chief, Lieutenant Colonel Sweeney. The drawings included ruined churches, damaged villages, the big guns at Reherry, and the soldiers' mess, among others. They were quiet yet disturbing scenes, reflecting the fact that the dough-boys were in a transitional phase in forward zones, displaying a youthful exuberance against a backdrop of ruins. In just over a month's time, this situation would change as the AEF's grace period of training came to an end and there was no choice but to become fully immersed in the bloody fray. However, for one official artist—Harry Townsend, who would arrive in France on April 30—the war would come to him most immediately.

# 3

# A BROTHER
# GOES TO WAR

A RECENT DARTMOUTH COLLEGE GRADUATE. A bright future in corporate America. A carefree existence in New York City. Yet, he wanted more out of life; he wanted adventure and romance. So, in July 1917, Henri "Hank" Townsend journeyed to Canada, where he enlisted with the Royal Flying Corps (RFC).

While at Camp Bonden in Ontario training as a pilot, Townsend, who was one of a small group of Americans, wrote to his old workmates: "For the past month I have been flying various types of machines, each a little faster than the former, gradually working up to the actual machine I will fly at the front. The main thing is the trick of landing these fast machines, that come down at sixty and seventy miles an hour."[1] It wasn't the safest of occupations even without German anti-aircraft guns taking aim. After all, the world was only in its second decade of air flight; it was still very much a matter of trial and error for the pilots. Not so unexpectedly, the pilots tended to be the wild ones, the risk takers, the ones with such zeal for life even while they taunted death. They played hard, too—drinking, gambling, and chasing girls. It was all part of the game. It was about staying sane.

After a romp in Canada, for the successful pilots like Hank Townsend, it was on to Lumberry, Scotland, in the fall for advanced training at the RFC's fighting and stunting school. In March 1918, Townsend was transferred to France, where he was assigned as a bomber pilot in the 103rd Aero Squadron, one of just two Americans in the group. The other Yank was Rex Willey, with whom he'd trained and become quick friends—Willey affectionately dubbing his new buddy Old Towney. Between bombing missions, they took long walks together to discuss the future that lay ahead of them and to reflect on the past. Dreams of tomorrow began to fade, however, as their comrades were shot from the sky with regularity or simply crashed in unreliable machines. Even the famed German ace with eighty kills to his credit, Baron Manfred von Richtofen—"the Red Baron"—was shot down on April 21, 1918, over French territory. He was subsequently buried at Bertangles, France, with full military honors in spite of being the enemy—there was a bond between these airmen that transcended the war.

Henri Townsend soon realized that he, too, would be shot from the sky; yes, it was inevitable. In contemplating his impending death and ruminating over his life, Townsend suddenly felt the need to explain his actions in the last year, including the flight to Canada, among other recent events, which had roiled his family and were causing him serious guilt and grief. There was only one person he felt comfortable speaking with: his older brother, Harry, who was scheduled to arrive in France in late April. He would make sure that a letter was waiting for Harry at GHQ in Chaumont—a letter that would serve as a confession.

Harry Townsend was looking forward to a reunion with his younger brother, who had so impetuously run off to join the RFC. Always the protective big brother, Harry had encouraged him to go to college, and then insisted he move in with his family in New York City to save money while paying off his college loans. Even though they were under the same roof, Harry had not foreseen Henri's flight to the RFC. Then, while he was in Canada, just before shipping overseas, Henri unloaded a personal bomb on the family: he had married a girl he had met before joining the RFC. This apparent elopement was another reason Harry, who shared a strong bond with Henri, was desperate to sit down with his younger brother and gauge his emotional state. He wanted to simply make sure his brother was content.

While Henri's actions were impetuous, Harry understood them because he himself had chosen an alternate course in life. Born in March 1879, Harry Townsend was raised in the small Illinois town of Wyoming, where his father was a farmer and a merchant with a peddling wagon. As a boy, Harry helped him sell supplies to the surrounding farmers, but then, as a teenager, Townsend first demonstrated his artistic skill by making money as a sign painter for local businessmen. Certain he didn't want the life of his father, after high school he enrolled in the Chicago Art Institute in hopes of finding spiritual fulfillment and adventure. With little support from his family, emotional or financial, Townsend rode his bicycle to Chicago.

Townsend continued his journey when, in 1900, the twenty-one-year-old traveled to Wilmington, Delaware, to study under Howard Pyle, the father of American illustration. The respected Pyle, then in his late forties, imparted to his students his fervent desire to capture drama and basic human emotions, and to tell a story with such vividness that his audience was drawn in as eyewitnesses. An avid student, Townsend quickly developed an instinct for capturing the action of the moment, which would pay handsome returns during the war. After several years under Pyle, Townsend studied briefly in Paris and London and then launched a prominent career as an illustrator for *Harper's*, *Century*, and *McClure's*, among others. He was also an accomplished painter in oils, watercolors, and pastels, and he, along with his family, moved to France in 1912 to be close to the more progressive art scenes in London and Paris. But then the European War forced Harry, his wife, Cory, and his young daughter, Barbara, to return to New York, where they took an apartment on Waverly Place and settled into the Greenwich Village scene.

Harry Everett Townsend

Once the United States entered the war, in April 1917, Townsend volunteered for the Division of Pictorial Publicity, as had Wallace Morgan, and the group commissioned him to design and draw war posters.

His work was highly regarded, which led to his recruitment as one of the AEF's official artists.[2] Townsend jumped at the prospect; it was a fantastic opportunity to develop as an artist and to explore the emotional depths of himself and his craft. He was forever looking for that "aesthetic thrill" that was "peculiar, mysterious, haunting, personal and intangible."[3] The war, more than any subject imaginable, would provide him with aesthetic thrill.

So, the thirty-nine-year-old left Cory, his wife of almost fourteen years, and his young daughter, Barbara—she almost seven—to accept a commission as a captain on March 21, 1918. It was a brutal decision to leave his wife, with whom he had a very loving relationship. Compounding the difficult situation, Cory would be forced to relocate to Chicago, where she would need support from her family. Despite the support, the move would be disruptive for their young daughter, who was attending grade school and had her friends. Sacrifices were necessary, however. And there was young Henri to track down. Harry Townsend shipped out in April, in a spring snowstorm.

When Townsend reported for duty at the AEF's General Headquarters in Chaumont, France, on May 1, he was greeted with a pleasant surprise: a letter from his brother. As he read the first paragraph, a look of despair spread across his face. The letter was intimate and grave; it concerned serious private matters. Henri opened by admitting he had certain troubles and worries that he wanted to talk over in person, that he was keenly looking forward to seeing Harry. He knew the family had been waiting to hear from him concerning his marriage, which he had "so stubbornly" kept from them, and he "wanted to set himself right" in their eyes. This alone had become such a burden to Henri that it was "a poignant grief."

As he explained it to Harry, when Henri met his future wife, Dwight, they were immediately attracted to each other—she the "sweet pipes" and he "Pan"—they so very naturally belonged together. Even though they married rather suddenly, Henri continued in the letter, they recognized that they should have financial independence from each other in case the marriage didn't work. But that notion quickly changed—and the reason hit Harry Townsend hard—because Dwight was pregnant with their child. In July 1917, Dwight had become pregnant and just recently, in late March, she had given birth to a girl, whom they had named Stephanie. What truly baffled Harry was that while all these momentous events had been occurring, his younger brother had never dropped a hint of it. To the contrary, while in Canada, Henri had continued to tell him that after the war he would return to his room with them at Waverly Place. But now, in the letter, Henri admitted that he hated himself for lying; he was guilt ridden for living two lives. Full of emotion and remorse, he asked for their forgiveness.

The guilt was all the more searing because, as Henri stated, Harry and Cory meant so much to him and had done so much for him and he dearly loved them. He recalled what an uplift Harry had been, how he helped him better himself and how necessary they were for each other to sustain their ideals, especially now that "we are here in this awful conflict." Rambling now, Henri spoke of how much he loved his mother, his brothers, and his sisters. He spoke of his love for Harry and Cory's Barbara, and how it was "beyond words to express." He always wanted to be a part of Barbara's life and was already laying plans for her college education. This desire alone burned "like a benison"—a blessing—in Henri's chest. He divulged that he had gone so far as to take care of Barbara in his will—a debt to be repaid to Harry—by leaving her $500. He had wanted to give Barbara more, but circumstances had changed with Stephanie's birth. Henri hoped Barbara and Stephanie would grow up together; he longed to see both of them; and if anything should happen to Dwight, he wanted Harry and Cory to care for Stephanie. This last sentence stopped Harry cold. His brother was talking like he was already dead.[4]

Over the next couple of days, as Harry awaited his orders and made plans to see his brother, he could not bring himself to read the letter again because it was "too full, too intimate and too wonderful and too sad." Unable to bear the thought of someone else reading it if something should happen to him, Townsend destroyed the letter. And months would pass before he gathered enough strength to tell his wife about Henri's confessions. In those days of limbo, a second letter arrived for Harry, this one from Rex Willey, his brother's buddy, the letter dated April 28. He could not get past the first line. He broke with grief. He felt as though he had taken a bayonet in the stomach. The first line: "I am very sorry to have to tell you that your brother was killed on the 23rd." Killed one week before Harry's arrival. One week.

Pulling himself together, Harry struggled through the remainder of the letter:

We left on a long bomb raid that evening and although we were severely "archied" every one apparently returned safely before dark. Your brother was one of the last to land and for some reason, which will always remain a mystery, his machine came down in flames from about a hundred feet just before he reached the aerodrome. He was thrown out in some way but the observer was killed outright. He died an hour and a half later without regaining consciousness.

I had the pleasure of meeting you when you visited him at Bonden and he and I have been together ever since although all the rest of our little group of Americans were gradually split up during our long stay in England.

I was unable to communicate with you before this because he had told me you were on your way over here so had to wait until you sent your address to him. I took the liberty today of opening your note to him which you wrote from London.

Old Towney and I were the only Americans in the squadron and having been together since last July we felt more or less drawn together with our mutual intensity. It is needless to say I miss him. He is posted in the casualty list as "died from wounds."

I packed up his trunk and other belongings and they will be forwarded to his next of kin thru the regular channels. Looking thru some of his correspondence I found that he was married. A fact he had told none of us, however there was no record of his wife's address so I could not communicate with her. In the squadron records he gives his next of kin as his mother, not mentioning his wife at all.

Allow me to assure you of my sympathy in his loss, Mr. Townsend, and please don't hesitate for a moment in calling upon me, if there is anything I can do.[5]

Henri's Dartmouth College friends took his death hard, too. "God damn!" wrote Dan Chase to buddy Pat Maloney, another aviator. "It's just beginning to sink into me now. Next to my father and mother, and yourself, I believe that his clicking it leaves the biggest hole in my life. I loved him." An artist aiding in the propaganda effort, Chase thought he could steel himself against such tragedies but could not:

My profession makes me rather critically analytical of all emotion, but all this afternoon I've been plugging along muddy country roads, with something beside rain on my face. . . . and find it impossible to think that he's underground. Damn this war.

I'm trying to nerve myself up to writing to his wife and finding it a hard job. We ought to do something for her, kid; there's nothing we can do just now but make clumsy condolences and lay ourselves wholly at her disposal. But later on we may find a chance to come through. According to the Herald the lad leaves a six week old daughter. Christ, but isn't that tough all around? I wish to God that we could figure some way of filling Hank's place in a faint and shadowy fashion; perhaps we may, in time.

To end his letter, he mustered what faith he had: "Do you suppose we shall, in some great inn beyond the grave, pull up leather bottomed chairs before a big fire and read poetry far into the night? I hope we may."[6]

Harry Townsend had come to France with the greatest opportunity as an artist, only to have his life ripped apart. Their mother would take Henri's death the hardest, however, for as Townsend put it to his wife, he had always been "sort of a favorite of hers and he was always so sweet to her." He hated to think of his mother, widowed years earlier, and the heavier burden she would now shoulder.[7] Townsend flashed back to before his little brother had shipped overseas, to when they had sat together in Henri's bedroom. How quiet and sad his brother had seemed. He told Harry that he had been keeping a diary, had been writing poetry in it, and if he didn't make it through the war safely, he wanted him to take the diary for safekeeping. Paralyzed by the thought of his brother being killed, all Townsend could do at the time was to encourage his brother to keep writing.[8]

As Townsend reflected on his brother's death, he was troubled by the fact that Henri had apparently made it back from the mission in one piece—surviving the "archies," the German anti-aircraft guns—only to have his plane burst into flames just short of the airfield. Why had this happened? If Harry could understand *why*, if whatever happened could be explained—in a desperate but understandable line of logic—it would allow him a measure of acceptance and peace. *Why* was the refrain for millions of families, and *why* could never be answered, not really. Regardless, Townsend petitioned British HQ to permit him to visit the 103rd Aero Squadron and investigate the circumstances of his brother's death. They agreed to the request, but then the powers that be just as quickly reneged; without explanation, the door was slammed in Townsend's face.

Whatever Townsend needed to know would have to come from his brother's buddies: Willey and two boys by the names of Cunningham and Westing. But before he could meet with the aviators, Willey and Cunningham would be dead and Westing a prisoner. "It's strange how short a time the four of them lasted in the game," Harry would later write despairingly to his wife, "and I can't quite make it out except that as lots of have grown to believe that the R.F.C. or now the R.A.F. is play-ing the game much harder and more effectively than the other allies. There seems to be no doubt of this, their bombing campaigns systematic and final are stupendous, so it is natural that their losses should be in proportion, I suppose."[9]

Over the next months, Harry Townsend's belief in man and God would be sorely tested as the war would change him dramatically. As a tribute to his brother Henri, he would focus a good portion of his work on aviation—dedicate himself to it—and he would eventually take to the air in spite of his wife's warnings. All the while, he would be haunted by his brother's death, the simplest of scenes or words reminding him of the tragedy. And when it came time to face his own mortality, he would have to choose between retreating like a coward or pushing forward.

# 4

# LAST PEACEFUL
# FORAYS

HARRY TOWNSEND WAS NOT THE ONLY ARTIST leaving behind a family. It was a quiet winter evening at the Dunns' comfortable and spacious residence in Leonia, New Jersey, where Harvey Dunn and his wife, Tulla, were having dinner with her brother Sonnin when the telephone rang. It was the War Department; they had approved Harvey as an official artist and wanted to know how soon he could ship out. "Two hours!" he said. For Tulla, it was an unreal, dreamy kind of night as she attempted to grasp that her husband was going off to war. It was made all the more surreal by a dramatic display of the aurora borealis in the northern sky, an omen left open to interpretation.[1]

Born March 8, 1884, during a blinding blizzard in Dakota Country, Dunn was shaped by the rugged frontier, high plains life. At six one and two hundred pounds, he had "huge, ham-like" hands, but long, smooth fingers deft enough to take apart and put together a car

49

engine.[2] "He was a whale of a man, a veritable pioneer hulk of a man," a longtime friend, Grant Reynard, observed, "with a head reminding you of a cross between an Indian chief and a Viking. He looked as though he could easily bite a spike in two with one crunch of his broad jaws. . . . It was years before I came to know that he was as gentle as a lamb under that steel frame, and as sensitive in emotion as the artist he was. To discover this was like finding lilacs in a boiler factory."[3] The United States's most famous illustrator, Norman Rockwell, considered Dunn to be the "personification of a great man, stalwart in appearance and majestic in manner."[4]

In contrast to his very physical presence, from a young age the sensitive Dunn was intrigued by the arts. As a boy he sketched with his mother, Bersha, and at grade school he sketched endlessly on the blackboard, rendering gnarled cottonwoods and steaming locomotives, among other subjects. Eventually his teacher was forced to confiscate all chalk. While his father couldn't understand why a strong, strapping boy would want to make pictures instead of working the land, Dunn left home to study at the Chicago Art Institute. There, a group of his fellow artists urged him to quit because they had concluded he didn't have adequate talent; instead, he was ever more driven to excel and went on to study under Howard Pyle in Wilmington. While there Dunn met Tulla Krebs, who lived across the street, and, displaying a marginal romantic streak, he proposed to her as they swayed aboard an open trolley car. At their 1908 wedding, another famous artist, N. C. Wyeth, was his best man. Eager to start a family, they soon had a son, only to lose him in infancy. In 1911, they had another boy, Robert Kruse, and in 1912, a girl, Louise. So, Harvey Dunn would be leaving his wife and two children.

After being commissioned a captain on March 7, 1918, the day before his thirty-fourth birthday, Dunn, according to his friend Dean Cornwell, was in a "state of maximum exuberance" as he made preparations to ship out.[5] He knew most of the artists he'd be joining; after all, Harry Townsend, George Harding, and he had studied under Pyle, and most of the eight had gravitated to New York City. Prone to being egotistical and volatile, Dunn did rub some of his peers the wrong way. He referred to Wallace Morgan's Bohemian crowd as the "velvet pantaloon artists" and would never be caught dead wearing a beret.[6] He preferred workingman's clothes and a slouch hat. Like the adventurer Harding, Dunn, who relished fast cars and wasn't adverse to placing himself in danger, was cut out for war. As a result, his bold and dramatic World War I paintings would become the most popular of the artists' work.

Dunn arrived in France feverishly determined to paint the war as it was: "the shock and loss and bitterness and blood of it."[7] Certainly, it would not be the peaceful, cultured country he encountered in 1913, when he had toured Europe with his father-in-law and brother-in-law. When he and fellow Pyle protégé Harding connected in Paris on May 2, shortly after both arrived in France, they discovered the City of Light blackened at night in the futile hope of thwarting German bombers. Three days later Harding had a taste of the more personal consequences of war when he met a peasant woman who had lost four sons and had not heard from a fifth for eight months. The encounter left Harding sitting on a terrace with a bout of homesickness, and thinking of his wife, Anita. "I never knew I could love her the way I do," he jotted down in his diary.[8]

Harvey Thomas Dunn

As for Dunn's introduction to the war, he could not have imagined the bureaucratic bungling that greeted him at GHQ in Chaumont. When he reported for assignment, they mistakenly placed him in command of an infantry company. For a man who didn't even know how to properly salute, it was a rather confounding situation. Of course, it was going to take days for the bureaucrats to untangle the mess, so the only option for him was to place himself on sick call until he could be reassigned.[9]

When Dunn finally arrived in Neufchâteau on May 6, those artists who had never met him were immediately impressed by his size and his personality: he was both flippant and sentimental; he was both self-assured and at times withdrawn. Dunn did everything with flair—he smoked cigarettes dramatically and punctuated his rich, vibrant-voiced discourses with dramatic pauses—an exuberance that his fellow artists would find both annoying and endearing.

By mid-May, all eight official artists—Harvey Dunn, Ernest Peixotto, Harry Townsend, Wallace Morgan, George Harding, J. André Smith, Bill Aylward, and Jack Duncan—were settled in Neufchâteau. Like

Harding, the forty-two-year-old Aylward was a world traveler who had toured the Orient and spent years in Europe. He, too, had since settled down, had a wife and a five-year-old daughter, but couldn't resist the allure of war. Having studied at the Art Institute of Chicago, the Art Students League in New York, and then under Howard Pyle, Aylward was well acquainted with his comrades. As for the thirty-seven-year-old Duncan, while a top illustrator, he was best known for his grandfather, a renowned Shakespearean actor. A native of Indianapolis, he moved to New York to study at the Art Students League and never left the city, except for his field assignments for such magazines as *Scribner's*, *McClure's*, and *Harper's*. And so the AEF's "Eight" came together, each with their idiosyncrasies, each driven to make good, and each inspiring the other—in one way or another.

William James Aylward

There was another American artist of note—the country's preeminent painter at that time—who would also take the stage in France: John Singer Sargent. At age sixty-two, this grand old man—who had befriended such literary giants as Edith Wharton and Henry James, who hobnobbed with Britain's royalty, and who made a fortune painting portraits of those exclusive members of high society—was determined to see the war. Tall but exceedingly overweight—his weight hidden behind well-tailored suits—with intense blue-green eyes fading somewhat and a full gray beard discolored by nicotine, his soldiering days were long past. Yet, Sargent temporarily halted a major mural project he had been commissioned to do by the Boston Public Library, and in May 1918 boarded a transport ship bound for England.

Of course, the foremost question was why this venerable painter would desire to subject himself to the dangers of war. Sargent had very personal reasons. On Good Friday 1918,

Walter Jack Duncan

he had received a telegram with devastating news: his niece Rose Marie
Michel, who had lost her husband to the war, was killed in the church of
Saint-Gervais, place Lobau, Paris—one of seventy worshipers killed by a
German bombardment. She was only twenty-four and a favorite of his,
having modeled for him on numerous occasions. "I can't tell you . . .
how I feel the loss of the most charming girl who ever lived," Sargent
wrote to his sister Violet, who was living in London. "And what a death.
I hope it was instantaneous." He then proclaimed, "I ought to be with
you instead of over here," and subsequently, he prepared his will and
sailed for England, where he kept a residence in London on Tite Street.
After a short visit in the city, he went to France to witness the conflagra-
tion that had killed his niece.[10]

When Sargent eventually took to the battlefield in July, the experiences of this celebrity would provide both a stark contrast to those of the
AEF's artists and confirmation of what they were already discovering:
that war was a grim business.

As André Smith soaked in the atmosphere at the Press and Censorship
Division HQ—which included journalists, photographers, and illustrators—he realized that the war had become a true spectacle:

During the first few months of this mad conflict the war had not
had time to grow self-conscious. It was not until it had settled into
the trenches, recovered its breath, put on new uniforms and steel
helmets, used gas, dropped bombs and felt reasonably sure of
being something greater and more destructive and more expensive
than anything in the world's history, did it become fully conscious
of its importance and call upon an astounded and shocked world
to come and regard it. And so it happened that the journalists or
war correspondents, who at one time were the only "outsiders" to
enjoy orchestra seats in the theatre of war, were now being
crowded by the arrival of novelists, poets, historians, propagandists, artists, sculptors, photographers, and moving-picture men
(not to mention a liberal scattering of miscellaneous scientists). All
these spectators were allowed to view this "Big Show," record it,
picture it, criticize it, and glorify it, under the sanction of govern-
ments that made them their official, semi-official, or unofficial
representatives.[11]

Smith found Neufchâteau itself to be a sleepy town that, being a "rather compact clustering of houses" constructed mostly of gray stone centered on a hill, was an easy target for German aviators.[12] The town offered little in the way of culture; its purpose was purely logistical as it was halfway between the front and GHQ in Chaumont. For a social outlet, the artists would spend their evenings crowded into Club Lafayette—with the hundreds of other officers—for dinner and then a smoke in the adjoining café.

HQ assigned the artists billets in private homes regardless of whether the houses had studio space or the potential for it. Townsend found himself with a refugee family, the Bathoses—Henri, his wife, his teenage daughter, and his boy of about twelve—who had been living in Nancy, but abandoned their home due to the constant air raids. Their house in Neufchâteau was relatively modern; while sparsely furnished, it had a shower, a fine marble fireplace, hardwood flooring, and a large garden, where there was a hutch filled with rabbits and six chickens. Townsend's room boasted a south-facing French window, so he overlooked the town and the valley beyond. He paid 1½ francs a day in rent, although he was reimbursed by the government. Included with his rent, the family was willing to serve him breakfast if he could manage to squirrel away valuable coffee and sugar from the quartermaster's supplies.[13] This marginally underhanded task he managed without reprisals.

With any serious U.S. military action still several weeks away, the artists' chief, Lieutenant Colonel Sweeney, thought it was best for them to continue to orient themselves to the countryside and the deployment of the AEF's divisions in northeast France. At the moment, American units were still training and moving into forward defensive positions to relieve their French counterparts. To clarify the artists' mission, Sweeney also issued a memo in which he made five points: (1) The artists had to keep in mind that their work was for both historical purposes and use in American publications, to be distributed by the War Department; (2) the artists had to decide which sketches they wished to save for future, more finished pieces and what should be released immediately; (3) they were expected to submit pieces on or about the first of each month; (4) after being approved by the censor, each piece would be photographed by the Signal Corps before the original was sent on to Washington; (5) on the first of each month, the artist had to prepare a brief report of what he had done the previous month.[14] Apparently always seeking a crisis, the General Staff in Washington now demanded to know how many drawings the artists could send back on a monthly basis. Not expecting such a question, the wary artists perceived that the tone was suddenly changing: it was as if their artwork was about to become another statistic like monthly casualty counts.

Smith, who would quickly take a contemptuous attitude toward the bureaucracy, didn't hesitate to complain to Major Banning, chief of the Pictorial Section of the Historical Branch for the General Staff in D.C. What irked the artists, he explained, was that the AEF was apparently demanding "from all of us the same procedure and did not take into consideration the individual difference both in the method as well as our particular lines of work." Certainly, artists have very individualistic approaches to their work; however, caught up in the voracious hunger for propaganda, Banning would show little sympathy.

A month later, the artists' assistant chief at G.2.D., Lieutenant Colonel E. R. W. McCabe, issued a clarifying memo: the artists were to cover the troops in the trenches, the troops in training and reserve, and lines of communication. As long as they covered this material, they were to be "allowed considerable latitude." Assuming an independent attitude, the artists took it upon themselves to specialize in various aspects of prosecuting a war: Dunn and Harding would focus on the combat scenes; Townsend on aviation and artillery; Peixotto, Smith, and Aylward on the setting, that is, the ruined landscapes and villages; and Morgan and Duncan on daily life of the soldiers.[15] As illustrators, the men were accustomed to working fast, the pressure of deadlines, and long hours, so they thought they were prepared for depicting the war. But the massive scale of it all surprised them. A taste of what they were about to encounter when the doughboys finally engaged the enemy en force was provided when the artists toured the Verdun sector, a place made famous by the bloody battles of 1916.

The Verdun legend took root in February 1916 with the Germans seizing Fort Douaumont, one in the ring of forts protecting the city of Verdun, itself a strategic gateway into eastern France. Over the next ten months, the frenzied French threw almost 2 million men at the Germans to win back lost ground, and both sides fired a combined 40 million artillery rounds—indications of Verdun's significance. The only

*The Machine Gunner* by Dunn. The heroic
pose of a marine is depicted.

breaks in the vicious fighting were momentary or when the munition
dumps were empty. At the end of the extended battle—which resulted
in the French retaking Douaumont—France had suffered five hundred
thousand casualties and Germany close to four hundred thousand.[16] It
had been relatively quiet since, both sides hunkered down in a network
of trenches. Now the AEF's 2nd Division—regulars and marines—had
moved into the area for training purposes, and were, for the moment,
under French command.

From Neufchâteau, Verdun was almost directly north, but to drive
there in their two assigned motorcars the artists had to sweep to the west
to avoid the Germans occupying the Saint-Mihiel Salient. Into the field,
Dunn brought his sizable wooden sketch box, bigger than most men
could have handled, which he carried on his back. Designed specifically
for his battlefield work, it had two rollers with paper mounted on its

*The Engineer* by Dunn. This piece better typified the doughboy
weighted down by his pack.

frame so he could open the box, make a sketch, and then turn the knobs
to scroll to fresh paper for the next sketch. Over the coming months he
would fill dozens of rolls of paper. He also brought along a harmonica—
a Hohner "Marine Band" model in C—which he would play for the
marines and regulars to relax them. Of course, fraternization between
officers and grunts was frowned upon, so Dunn would find himself
being reprimanded—not that he paid attention to what he considered
ridiculous regulations.

On May 9, 1918, the artists arrived in the vicinity of Verdun, where
the marines were holding the line.[17] The roads were filled with American
artillery trains and trucks loaded with marines dressed in their olive drab.
"Superb fellows they were," Peixotto observed, "these 'leather-necks,'
these 'hard-boiled guys,' as they liked to call themselves."[18] Some 20

percent of the 5th Marines and 10 percent of the 6th Marines were classi-
fied as "old-timers"; in other words, they'd been in the service for over a
year, with a number of them having been pulled from duty in places like
Cuba, Haiti, and the Dominican Republic, where they had indeed
become hard-boiled under the scorching sun. While now in a quiet zone,
the marines would soon find themselves in very hot place called Belleau
Wood, and they would produce their share of Medal of Honor recipients.
Gunnery Sergeant Ernest Hoffman, for one, would distinguish himself in
less than a month's time when he would charge twelve Germans armed
with five light machine guns crawling toward his fellow soldiers. Hoffman
would bayonet two of the enemy and chase off the others.[19]

Intent on entering the Verdun trenches, Peixotto ordered his driver to
the 2nd Division Headquarters in Sommedieue, where he hoped to
receive permission to move forward. After they parked the car in the
village square, a guide led Peixotto—along with Morgan—toward a

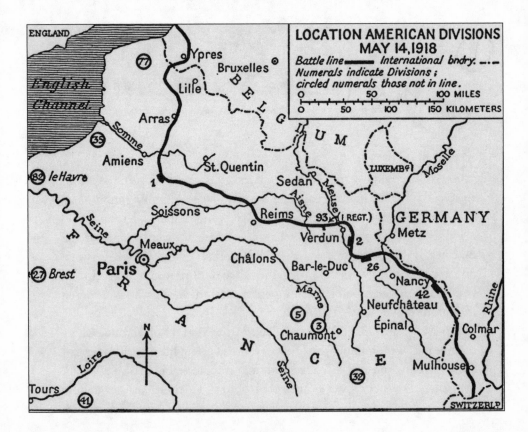

dense grove of pine trees. Peixotto wondered just where they were going because no structures were visible, but then, under the natural camouflage, a group of wooden huts harboring the HQ materialized. Encountering no complications, the artists received permission to move forward to within seven miles of Verdun, to 4th Marine Brigade Headquarters, where they were to report in to Brigadier General James Harbord. A handsome, stern-looking man, Harbord had enlisted as a private in 1889 and later befriended General Pershing. Having known Harbord for almost twenty years, Pershing made him his chief of staff in France; however, Harbord wanted a field command, so Pershing awarded him the 4th U. S. Marine Brigade. As Peixotto now studied the brigadier general surrounded by intimidating elements of war, the one thing that stuck in the artist's mind was that among the ubiquitous, sticky mud, General Harbord's riding boots were immaculate.

Peixotto and Morgan received permission to move forward to the Verdun trenches, but it was growing late so they had to spend the night at a battalion's headquarters situated in an old quarry in the Côtes de Meuse, a series of flat-topped hills with the land carved out in between, the landscape particularly angular in the quarry. Intrigued by the natural and man-made lines, Peixotto sketched the rows of sandbags that protected the barrack roofs, magazines, and dugouts embedded in the walls of the quarry. And beyond, always below the horizon, the first-line trenches—held by companies of the 6th Marines—wove through the destroyed village of Haudiomont. Here they encountered Major Berton W. Sibley, commanding officer of 3rd Battalion, 6th Marines, who were slowly making their way west, toward the active part of the front.

Peixotto chose to billet with a Lieutenant Noble, who, at the relatively tender age of twenty-four, had a company of 290 men in his charge. The first thing Noble did was eye this strange bird of an artist-soldier from head to toe and immediately determine that Captain Peixotto was not fit for the trenches. His soft shoes in particular would not do. So, Noble fitted Peixotto with rubber boots, a tin hat, a gas mask, and a trench cane. Only now was this green officer of the AEF ready for a quick evening tour. "The men, as we passed, stood flattened against the platted revetments, watching," wrote Peixotto. "Every little while the *pap-pap-pap* of a machine-gun sounded startling close, for the Boche trenches at certain points were only a hundred yards away, and at others were even connected with ours by bits of abandoned *boyaux*, now choked with barbed wire." At the German's deepest outpost, their machine guns were clattering constantly.

"They're at it early to-night," observed Noble. "I wonder if there's something doing."

Such commentary and the thought of being caught in a raid—as the mud clinging to his boots made his feet as heavy as lead—did little to steady Peixotto's rattled nerves.

They returned to Noble's dugout located in the small cellar of a razed house. A door from an old Brittany armoire, which would have made a handsome antique, was pulled over the entrance. Behind it was a blanket hung to block any light from leaving the cellar as soldiers came and went at night. Spartan to the extreme, there was a chair, a bed made from a few boards and straw, and spread across a table were maps, photographs, and papers, as well as a crudely made candlestick. "I'm going to let you live my life to-night just as I live it," said Noble. So Peixotto settled in for what proved to be long, tense hours, even though they did not come under fire. Not until midnight did they serve dinner—cooking was only done at night—which consisted of a steaming bowl of soup filled with vegetables and meat, along with canned peas, thick slabs of buttered bread, and a cup of hot chocolate. Into the early morning hours, order- lies came and went with orders—orders concerning rockets and signals, orders for tomorrow's march—intelligence reports, and company papers to sign. There was no time for sleeping or relaxing.

Anxious to see dawn break over no-man's-land, when the light would be most dramatic and stir his imagination, at 3 A.M., Peixotto accompa- nied a runner into the trenches. Once in a while, the runner's bayonet would catch a flicker of light, the glint ominous, the tension palpable in the darkness. "Suddenly a gun went off quite near me; then others up and down our line," wrote Peixotto. "Rifle-shots are contagious at night. Why did he shoot? He thought he saw something moving in the dark- ness." Now in the ruined village of Haudimont, they entered an observa- tion post—a destroyed building—and climbed the rickety steps to a platform behind a fractured stone wall. Peixotto put his eye to a peep- hole. Even in the lingering blackness, the images were vivid: along a white road two blasted trees stood like sentinels; a field was pitted with shell- holes; barbed wire had shaped itself into thickets; and the revetments of the trenches were braided together. In this supernatural setting, in the cold and still air, between the sporadic *pap-pap-pap* of machine-gun fire, songbirds began to fill the wasteland with morning carols. And then a gray cat on the hunt for breakfast climbed along a fallen beam below the artist. Not until the sun was in the sky did "the witchery, the dread of the night" disappear for Peixotto. In the soft morning light, he quickly sketched the observation post, a cavernous, bombed-out home, with crumbling rock and exposed beams. Then it was onward to a deeper level of hell, a descent into the absolute desolation of the Verdun battlefield.

Peixotto and Morgan retreated from the Haudimont trenches and motored as far forward as they could to the northwest of Verdun, before continuing on foot into the hills, into the 1916 battlefield. "As we advanced the spectacle was terrifying," wrote Peixotto. Two years after the bloody battles the land remained covered with body parts and weapons: "Shell-hole overlapped shell-crater; the earth was ploughed and torn, blown up and smashed down again. Every step was a pitfall. Weapons of every description, grenades, canteens, shells, casques, accou-trements, bits of uniforms stained with a putrid red-brown varnish, and in certain shell-holes whitening bones sticking out of the stinking water, and in one a boot floating with a foot still in it. Though it was Maytime, the only vestige of green that Nature could bestow was a few blades of grass on the edges of the new craters." What here could be sketched that was glorious when everything was heinous?

A French officer beckoned Peixotto and asked with sardonic grimness, "Do you know where you are? No? You're in the village of Fleury." What was a village, that is; it would never exist again, except on a tourist marker for future generations. Yes, as Peixotto looked around, he could not find a trace of Fleury. Usually, in these destroyed places there was a bit of church left standing, or a segment of stone wall, or a road. Not here. As Peixotto raised his eyes to the horizon, everywhere was the same: "Not a tree; not a green thing. Hills as bare as the palm of your hand. Where once had been orchards, vineyards, and well-kept woods, now were lunar solitudes, vast stretches of desert, utterly devoid of life."[20]

Also determined to visit the forward trenches, on May 14, Harding departed for the village of Mandres, where units of the 101st Infantry Regiment, 26th Division, were positioned. On the road there he absorbed the many sites: a camouflaged airdrome, ammunition dumps, observation balloon stations, evacuation hospitals, and the bucolic canal paralleling the road with old wooden boats being pulled by mules. Two airplanes roared overhead, prompting Harding to jot in his diary, "The terrific sound of motor is terrifying . . . looks like the swallows flying low." Outside of Mandres he checked in with the CO and arranged for a runner to take him into no-man's-land, or "Hell's Half Acre" as it was called here. In the trenches, Harding visited a bunkerlike "observation fort" that had a low ceiling, gas curtains, maps pinned to the walls, and long slit windows with mounted telescopes. While here Harding watched with excited anticipation as an American pilot attacked a German observation balloon—only it was the American who was blasted from the sky. Paying no attention to grammar or punctuation, he quickly wrote in his diary, "German observation balloons up, French Amer plane which hid behind cloud and then shoot over German lines with anti aircraft shots all around plane comes down 2 Amer aviators killed."

After pulling out of no-man's-land, Harding next joined K Company of the 101st in the trenches. When he and his guide approached the CO's dugout, the sentries called out, "Halt, who goes there?" and then brandished their "bayonets within 2 inches of ones stomach." Quickly the runner whispered the password and they were permitted entry. That

*In the Front Line at Early Morning* by Dunn. Life in the frontline trenches was filled with hours of boredom, but there was also the fear of raids, gas, and sporadic shelling; Dunn sought to capture the anxious boredom.

evening Harding discovered that the trenches were hardly safe even in quiet areas, for shortly before 7 P.M. a Boche plane roared in and sprayed them with bullets. Not until 9:30 P.M., once darkness had fallen, did Harding venture farther forward, through narrow trenches lined with men grasping their guns and gas masks. While mingling with the soldiers, he heard stories of the sporadic enemy barrages and the black comedy of being caught at the latrine with trousers around ankles when shells came over. He met a nervous lieutenant who was greatly worried about gas, a worry for which he could hardly be blamed; as Harding noted after their talk, "In long gas attack men can't drink, eat, and only whisper—glasses cloud—it is hell." While the artist didn't consider the lieutenant cowardly, it was clear to him that the troops were not yet ready for battle.

Going out on patrols and small raiding parties worked toward steeling the men against what was to come; however, it didn't help their psyche when some soldiers simply went missing while on these modest missions. In fact, as Harding made his tour of the forward trenches, they stumbled across forsaken American and German bodies stuck in quicksandlike muck. And there was the incessant, unnerving sound of guns, a forbidding reminder of how close the enemy was: "All the while to our left the sky and landscape lighted up with star rockets from French and putt, putt, putt of French machine gun—a German signal in their lines, and the wonderful night—the sky filled with stars." There was still natural beauty to behold; however, as the firing of guns and screech of shells became more insistent with dawn arriving, Harding retreated to Mandres: "At 3:30 walked through town and saw ghostly ruins on the early morning mist." Like Peixotto, he was discovering a bewitching, disturbing landscape.

With daylight, activity heated up as both sides harassed each other, and Harding watched two men die on the road before him. Taking out another sheet of three-by-five-inch paper, he scrawled:

The screech of shells again
The buzz of airplanes, the
mist in valley—the bright
sun overhead. . . .
ambulance shot through
2 men killed driver escapes.[21]

. . .

In the middle of May, a number of the other artists also visited with elements of the 26th Division, which had recently pulled out of Seicheprey, where the enemy had inflicted damage on them during the night raid of April 20. The division settled into areas surrounding Boucq and Ménil-la-Tour, the latter an ugly and dusty crossroads village that typified a Lorraine farming community.[22] It was void of architectural charm, houses and stables standing wall-to-wall but with room along the fronting road for a "treasure-pile of manure," Smith enjoyed remarking.[23] The adjacent barracks and supply depots built by the armies did not add to its beauty.

On May 22—a sunny, delightful day for driving through the countryside—Harry Townsend, thankful to start working to keep his mind off Henri, set off for Ménil-la-Tour. He was accompanied by Peixotto and the provocative Dutch artist Louis Raemaekers, their friend who had been creating emotional pictures of war victims and drawing searing cartoons of the Germans. His characterizations of the enemy as tyrannical oppressors bent on the destruction of civilization were so scathing that the Germans had put a 12,000-guilder bounty on his head. After lunch in town, a Captain Maris, who was in charge of an artillery battery, took them out to his position, which was adjacent to a twelfth-century château. On the road there, the artists realized they were under Boche balloon observation—the balloons hanging in the distance, omniscient and ominous—which actually gave them reason for a good chuckle: it was amusing to think that the Germans could have killed Raemaekers right there and then, if they'd only known.

Although the château had taken a few hits from the Germans, it was still in fine shape, with its heavy timber supports and parapets that once protected the crossbowmen. In complete contrast with this ancient edifice, gleaming modern artillery surrounded the castle and trucks filled its courtyard, a section of which had been turned into a corral holding some eighty-four asses. Tucked under a high road bank, out of sight of the Boche observation balloons, Maris's battery entranced Townsend just as the guns had Peixotto. "How wonderful they looked," wrote Townsend, "and how wicked—yet human—they seemed. They seemed alive but oh so patient and ready to be up and 'at them.'" So Townsend could make a sketch of it, Maris's men elevated one of the guns slightly. "What a thrill goes thro one at the sight of these monsters—conscious of their own power—lying there, serenely waiting—waiting for what, tho?" he continued in his diary. "Will it be first a German bomb—or will they manage to keep their position secret until after they have gotten in their own deadly work and have served most of their usefulness?"[24] These unknowns, this trying to imagine the dire consequences of war, were maddening to Townsend. Before they left, Maris hinted that in ten days' time or so, the guns would be moved forward for action. The anticipation of all-out battle was turning to an impending inevitability.

"On our way back," Townsend wrote in his diary, "we stopped in places along the military road under observation by Boche balloons, to search out with our glasses various well-known spots on the front— Seicheprey (where so many of our boys in an uneven fight went gallantly, tho perhaps foolishly, to their death—held under long gas concentration), Flirey, Beaumont, and Foret-du-Bois-le-Prêtre."[25] Why did Townsend feel somewhat cynical and doubtful about the relatively minor skirmish at Seicheprey? After all, it was being touted as a victory back home; it was spurring war bond sales. Townsend was referring to the apparent order to hold Seicheprey at all costs, which meant green boys going up against seasoned German troops. In fact, historians point to evidence that the doughboys there had required more training, and that it was a humiliating experience, even though they did indeed hold the town.[26] To gauge the soldiers' reaction to the skirmish, Townsend interviewed men with the 102nd and 103rd Infantry. As it turned out, the soldiers were solely concerned about the quality of their gas masks; they were cursing the English type and praising the French. According to soldiers in the 103rd's Company C, they suffered 20 killed as well as more than 130 severely gassed, a number that would have been far reduced if they all had had the gas mask. Other than that rather poignant concern, they had no complaints.

Unfortunately, on the return trip to Neufchâteau, the artists' car experienced three blowouts that left them with no spare tires. Naturally, there was no telephone nearby to call for help, so, making the best of it, they ate a hearty meal in a local inn while waiting for relief. As the artists endured their forced respite, they watched RAF planes taking off and landing at a nearby air base, the pilots flying on bombing runs deep

*On the Gas Alert* by Townsend. A prolonged gas attack was most feared; removing your mask for a bite of food or a drink of water could result in death.

into enemy territory. In the distance Townsend could see the "flicker of bursting shrapnel from archies," which was "weird and exciting." The very sound of the planes sent Townsend reeling back to memories of his brother: "How it brought dear old Henri back to me tho—for it was to me as tho the throb of his motor mingled with the rest. Then I'd try to realize the facts as I knew them, but no picture would come, and oh it seems he must still be here—doing his work that he knew and loved so well."

While haunted by Henri's death, Townsend remained mesmerized by the air machines. Always fascinated by mechanical devices and technology, he had paid his way through art school in Chicago by repairing McCormick reapers in the summer. Determined to focus on aviation, in a couple of days he would journey to Toul, where the 94th and 95th aero squadrons were based. At the airfield, the big news would be the appearance of what were apparently armor-plated German planes and the recent death of the American ace Raoul Lufbery.[27] On May 19, the thirty-three-year-old pilot had been dueling with a German Rumpler when his plane burst into flames. From two hundred feet, "Luf" fell from his craft and was impaled on a picket fence in the town of Maron, France.

Still on the road to Neufchâteau, the artists took a break in the town of Andilly, where Townsend learned that Elsie James—a well-known vaudeville comedian and the "Sweetheart of the AEF"—was to provide entertainment that night, so Peixotto and he decided to stay for the show. After a regimental band played a few tunes, her opening act, Elsie performed in an elevated boxing ring that the doughboys used to burn off energy. She started off slow: it was a cold night, and Elsie didn't want to take off her jacket, which hampered her performance. But then, once she started in on a few stories and song, she forgot herself, tossing her coat aside to reveal a thin black dress. The men roared with approval. Immediately after the show, she was whisked away to another event, her third of the evening. The officers went on to enjoy a dance, which explained the presence of the fifty nurses seated up front, the nurses imported for the event. Unable to stay for two-steps and waltzes, "Hard luck!" was all Townsend could note in his diary.[28]

As for other entertainment, Townsend soon realized that baseball remained popular even under the arduous conditions near the front, where the boys playing ball in their gas masks were a "droll sight." More surprising, among the doughboys there was professional talent, a discovery Townsend made on a May 24 visit with the 42nd Division near Baccarat.[29] When Townsend attempted to locate the 166th commander, Colonel B. W. Hough, to inform him that he would be sketching in the vicinity, he was told that the colonel was playing baseball. Already a fanatic fan of the game, Hough was further inspired because, under his charge, he had one Hank Gowdy. A major-league catcher for the Boston Braves, Gowdy was the hero of the 1914 World Series, during which he batted a remarkable .545 and led the team to victory. In 1917, Gowdy volunteered and brought his leadership to the battlefield. "Every outfit ought to have somebody like Hank," Colonel Hough commented. "The boys idolize him and he gets them all stirred up with his baseball stories. He helps 'em forget about the terror of war."[30]

. . .

Toward the end of May, Harding returned to the Beaumont-Seicheprey area on what would be a last visit with the 101st of the 26th Division before all hell broke loose. When passing through earlier in the month, he had caught wind of a raid that was planned for May 30, and he was determined to witness the event. It was being led by Major James F. Hickey, who had been given three hundred men for what would be the division's first large-scale raid. After having some grub at mess, Harding joined the other officers at an observation post overlooking the trenches. As darkness fell, there were no lights and all was quiet save for an Allied battery to the left, which was retaliating against an earlier German artillery attack.

At 2:30 A.M., the American artillery opened up. "Then it started in a perfect rain of fire from the sides and rear a half circle—the moon overhead like a star," the artist, who had retreated to the safety of a dugout, wrote in his diary immediately afterward. "The horizon like a dawn of red sky—like a thousand thunderstorms approaching—The noise like bursts of fearful thunder—yet we heard the whistle, whine, and screeching of shells—" As the Boche retaliated, a nearby camouflage net caught fire, and one shell hit so close to Harding that he instinctively ducked, for whatever good it would do. Just as quickly as it started, the batteries fell silent: "All this stopped and we stood in silence. The song of early morning birds. . . . and the raid was on."

At dawn, the raiding party, with white bands on their sleeves to distinguish them from the enemy, returned from the enemy's trenches; they had reached the Germans' second line. Harding noted that the lucky ones came out with trousers torn from barbed wire; the unlucky ones came out on stretchers. One boy had a thigh wound, another was missing his left hand, another had fourteen pieces of shrapnel lodged in his body. Their hair was disheveled; their eyes wandered. The aid station was crowded. Ambulances flew to and fro. Harding watched as one shell-shocked soldier started wrestling with an orderly and a chaplain, yelling, "I'm a Canadian. You're no Kamarade of mine, no mercy for you and let me go." Despite the abuse, the chaplain attempted to soothe the "now raving idiot."

After all the training, effort, risks, and casualties, all the men managed to bring back with them was "one little 17 years old prisoner—scared to death—poorly clad, round pink face, major leading him, crowd laughing." Yes, Hickey's Raid had become a bit of a tragic farce. The tragedy would climax at four o'clock that afternoon when some of the men, who only hours earlier had been behaving like a "carefree crowd" as they sipped hot cocoa supplied by the YMCA, started suffering from the effects of gas, apparently thrown over by American batteries. Someone was to blame, Harding surmised at the time. In fact, during the subsequent investigation, it was determined that American batteries had launched gas into the village of Lahayville, just over a thousand yards from where the doughboys had conducted their raid. It then drifted toward them and settled into the trenches, silent and lethal. While there were no recriminations against personnel, it was concluded that no one should go within two thousand yards of gas without masks; meanwhile, the French had claimed going as close as five hundred yards to exploded gas shells was perfectly safe under any conditions.[31]

To return to Neufchâteau, Harding hitched a ride in a rations wagon that rattled so loudly—the only suspension spring was under the seat and the roads were fiercely rutted—he would not have heard a shell explode right next to him. Some of the roads they covered were exposed to German observation, Harding noticed, with warning signs wisely posted on these stretches. The soldiers had their own names for the more harrowing spots the enemy took aim at, such as "Deadman's Curve," "Prayer Corner," and "Suicide Stretch."[32]

One of the last peaceful tours Peixotto took through AEF-occupied zones was to visit the 32nd Division in the Haute Alsace, a sliver of southwest Germany the French had managed to seize. The 32nd, which was an amalgamation of the Michigan and the Wisconsin National Guard, had arrived in France in February 1918, and three months later relieved French troops in the Alsace. They were the first U.S. troops to set foot on German soil and the first to contend with Germanophiles. However, any petty annoyances or disturbances caused by resident Germans would soon prove negligible as the division would fight in three major offenses and suffer nearly fourteen thousand casualties.[33]

Late in the afternoon they motored through a mountain gap separating the Vosges and the Jura mountain ranges and arrived at 32nd HQ in La Chapelle-sous-Rougemont. There Peixotto met Major General William G. Haan, a seasoned soldier with silver close-cropped hair, a prominent nose, and a fleshy face, who had trained this division back in Waco, Texas, and who would lead it into battle. Haan's aide-de-camp guided the visitors to forward observation posts in the towns of Ammertzwiller and Burnhaupt-le-Bas, under the vigilant eyes of resident Germans. At the outposts the artist climbed into reinforced steel boxes with slits through which he surveyed yet another devastated no-man's-land. Just as Peixotto was returning rearward, his car came under artillery fire—Peixotto's second such experience—as the Germans attempted to locate American positions. Eager to accommodate, dough-boys fired back with 240s. Having not heard these big guns before, Peixotto was surprised by the intensity of their roar, which set his ears ringing. It was clear to him that both the officers and the soldiers were straining at the leash. They were ready to do battle. They would not have to wait long. In a week's time, the German spring offensive that had been battering the British would take a change of direction and sud-denly break through the French lines protecting Paris.

Just five days before the Germans broke through the lines north of Paris, on May 25, Peixotto, along with Morgan, was again in the Alsace sketching elements of the 32nd when a motorcar carrying blue-uniformed French officers pulled up. The officers asked who the artists were and what they were doing. After receiving an explanation, the Frenchmen enthusiastically complimented their work and continued on. A short while later, in the village of Soppe-le-Bas, Peixotto and Morgan were standing on the front steps leading to 126th HQ when a scowling lieutenant colonel approached them in a forceful manner. He demanded to know who they were, so again they explained that they were official artists and displayed their passes.

"My God," Lieutenant Colonel Waldo exclaimed, "as if we didn't have enough trouble! They send us artists."

Peixotto attempted to enlighten Waldo—his first mistake—on the uses of their work, how it would aid the war effort and serve as a histor-ical record.

Belligerent to the point of being offensive, Waldo insisted that the use of artists "was no way to win the war."

Holding his ground, Peixotto then attempted to justify the artists' presence by telling Waldo that France and Great Britain had issued sim-ilar commissions to artists.

"That is why they are not winning the war," Waldo said smugly.

Neither Peixotto's captain bars nor his papers and passes held water with Waldo, who was so critical of the AEF's policy that Peixotto decided to report the incident.

On returning to Neufchâteau, Peixotto told McCabe, their assistant chief, what had transpired and he brought it to the attention of a higher authority. A formal investigation was initiated, and Brigadier General Louis C. Covell of the 32nd Division went into the field to personally interview Waldo. Naturally, the boorish Waldo stated that he didn't know what Peixotto's official capacity was until after their debate and he was sorry if it appeared he was being critical of AEF policy, because that was not his intention. He thought Peixotto was making the drawings on his own volition. On receiving Covell's report, Haan then wrote to GHQ that the "unpleasant incident" was "very much regretted" and Waldo had been "talking without meaning offense." Nevertheless, Haan admonished Waldo and sent his personal regrets to Peixotto. Meanwhile, through it all, a contemplative Morgan was appalled by Waldo's attitude; the artist truly believed the only hope for humankind and peace lay in the fields of science, religion, and fine arts.[34] It would be awhile before the artists again encountered the 32nd, and, when they did, the division would be in a bloody battle as it attempted to dislodge the Germans from the village of Fismes.

While Peixotto was still enmeshed in the Waldo debacle, for very personal reasons he found himself both excited and fearful: his wife, Mary, had managed to find passage to France. It portended either better days or disaster. Back in April she had written him the letter in which she reflected on their life in France before the war; she expressed concern over Peixotto being lonely at his Neufchâteau studio, for she knew how it felt to be "dreadfully lonely. . . . It is a constant dull pain;" and she hinted of her desire to return to their home in Samois-sur-Seine.

Determined to go to France—for her own sake and for her husband's—Mary enlisted the help of Peixotto's brother Percy, who was connected to the State Department. After pulling a few strings, the end of May found her in Paris, where she would stay several days before going to Samois-sur-Seine. There she would go to work in a hospital for wounded soldiers. "Someone is surprised," she wrote him giddily on her arrival, "but it all happened so suddenly." Fearful of how his fellow artists might react, she warned, "Don't say anything to your American Camrades about Mary's arrival. It might make them unhappy—and for what good." Later they could be told. Also, she asked her Ernest not to disrupt his work for her—they had to be patient in arranging a reunion.[35] While there would be certain benefits to having his wife relatively close at hand, it was a complication Peixotto didn't need; put simply, he would worry about her safety.

As if on cue, as Mary was moving into their old house, on Thursday, May 30, the Germans broke through the French line along a thirty-mile front between Soissons and Reims, located northeast of Paris. Initially, in hopes of drawing French troops away from supporting the British to the west, on May 27, German general Erich Ludendorff had launched this drive. When the unprepared French failed to blow the bridges on the Vesle River, they allowed the Germans to easily take Soissons and, within just a few days, push south to the outskirts of the town of Château-Thierry, which straddled the Marne River. As Ludendorff's troops unexpectedly and all too easily overwhelmed the French, the feint became a legitimate thrust for the City of Light.

While this lightning strike was creating a salient that brought the enemy within fifty miles of Paris, Pershing hurried to meet with Foch and agreed to bring American divisions into the Château-Thierry area for support. Once the line stabilized, they planned to counterattack this vulnerable German bulge, but first the line had to be stabilized. Meanwhile, with Paris suddenly within striking distance, the residents evacuated the city in droves, and there was serious talk of abandoning such outlying towns as Samois-sur-Seine. "Those were dark days—in many ways the darkest of the war," Peixotto observed. "While hoping for the best, everyone feared the worst."[36]

# 5

# A GRIM HARVEST ALONG THE MARNE

WITH THE GERMANS THREATENING PARIS and the AEF about to enter the fray in full force, Peixotto was desperate to see his wife, Mary. Who knew when he'd have another chance, or—having already come under artillery fire—if he'd even survive to again see her. After receiving permission, on June 1, he boarded the train bound for Paris, where he would find transportation to Samois-sur-Seine. When the train departed Neufchâteau, it appeared the journey would be pleasant enough, just he and a colonel in the compartment. Then, at Troyes, a full 105 miles east-southeast of Paris, they encountered the first wave of refugees—"forlorn-looking derelicts bound they knew not whither"—who feared being caught in the German onslaught. Running south and then westward to Paris, the refugees held hope that they would find protection in the great city, or they would continue southward to escape the enemy's bombers and artillery.

After a long delay, the train made slow progress to Romilly, where the flood of refugees increased dramatically. As the train pulled into the station, the people stormed it, clambered aboard, and crammed themselves and their pathetically small personal bundles into any space available. Then, closer yet to Paris, at the Nogent station, it was "the same sad picture—" Peixotto wrote, "the platforms a confused and swaying mass of humanity laden with every conceivable object: bedding, bird-cages, clothing, boxes, bags, and household articles piled into baby-carriages." Through the pervasive fear and despair, Peixotto could feel the presence of the Germans.

As Peixotto's train crawled toward Paris, it encountered outbound troop trains rushing soldiers to reinforce the shattered French defense hanging on along the Marne River. With the rail lines jammed, everyone at a fever pitch, it was 1 A.M. before Peixotto's train even reached the Paris suburbs—more than seven hours late. Just as he was congratulating himself for nearing the end of a long journey, the train was shunted off to a siding, which, Peixotto knew, didn't bode well. "Suddenly the heavens lit up," he wrote, "streaked with the tall shafts of search-lights. Innumerable new stars and constellations blinked and twinkled in the firmament and the barking voices of the antiaircraft guns told us we were in for an air-raid." He watched as the lights came nearer; it was like watching an approaching storm; the flash of lightning followed momentarily by thunder; the lightning coming closer, the thunder following more quickly. The anti-aircraft batteries barked. The train shuddered. The din grew louder.

Two women in the compartment started crying hysterically: "*Que voulez-vous; nous sommes des femmes!*" What do you want; we are women! But these innocents should have expected no different; they were not immune to war's effects. Even as Peixotto tried to reassure them, he, too, was terrified. He knew full well that nothing but a thin metal roof separated them from the falling bombs. And then the storm passed over, the flashes and grumbles growing more distant. That wasn't the end of it, however; a second raid soon approached, the crescendo building, coaxed quickly to a climax. There would be two more, a total of four attacks. It appeared the Germans were indeed intent on taking Paris.

Not until 3 A.M. did Peixotto's train pull into the Gare de l'Est, where he emerged into "the Stygian darkness of unlighted streets."[1] Later that morning he set out for Samois-sur-Seine, where, on his arrival, he looked for Mary at her place of work—Hôpital Auxiliaire 312 d'Héricy—but she wasn't there. No, instead she was at church, along with the congregation, celebrating God while the village elders considered evacuation. When Mary turned to see her husband in the church, it was a sublime moment: "You appeared like a knight of old before his lady while at prayer," she later wrote him. She felt so ardent, her heart throbbing after months of separation. The whole congregation sensed her emotional reaction and shared her ecstasy and exhilaration.[2]

The first U.S. troops to arrive at the tip of the German drive to the Marne River, at Château-Thierry, numbered all of fifteen doughboys from the 3rd Division, 7th Machine Gun Battalion. There were two stone bridges in town the enemy could cross in their push to Paris, so it was absolutely critical for the doughboys to thrust themselves into the breach at this pivotal location. Company A, led by Lieutenant John T. Bissell, lugged two Hotchkiss 8mm machine guns over the river and helped cover the retreat of fleeing French colonials, the Germans having flanked their left side. Once forced from their position, which occurred around 1 A.M. on June 2, Bissell and his crew attempted to fall back across the town's western bridge. However, the Germans, under the cover of thick white smoke, had already fought their way to the middle of it, forcing a French demolition crew to blow it, sending both attackers and defenders into all of eternity. For the moment, no one knew what had happened to Bissell.[3]

Amazingly, on the day Peixotto was visiting Mary, Bissell and thirteen of his men returned safely. Once night descended, they, along with other trapped American and French soldiers, crossed the second bridge, on the east side of town, which was still controlled by the Allies. Meanwhile, elements of the 3rd Division, under Major General Joseph T. Dickman, continued to filter forward to replace the shattered French, who were moving to the rear. It took an inordinate amount of time as the light Ford trucks ferrying the soldiers were overloaded, often driven by inexperienced drivers, and, in some instances, out of gas. Despite these impediments and coming under heavy enemy fire, they managed to dig in on the southern side of the Marne River.[4] The 3rd Division now stood between the Germans and Paris.

. . .

Although happily married and trying hard to be domesticated, the artist George Harding remained a risk taker. He was determined to get into Château-Thierry before the lines stabilized, to analyze how dire the situation was, and to capture the doughboys' first truly critical engagement. It was hardly what his older sister, Charlotte, also an accomplished artist, had envisioned all those years ago when she had so encouraged him to join her field of interest. On June 5, Harding, along with Aylward, Dunn, and Duncan, departed Neufchâteau for Château-Thierry, a journey into Dante's inferno.

The drive through the pastoral countryside provided no intimation of what was to come; for Dunn, the rolling fields and wagon trains reminded him of the upper Midwest plains, but soon nothing would vaguely resemble his home territory. "We went through wonderful country," Harding wrote in his diary, "fields valleys . . . whole fields red with poppies . . . daisies—wild roses—"[5] A caravan of French trucks rushed by, kicking up dust from the dry, crushed white rock roads; clouds rose and covered the "trees and fields like a white frost. Pass a platoon of French cavalry with a hundred Boche prisoners just captured over near Belleau. They are stolid types, some like professor with glasses, or short and stocky, all with coats off, shirts open, hands swinging, and all covered white like the fields." And then, as the artists neared the town's outskirts, the wonderful country suddenly changed: fields once red with flowers were now wheat fields on fire.[6]

Before coming under observation from Boche balloons, the artists' driver pulled the motorcar into the woods and they pushed forward on foot, until, from a point still three miles away, they were looking down on Château-Thierry, the town nestled in the river valley, the surrounding hills a great amphitheater. Laying in the grass, Harding watched shells fall on the town; he could see the blown western bridge, shattered and crumpled in the water. On the near side of the city, French and American soldiers were dug in; on the far side were the Germans. There were streams of anxious refugees, as the civilians in the Allied-occupied half continued to be evacuated. There was general panic. There was frantic chaos.

This scenery was the kind of truth Dunn was aching to explore. "War should always be painted from the point of view of the civilians," he declared; he wanted to live the war like the despairing refugees streaming southward.[7] He wanted to feel the anxiety of the soldiers as they threw themselves into the breach in spite of the dangers. The risks he would take at the front were necessary because he wanted to ensure that his audience would truly sense the experience of war. To record his impressions, Dunn had his burdensome sketch box; however, he was not interested in realism—making pictures of precisely what he witnessed. Rather, he would use his impressions to allow images to form in his mind; he would allow his creativity to shape reality, to make his statement on canvas. "The idea of the two old soldiers talking together is good but is not successful because they have no foil," he later explained as example. "In all things there must be contrast. Instead of keeping the old soldiers in the foreground it would have been better to have a little child all dressed up in fluffy ruffles rolling a hoop, perhaps, in front of them."[8] This contrast would add meaning; now there would be the innocent victim of man's inhumanity or hope instead of weary resignation. It was time to seize the truth of human existence.

Still pushing toward the outskirts, the artists encountered a startling sight: a big water main had been broken open by an artillery shell. "It was in the woods and nicely screened," Dunn explained in a letter to his parents, "and the water was spouting up beautifully, so some of the fellows took a bath. Personally, I didn't think we needed one, so looked on and explored some dugouts in the neighborhood."[9] Refreshed, the artists moved forward to within two miles of the town, where they came upon a machine-gun battalion's HQ. A Major Scott assigned them a lieutenant to take them into Château-Thierry itself, to the post commander of the 7th Machine Gun Battalion. Their driver followed French machine gunners roaring into town in a sidecar, but then the enemy caught sight of them. "Germans spotted car and shelled road 200 yards ahead of us all the way to town," Harding wrote. "We met Frenchman who yelled faster faster as cleared open spaces in road." As shells fell around them, they pulled under a tree grove and jumped into a ditch. Harding found himself caught in telegraph wire entangling the ditch and turned his ankle. Again moving forward, when they came to open areas, Harding wrote, they "ran with head down. Crouching—passed deserted houses—shelled, stretchers in ditch . . . automobile abandoned . . . helmets, then came to low place between road and houses—followed behind trees, tree to tree . . . houses on fire." As Harding looked around, it was if a tornado had swept through: houses were shattered, furniture in the streets, and broken tree branches scattered.[10]

In his trip around the world, Harding had encountered madness in
the marketplaces arising from an ancient past, cruel treatment of marginalized peoples in lands with no codes of law, and uncivilized human
beings still living the hunter-gatherer life, but none of that had prepared
him for the strife he would now witness. Determined to brave the current artillery duel and infiltrate the town, as recounted by Harding, the
artists and their guide cut into a neighborhood:

Keep to gardens and yards through lilac hedges—across ivy beds,
strawberry patches, lettuce and parsley. We separate to make the
break at irregular intervals across the road under direct observation
by the Boche. Machine guns pup-pup continuously. Beyond the
ridge behind us French 75's barking. Boche 77's coming in. The
front of a house falls. The intimate state of undress of a house just
hit by a shell. Rooms open up intimately—beds unmade—dishes
still on dining room table, pots still on the stove, curtains blowing
gently through the dust and smoke—flame. The French civilians
left in panic abandoning everything in most cases save the clothes
they wore.

While Harding kept under cover, he was astounded by the nonchalant behavior of a French general: "Down the road comes a French
Division General and two of his staff. He walks as if in Paris in peace-
time—cane in hand, helmet on, gas mask hanging. He vaults a low
hedge, picks a rosebud and puts it in his lapel buttonhole, picks two
more roses, and vaults the hedge again; gives one to each of his aides. He
does not see us fifty feet away walking behind a hedge. Maybe after three
years training I can do it too. Four shells in quick succession, then four
more bracketing the road. The French General sticks to the road."
Whether out of bravery or stupidity, it was clear that the French general
was snubbing his nose at the enemy, saying, To hell with you, Boche.

Harding located the machine-gun headquarters of a Captain Carswell
in a wine cellar—just one hundred feet from the Marne and just three
hundred feet from the Germans. Before ducking below, Harding studied
the remains of the western bridge: "Before going in I glimpse the blown-
up bridge, two maimed piers from which the arch springs—a gaping
wound in the center—like two shoulders each with the upper arm shot

off." In this war, even inanimate objects shared a human quality in their tragic wreckage. As Harding climbed down into the cellar, he encountered one soldier playing a violin and another playing a phonograph. Adding to the bizarre circumstances, a scowling sergeant was berating a corporal who was plucking a chicken. "If you'd a done what I said," he growled, "we'd have had that pig—now the French have it." Another soldier was milking a cow—the beast pulled and pushed into the basement for safekeeping. There was a certain common sense—efficient Yankee ingenuity—to the comic scene. Shelves in the basement were lined with champagne, wine, cordials, jams, and preserves—a veritable feast in the making. On a table flickering candles were stuck in empty bottles. While several soldiers were asleep on the floor, three U.S. officers were leaning over a map, discussing their plans to shift machine-gun emplacements during the night.

With holes having been blasted through the walls to connect the basements of the houses, Harding climbed through to the next cellar, where wounded men were receiving first aid. Cautiously, he climbed the stairs to the first floor. There a French lieutenant was looking over the books in the home's library as if considering what he might like to borrow—the surviving library a little piece of needed civilization. On the wall there was a map of the sector: pins with French colors marking their line and pins with German colors marking theirs. On the front door Harding discovered a scrap of paper: a note left by the owners saying they had fled to Montmirail.

That night on the Marne in the first week of June everyone was anxious and trigger happy as officers on either side continued to strengthen their lines. Mere shutter creaks set off machine-gun bursts. Meanwhile, the big guns continued firing regardless. "Toward Belleau Woods a barrage is being laid," Harding noted. "In front of us toward Mont St. Père on the other side of the Marne a couple of rockets go up, a sickly green line and then burst and silhouettes, for a few seconds, the shambles of what was once a farmhouse and mutilated trunks of trees— limbless but each limb on the ground mutely pointing to where it once belonged."[11]

As Dunn took in battered Château-Thierry, he could still feel the presence of the people in the abandoned buildings. In a letter to his parents, he wrote:

Then we went on and into a town where beautiful homes with furniture and clothing still in them were shot to pieces and ransacked, while still there clung to them homelike smells, and many traces of the careful labor of loving hands.

In some rooms that were still untouched except that the concussion shattered windows, the sound of the shells which came over every once in a while, seemed very unreal. Then the silence of the late afternoon would settle like an oppressive thing—no sound anywhere in the city—even the branches of the trees hung without motion or rustle of the leaves.

Bill [Aylward] and I sat in a beautiful drawing room and sort of held our breaths, for as I said to Bill, there seemed to be a regretful presence there.

To fully develop ideas for rendering the war, Dunn would spend a week at the front. The hardships in the trenches hardly affected this pioneer's son. In Dakota Country, he had helped his father clear the fields of rocks, he had plowed and planted, and by age fourteen he was as strong as a grown man. But he also comprehended that not every man, every soldier, should be expected to be as strong as the next. When his father had forced his younger brother Roy to work as hard as Harvey, it resulted in Roy suffering a debilitating respiratory attack. Rather than denigrating his brother, who was only a year younger, an angered Harvey punched his father square in the nose. Yes, he knew each man had his own limits, and he would bring that sensibility to the front; he would portray the soldier's vulnerability.

Not at all interested in a hotel behind the lines, Dunn stayed forward at night and followed the lead of the ripe doughboys: he did not bathe and he did not change his clothes. "I slept what sleep I got on the floor," he wrote to his parents, "one night in a school house, under a map of France dated 1789, so I might almost say I was covered with the dust of centuries—the rest of the time I slept on the stone floor of a wine cellar and in the corner of a barn." From the shelter of one building he soaked in the details of an artillery attack, which he found difficult to describe to his parents: "From a window in a shattered house I watched the bombarding of a city a mile away, the shells making their devilish and wonderful chorus as they droned by overhead, and the city disappeared in various colored smoke and gases. There is no use trying to tell you about it. Just can't be done, that's all!" For once, the blustery and garrulous Dunn was subdued by what he witnessed.

On exiting Château-Thierry, the artists and the doughboys followed a route that took them along stone walls, through clumps of trees, and across exposed wheat fields. "We then crossed into another clump of trees," Dunn continued in his letter to his parents, "and Fritz saw us and just trotted a couple of small shells of shrapnel and gas over. They fell short and we continued on our way, but the Lieutenant got lost and we found we would have to cross the hill with no cover on it, or go back the way we came. We said: 'Go ahead,' as the Lieutenant told us that the cherries were ripe on some of the trees on top of the hill, and they were remarkably big and good." Considering they were within easy range of German gunners who would relish an opportunity to fire on American officers, they didn't pause for long to eat the cherries. "I went over that hill in short pants, now I tell you. Of course it was a fool thing to do not the short pants, I couldn't help that—but going over that hill, as we were in easy range for half an hour before we reached cover," a flip Dunn wrote. "Then a Boche plane came over but paid no attention to us. I tried to make myself look like the trunk of a tree, but felt it to be a miserable failure. Fritz sent some more little bangs over, perhaps to hurry us up, but there wasn't any hurry in us; we just kept plugging along." In an exasperating conclusion to the trip, a bee stung him on his face and one eye swelled shut.

After this Sunday stroll in the park, in a rear location Dunn and Aylward were relieved to happen across a wine cellar converted into a dugout, in which they hunkered down for the night. Exhausted, Dunn fell into a deep sleep: "They told me next morning that the artillery shook the building all night, but I slept through it all." In a reflective mood, Dunn concluded his letter, "No, thanks, the exercise may have been good for me, but the experience was unpleasant, even if I did get a magnificent view of the whole shebang. Bill said he felt like a statue in a public square."[12]

Harding also retreated out of town for the night, finding a billet in a stable; for bedding all he had was his raincoat. The next morning after breakfast he again made the mad dash into town, this time following French soldiers through a trench, under a culvert, and then through a second trench—all the while under shell fire. He entered a château that was now a forward headquarters; it was also filled with loot, from swords to fine china, collected by soldiers. In the kitchen men were cooking on a gas stove, with garden flowers on the table, and in the billiard room men were playing billiards. In the yard, at a chicken coop, Harding could see that many of the chickens had had their heads blown off, yet, using the chickens, French soldiers bartered for whatever other food could be had. Yes, it was another surreal day in wartime.

A lieutenant gave Harding a tour of their machine-gun emplacements, and through glasses they watched German soldiers moving about across town. In spite of the regular bombardments thrown over by the enemy, as Harding toured the Allied controlled zone, he made his sketches. Invariably, whenever he set up with pad and pen, doughboys looked at him suspiciously and officers insisted on seeing his papers because they were convinced he was a spy. Germans had been taking uniforms off prisoners and dead doughboys and infiltrating the ranks; certainly, an artist was a perfect cover.

Townsend, Morgan, and Peixotto also intended to visit Château-Thierry to capture the action, but not until after Peixotto returned from visiting his wife and Townsend patiently finished a drawing of troops shipping

*The Hurry Call—Night of May 30, 1918, Toul Sector* by Townsend. In Neufchâteau, on May 30, Townsend captured ambulances and troops rushing to the front.

out titled *The Hurry Call—Night of May 30, 1918, Toul Sector* (see previous page). On June 4, a day when the 3rd Division was still digging in and repulsing the German thrust, Townsend, along with Peixotto, Morgan, and Captain Franklin Pierce Adams, a newspaper reporter working for the *Stars and Stripes*, departed for Château-Thierry in brilliant sunshine: "In front and behind us the road is a long white ribbon in the sun," Townsend wrote in his diary, "strait and inexorable as Fate."[13] Fate was with them on the road: convoys of heavy guns and supplies, of trucks and troops, intent on meeting their enemy.

Whenever there was room to pass, the artists in their National motorcar roared forward. They roared past prison camps where the Boche stared with vacant looks; they roared past "coolie" road repair crews who straightened for a look; they roared past wizened farmers behind their oxen in the field and young girls doing men's work. And then there were the scarlet poppies pushing up through the dust for a breath of air. Their path took them through towns and countryside that had witnessed the first Battle of the Marne in September 1914, the last time Paris had been seriously threatened, when the Germans had pushed to within thirty miles of the city before retreating to the Aisne River. "In fact," Townsend noted, "on much of the way up we passed over the old battlefields—marked here and there with reminiscent crosses, faded and dust-covered now—the once brilliant French *cocarde* on each washed with the rains and almost obliterated with the sun—and on top of all the dust. The places the very thickness of the tiny graves tells a muted story of the fierceness of the old battle. Dust! Dust are they indeed now. In a world of dust!" The crosses seemed to go on forever as the battles must have; the German graves as well tended by caretakers as the French. "Somehow it seems a wonderful resting place," Townsend wrote to his wife the next day, "there in the lovely fields in which one died—knowing that one would be cared for." He hoped that his mother would not insist on having Henri brought home, that Henri would be left in this peace with his comrades and honored by the villagers' memories.

It saddened Townsend to think that in the fierceness of the new battles these old battles were already being forgotten. Except for the crosses and except for those who knew the land before, knew that the once rolling hills had been flattened by merciless artillery, there was no evidence of the actual battles. The violence of the past, present, and future was all too haunting for him:

For the steady, the fierce incessant streams of camions loaded with every sort of munition of death—tearing frantically over these strait, heartless roads—as well as their same kind, empty, hurrying back—have beaten and churned their surface until the whole countryside is a veritable inferno of noise and a wilderness of dust, white and cutting as the alkali of the plains. . . . Dust, dust, dust! Till the human element in the great struggle forward and back, white with it all, seems to peer out at one with great cavernous eyes like ghouls, and the sudden opening of mouth creates at once a strange elemental mask, almost terrifying in its mystery.[14]

Also impressed by the ghostly scenery, Peixotto wrote, "Chains of camions, making an infernal clatter and din, thundered along at lightning speed, enveloped in sickening clouds of dust. Under the deep hoods their drivers' faces appeared, covered with a whitish mask of limy powder, spread thickest on their eyebrows and beards and in the wrinkles of their foreheads, until they looked like some strange creatures of the Nibelungenlied or men in the legends of the Norsemen."[15]

As they closed in on Château-Thierry, they encountered endless columns of French and American soldiers to be thrown into the line. There were even French lancers on magnificent horses who echoed the "knights of old" as they passed through a quaint town. In contrast to these knights, Packard and Mack trucks rumbled by at full speed, as did officers in fast cars and the ambulances—driven by dusty blond Englishwomen—filled with the wounded. And then there were "long trains of refugees for many miles," Townsend observed, "grey in the dust, patient-faced, leaving their homes for the second time to who knows what fate. . . . Many of them were smiling as they waved their hands at us as we messed, and always were the children gay. Little did they seem to comprehend the meaning of it all. Lucky they!" Whole families were on foot, and, with fathers conspicuously absent, it was the mothers who shouldered the bundles. They pushed wheelbarrows and baby carriages "piled to the skies with stuff"; they had carts carrying a half-dozen children, along with chickens and rabbits in cages; and they towed their cattle. While they were escaping the inferno, many seemed nonplussed, accustomed to it, and some even shouted encouragement to the passing soldiers, including the artists. Yet, when Townsend made drawings of the adults, the images were somber, the women with pursed

*Refugees from Château-Thierry Section* by Townsend. Refugees fought their way against the troop trains as they sought to escape the Château-Thierry zone.

lips, the old men hunched under wooden boxes hefted onto their shoulders. Townsend's rendering of the column of refugees juxtaposed against the columns of soldiers, moving in opposite directions, reflected the stark harshness of war but also made for excellent propaganda.[16]

Townsend, Peixotto, and Morgan spent the night in Montmirail—just over 12 miles behind the front—in the Hôtel Verte Galante, the rooms 3 francs a night, a very modest price for comfort considering the conditions in the trenches. The owner, a nervous man with a sparse waxed mustache and a beard, served them a fine dinner and wine. In contrast, Malcolm D. Aitken, a private with the 5th Marines, with whom the artists had already crossed paths, wrote that they were "living on cold canned tomatoes, cold canned beef and Argentine Bully Beef (French ration, in red or blue #1 size can.) The red one always had a slice of carrot on the top and was in demand, for it was thought better chewing."[17] And there was coffee, but god forbid they could get a warm cup of coffee; no, it was lukewarm slop by the time it reached the trenches. Aitken and his buddies would spend nights in shallow trenches dug with their bayonets and mess kit lids; "our graves" they called them.[18]

As Townsend and company sipped wine in the hotel, they were joined by a group of cameramen from the Signal Corps who had just returned from Château-Thierry and briefed the artists on the situation. The French had been driven back with heavy loss, so much so that when the Americans had disembarked from their trains they first had to move the wounded French. And apparently the French doctors had taken flight, so an American nurse was forced to care for most of the wounded herself. "And our men had arrived in the nick of time," Townsend recounted, "hurried there, as we know, by every means possible to stem the tide."[19] The cameramen also described how best to proceed toward Château-Thierry, how far they could go safely by car, and where best to view the panoramic battlefield.

To observe the Château-Thierry action, the next morning the artists drove to within the vicinity of soon-to-be-historic Belleau Wood, which the Germans would overrun and where the doughboys would shed much blood. They were directed forward to a regimental headquarters near the village of Nesles, where a runner was assigned to guide them forward by foot. Before they departed, it was made quite clear that their safety could not be guaranteed.

Pushing through the fields and woods, Townsend and the others climbed a hill just above Nesles; they climbed closer to incoming enemy shells, as the area was now home to Allied artillery, which was under Boche observation from two balloons. "These [75s] are firing regularly," Townsend jotted in his diary, "and over our heads there goes the intermittent whistle and scream of the heavies that we have passed as they go on their errand over into Boche lines. It all is quite thrilling to me, for it's the first time I have been so near to actual conflict." As they walked forward under the cover of roadside trees, "actual conflict" quickly lost its appeal.

A Cadillac automobile came hurtling toward them and swerved off the road. It was the Signal Corps moviemakers—their faces livid and eyes wide with fright. "I shall never forget the looks on their faces," Townsend wrote, "as they came rushing down the road and pulled up in front of us and told breathlessly of it—of how taking their car up farther than they should have perhaps, and then scattering and going on afoot, they had been spotted by the balloons, and little further on had been shelled vigorously." The moviemakers had then beat it back to the car, but the Boche shells followed them. One landed right next to the car— it should have done them in—but it was a dud. "We were pretty nervous over it all," Townsend wrote. "I know I was, for it was all new to me."[20] Just then another shell came whistling over and exploded in a neighboring field before anyone could take cover. That was enough for the merry moviemakers; they hopped into their motorcar and roared off in search of shelter. So much for their advice on a safe approach to the battlefield.

Delaying their decision of whether to proceed, the artists talked with a group of French ambulance drivers parked under the cover of trees. Finally, Morgan decided he wanted to try for a position on a hill overlooking the town where he might make a quick sketch. Peixotto also wanted to move forward. Although Townsend was extremely nervous about the German balloons hanging ominously in the distance, he agreed. They split up, single file, Morgan going first, Townsend in the rear. Several times shells screeched overhead, the mere sound prompting the artists to throw themselves to the ground. Diving into one bramble-filled ditch, Townsend sprained his wrist.

After walking a half mile, Townsend froze, completely unnerved. "My poor heart was trying to beat its way out of its weakening cage," he reflected in his diary. "Go on I could not, however much I knew I ought. Here to do the war and showing yellow, it seemed! But then it seemed a physical impossibility. I tried a few rods farther and had to give up. My misery then at finding that I couldn't make myself go, willing as my spirit seemed to be, under pressure perhaps, this, along with the physical agitation I was undergoing, was considerable."[21] Now he knew how the doughboys felt when going over the top—the paralysis involved, the absolute fear. This experience was all the more searing and confounding for Townsend in light of his brother's death. How could he be "showing yellow" when Henri had fought so gallantly? Townsend was unprepared for the emotions he now felt. He learned that civilians cannot possibly understand the emotions felt by men in a combat situation: the terror, bewilderment, helplessness, and, for some, anger. There was no becoming accustomed to it, either; any and every moment of battle could result in a nerve-shattering breakdown.[22] Townsend scrambled

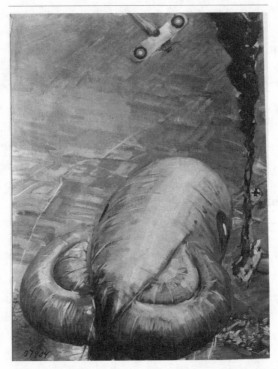

*Caught in the Act* by Townsend. Overhead, aeroplanes
throbbed across the sky as pilots dueled
and attempted to destroy the critically important observation balloons.

back to the French ambulance drivers, who were somewhat understanding and sympathetic, although they did point out that not one incoming
Boche shell had landed nearby.

Meanwhile, as Peixotto walked closer to the battle, a bullet zinged by,
snapping off the branch of a sapling just next to him. He remained in
the woods until stepping out into an orchard that offered a view to
Château-Thierry. From this point, a mile away, all looked relatively
peaceful in the valley. According to rumors, the town had been razed,
but there appeared to be little damage. At the moment, Allied artillery
was focused on distant hills beyond the city where German artillery laid
concealed. Incoming shell fire continued to whistle overhead, only the
shells didn't exactly whistle but rather made a "strange wabbly noise,"
according to Peixotto, a warning sound with which he was already too
well acquainted. Of course, Allied artillery responded to every enemy

*Northwest of Château-Thierry* by Townsend. American troops were exhausted from the grueling march to the front.

barrage; the guns would bark and then, in the hills behind Château-Thierry, there would be a puff of smoke where the shell hit.[23] Intimidated by the zinging bullet and only faintly stimulated by the vague battle, Peixotto beat it rearward quickly enough.

Only the more calloused Morgan, who in his early days as a newspaper artist had sketched suicides, murder victims, red-light cases, violent labor strikes, and train wrecks, was still out there, walking with his head down, resolute. He managed to push far enough forward for a good view of Château-Thierry, sections of which were actually on fire, the north side reduced to a no-man's-land. So, contrary to Peixotto's observations from a distance, the rumors of destruction were correct. Morgan made a quick sketch; but then, with little ground action to see—the main battle having already moved to the northwest of the city—he hustled back to the automobile. "You always lose your breath in running in gunfire," he said with a grin afterward, which aroused nervous laughter from the others.[24]

To follow the battle, the artists decided to relocate to the northwest, which would bring them closer to Belleau Wood. This time, as they moved forward, Townsend was "all keyed up—and overjoyed almost—at the thought that our guns and our boys were giving them such a hell as we all knew they were giving them." This time he allowed a somewhat perverse joy to displace his apprehension. As they closed in, they passed by troops hiding in the woods along the road while planes throbbed across the sky. Here Townsend sketched artillery trains clogging village streets and doughboys slumped against trees, rifles slung over shoulders and cigarettes dangling loosely from creased mouths.

Vigilance was absolutely critical because ahead of them, over the front lines, were six Boche observation balloons and the battle line was fluid, changing, no longer dictated by trenches. It was not a place to be caught flat-footed as the artists might. "We didn't have any desire to venture any nearer much as we would have liked to see the boys in action," Townsend wrote. "But it is dangerous down there—for in this fight up and down the lines—it's open warfare—not trench warfare. It's hand to hand fighting—from hill to hill or from tree to tree with machine guns, and their deadly fire in the open. But it's the kind our boys like. They hate the confinement of the trench and constant waiting. They go out into this with a shout and a rush—and while they suffer they certainly are getting results."[25] As the artists and the doughboys prepared to leave the area, two Boche planes roared in and fired on an American observation balloon. It exploded into flames. But not before the observer was able to jump from his rickety basket, his parachute opening immediately. It was quite a fireworks display as anti-aircraft gunfire exploded all around the retreating planes. A replacement balloon was immediately sent skyward.

That night the artists retreated to Viels-Maisons, where they enjoyed a decent dinner at the officers' mess and made plans to visit with the marines of the 2nd Division, the men they had befriended back in early May and who were moving through the area. In particular, they were eager to see Colonel Neville, Major Sibley, and Lieutenant Noble. Little did they know what these men would be experiencing the next day, a result of unanticipated circumstances that would inadvertently make heroes of the marines.

# 6

# QUESTIONED SACRIFICE
# IN BELLEAU WOOD

FROM THE RELATIVE PEACE OF THE worn-out Verdun sector, the 2nd Division had been ordered westward to relieve the 1st Division at Cantigny, a village located on strategic high ground well north of Paris. The 1st Division was in desperate need of some rest because on May 28, after a tense month of sitting opposite the enemy, it had attacked Cantigny. In the hours just before dawn, preliminary shelling commenced, followed by a full-scale bombardment to soften the German defense, and then, in the glorious morning daylight, the boys went over the top. They took and held this piece of real estate, but not without a price: two days of fighting resulted in 1,067 American casualties and 1,600 German ones, and the town itself was a complete loss. "At the end of the dispute over which of us should have Cantigny," observed the artist André Smith, who later arrived to make drawings, "there was very little of Cantigny to have."[1] While the 1st Division deserved a respite, the relief it so desired would not arrive.

*Lucy-le-Bocage* by Smith. After the battle for Lucy-le-Bocage, the only living creature found by the doughboys was a speckled hen.

Instead of continuing westward, on May 31, the 2nd Division received new orders and began a march toward a sector located west-northwest of Château-Thierry, where the situation was growing desperate. Comprised of over twenty-six thousand men with twin brigades of regulars and marines, they were now expected to assist the 3rd Division in plugging the holes in the riddled French defense along the Marne. As the men stumbled forward during a particularly black night, they could feel the ground under their feet vibrate from the pound of heavy guns. They could hear the thunder. They could taste the black powder. It was all the more infernal as French troops—the frantic poilus—stumbled to the rear, bloodied and proclaiming the Germans could not be stopped, screaming, "*La guerre est finie.*" Regardless, the Fourth Marine Brigade commander, James G. Harbord, set up headquarters in the ruined village of Lucy-le-Bocage, on the southwest side of Belleau Wood, which was a hot spot in the path of the German onslaught; in fact, the only living thing they saw there was a speckled hen running loose in the streets. "The Germans are shelling us pretty hard and the town is practically destroyed," Private William A. Francis, a twenty-year-old Texan with the

5th Marines, wrote in his diary. "A building on our right is burning, and as the flames light up the ground around us I can see dead Marines lying in the narrow road."[2]

Harbord conferred with a French general Michel, whose troops had been pushed back into the dense forest of Belleau Wood and the villages of Belleau, Torcy, Vaux, and Bouresches—all of which he would presently lose. Despite the thrashing he was receiving from the enemy—an impending apocalypse for the French people—Michel wanted to counterattack immediately. More even-tempered, the Americans wanted to form a line to stop the advance, hold it, and then consider options, which they did with expedience. In the center of the line were the 5th Marines of the 2nd Division, buoyed by Colonel Wendell C. Neville, who ordered his weary men forward at 3 A.M. Private Francis succinctly noted what they all experienced in taking up positions: "The woods we are going through is very dense, it seems impossible to make our way through, the limbs from the trees are hitting us in the face and the men are cursing like the devil. The line has been broken several times, it is very hard to keep closed up for men are falling into shell holes and old trenches and it is very dark. . . . The lines are so complicated that you are likely to run into the German trenches at any time." They were ordered to dig in; however, as Francis, a onetime store clerk, quickly discovered, a well-dug hole hardly protected you against artillery: "The Germans are shelling us very hard; a shell hit close by caving in our dug-out. A friend by the name of Burke was just killed, a piece of shrapnel taking his head off."[3]

Despite the fact that it was their line that had crumbled, on the night of June 5, the French again insisted on an American-led counterattack in the Belleau Wood area for the next day, demanded a counterattack that was blind, for no one knew for certain what the Germans had lurking in the woods. Not only that but the marines had neither trench mortars nor hand grenades in great number, both useful for knocking out machine-gun nests. The zone's French commander, Major General Jean Degoutte, had a simple plan: a two-phased counterattack that involved no strategy and all brute force. In the first phase, at dawn, the marines were to seize hillocks and patches of trees that faced the wheat fields stretching north to Belleau Wood. In the second phase, at 5 P.M., the marines were to rush across the wheat fields and take Belleau Wood, as well as the village of Bouresches, which sat on a strategic crest on the southern side of the wood. To record what would continue to be a

desperate battle to stop the Germans from marching down the Champs-
Elysées, the artists would infiltrate this zone and find out for themselves
just how hellish Belleau Wood was about to become.

While the first phase of the attack was under way on June 6, Townsend,
Morgan, and Peixotto—who had been on the outskirts of Château-
Thierry the prior day—pulled into 2nd Division HQ in Montreuil-aux-
Lions, just behind the lines. "As we arrive at HQ," Townsend wrote in
his diary, "a lone German prisoner is being brought in looking as tho he
really believed he was to be killed soon, as they are taught by their officers. This one was quite a young boy, and seemed so scared." He had
reason to be scared and would be interrogated with fierce diligence,
because the American troops were attacking and they wanted to know
what the hell they were up against.

   The opposing force was the 461st Regiment, 237th Division, part of
the elite German Army Group Crown Prince, but the actual numbers of

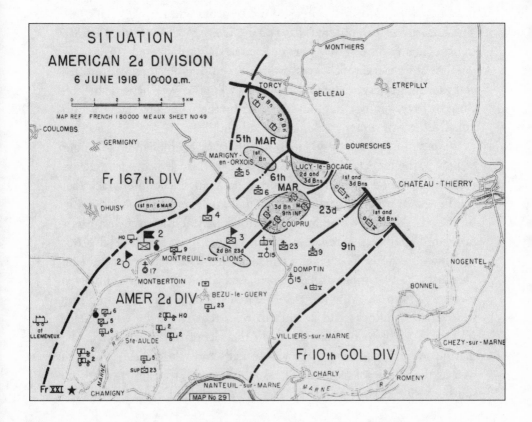

enemy troops involved remained unknown. In addition, the marines were also up against the wood itself. Belleau Wood was a little stretch that ran north-south, perhaps a mile in length and a half mile wide, with undergrowth made of small trees growing together in clumps to form thickets so dense they were impossible to push through. Towering above were birches, beeches, and oaks. The sloping ground was steep at points, running up to a ridge crowned with boulders—high ground the Germans now controlled. Between the thickets, the ravines, and the huge boulders, it was a veritable fortress for the enemy, with their machine-gun nests set up to deliver a devastating field of fire.

After the artists received permission to move forward, toward Belleau Wood, they drove down a road graced with big guns hidden in the woods on either side. It was into another nightmarish scene, yet

*Off Duty* by Dunn. Robust Midwestern boys were reduced to thin, ratlike creatures.

Townsend's nerves had steadied themselves: "Strange to say, I seemed a different person now. For some strange reason, I was thoroughly happy, gay in fact, and I seemed to get into the spirit of the Hell that we were then giving them." Why the change, why the awakenings of a blood thirst? There is, in war, a perverse delight in destruction.[4] Townsend was experiencing just that, for at his core, like other men, he enjoyed watching things destroyed.

The artists parked the car and continued on foot to a regimental headquarters, where they encountered a marine MP—a young man in desperate need of small talk to steady himself—who asked them eagerly where they were from. When he heard New York, the marine asked the artists if they remembered Johnny Baker, a successful jockey who rode at Belmont. They did, which pleased the young man—pleased him too

*Barbed Wire* by Dunn. In the attack on Belleau Wood,
American troops rushed across exposed fields.

much. Yes, the marine hopelessly desired to reconnect with his past life, with his boyhood, with his carefree life in New York. "He was one of those thin, rat-like creatures that the war has changed so many of our boys here into," Townsend noted. "One sees so many of them that have been thro much of the hardest of it. Thin faces, with staring eyes that look at you but thro and beyond; strange, patient, long-suffering eyes. Thin bodies trimmed down, as it were, to meet necessity. Thin legs that in their wrapped puttees give little mark for flying fragments or machine gun bullets. Fate seems to be trying to protect them as well as she can, till the thing is settled and they mean to see it thro."[5]

Townsend, Morgan, and Peixotto moved onward, along roads jammed with ammunition trains and troops, and through clusters of 75s that continued their steady fire. Just to their left an officer on horseback galloped across the field under exploding shrapnel. Just to their right a single shell killed twelve horses, their large bodies strewn about and bloodied. Above them observation balloons—the enemy's and the Allies'—filled the sky. And over the next set of hills, in a ripe wheat field, the doughboys were fighting their way forward to prepare for phase two of the counterattack.

With the first phase of the assault complete, at 5 P.M. the attack on Belleau Wood commenced. A half hour later, Major Sibley's 3rd Battalion advanced toward the woods, the two right companies cutting across the yellow wheat fields, where they were under direct artillery and machine-gun fire, while having little support from their own big guns. The marines would rush, halt, and rush again in a four-wave formation, rear waves stumbling over their dead comrades. They plunged ahead, as U.S. Secretary of the Navy Josephus Daniels put it, "until they, too, should be torn to bits."[6]

Bogged down on the edge of the woods and with casualties mounting, Sibley sent a runner with a message for the regimental HQ: "Unable to advance infantry further because of strong machine gun positions and artillery fire. Have given orders to hold present position at far edge of woods. Losses already heavy. Await instructions. Sibley."[7] Now under fire from all modes of weapons, the marines were being particularly hard hit by the Germans' trench mortars—these being four-foot-long aerial torpedoes packed with TNT. While consolidating his men and digging in, Lieutenant Noble's 83rd Company Headquarters

*The Hand Grenade* by Dunn. Dunn's artwork ran the spectrum of emotion from the heroic marines charging forward at Belleau Wood to the forbidding consequences.

was wiped out by a heavy barrage, only he and one other officer surviving. Throughout the night, chunks of earth and rock and tree splinters continued to spit through the air as bullets and shrapnel thudded all around the leathernecks.

On June 6 alone, the 4th Marine Brigade suffered over 1,000 casualties, with 228 men losing their lives.[8] Among the day's casualties was a friend of Townsend's: Floyd Gibbons, a newspaper reporter for the *Chicago Tribune* who had been imbedded with the marines. Gibbons and a Major Berry were cutting across a wheat field to inspect machine-gun emplacements when they came under fire. Berry was hit and went down. While attempting to crawl to the major's aid, Gibbons was also hit: two bullets ripped through his left shoulder and another pierced his helmet, going through his frontal bone and taking out his eye. It was an hour and a half before soldiers found Gibbons, conscious the whole time, with his eyeball laying on his cheek. "It must have been a strange and hopeless situation for a man to be in," Townsend wrote in his diary, "fearing to try to crawl back to his own relief and not knowing when other relief would come." The next day he wrote Cory that he thought

Gibbons to be a "fine fellow" and hoped his injuries weren't too serious. "But he need not have been quite so near the front," he observed. "But they are after stories for their papers—and are apt to want to go the other correspondent one better. They are a jealous lot."[9] Gibbons would wear an eye patch the rest of his life, a small price. As for the dead, their bodies would lie in the fields and woods for weeks under the hot June sun; they would bloat and ripen, until the war had passed by and the burial details took charge.

Having had their fill of the front by late afternoon, the artists returned rearward, fighting against the ammunition trains that continued to snake forward, man and beast, wagon and motorcycle fading into the twilight. At division headquarters in Montreuil-aux-Lions that night— while Noble and his men clung to edge of Belleau Wood—the artists washed down their food with champagne, and then indulged in song and stories with the other officers present. As they did so, they watched a German air raid against the town of Meaux; it was as though they were seated in a vast theater. The bombs, the anti-aircraft fire, the starry explosions. It was all very exciting . . . and safe, with champagne in hand.

The night was spent curled up with a blanket in their National motorcar, the artists managing to snatch some sleep until 3 A.M., when an emergency call came in to send trucks to the front. Apparently, the mounting casualties suffered by the marines were more than the ambulances could handle. All morning both trucks and ambulances rumbled by, transporting the wounded to the hospital, situated a couple of hundred yards down the road from where the artists were camped out. After breakfast, Townsend and Morgan walked to one of four field hospitals to visit with the wounded. "They certainly were a brave bunch," Townsend wrote in his diary, "and how the slightly wounded ones cursed to think that they were put out of the fight, and how eager they were to get back into it. The hospital was a pretty trying place, for they were coming in in terrible shape, some of them." Although surgeons worked around the clock, their aprons drenched in blood, many wounded died before they could be treated.

On June 7, Townsend, Morgan, Peixotto, and Smith found their old acquaintance General Harbord in a deserted farmhouse not far from

Montreuil-aux-Lions, where they received permission to drive forward to the regimental headquarters of Colonel Neville. He, too, was lodged in a farmhouse—"la Maison Blanche"—which had sustained shell damage and had a gaping hole in the roof, yet was still functional. As Smith made a sketch of the rustic interior, he reflected on the various headquarters he had encountered: "Army headquarters afforded an interesting study; they were as different as their distance from the firing line. The pomp and polish of General Headquarters faded into the less garnished military procedure and neatness as you went from Divisional headquarters to Brigade headquarters and so on down the lines, always nearer the bursting shells, into Regimental headquarters, and from there to Battalion headquarters and the zone of machine-gun fire and other forms of sudden death. Architecturally, the same progression was evident; you passed from a cluster of four-storied barrack buildings through rich men's chateaux, farm buildings, peasants' huts, to a hole in the mud twenty feet below air level." Fully exposed as he made his sketch of Neville's HQ, which was decidedly not twenty feet below, Smith was distressed to hear "that the Germans knew its exact location, and were in the habit of showing that they did."[10]

Neville was willing to give them a runner to take them into Belleau Wood, but he warned, "Go as far as you like, but be sure to keep fifty paces apart on the way out." So single file they set out through the "shell-torn fields and bits of woodland where the branches hung limp, snapped off by bullets, and where narrow paths were choked by fallen trees." They descended into a ravine that afforded some protection from the shells being lobbed over relentlessly. Scattered along the trail were piles of fresh earth marked by a stick or a helmet with a scrap of paper attached, a scrap of paper with a name scribbled on it—these were the shallow graves of men cut down indiscriminately.

They came upon a culvert, which carried the road across the ravine, its stone supports offering shelter for a first-aid dressing station. The men stopped to catch their breath and appraise the situation. As Peixotto gazed around, he pulled out his sketchbook: above his head was a great tree prone across the gully, cut down by a shell, and several wounded lay waiting to be carried to the rear, but it was the debris littering the ravine that caught his attention. There were bits and pieces of gas masks, cans, canteens, stretchers, rifles, cartridge belts, dented helmets, and bloody uniforms ripped off the wounded. There were tobacco tins, gum, cards, and torn letters from home. He reached down and picked up one scrap: on it a father had written, ". . . a son such as I have found you to be. God grant that you may be returned to that mother has and will be my constant prayer."[11] Where was that son now? Rather than the heroics of the marines, it was this scrap of paper that held Peixotto's attention and inspired his imagination. As J. André Smith sketched the scene, he, too, was drawn to the letters strewn over the ground, left by the wounded and dead: "letters . . . home letters, most of them which, in this dismal place of suffering and desperate need, spun their thread of contact three thousand miles away to where anxious people read bulletins and waited in dull suspense to have their fears abated."[12]

An ambulance pulled onto the culvert and the medics loaded the human freight as another company of stalwart marines marched forward through the ravine. The smell of blood and the bite of gray horseflies became unbearable for Peixotto. It was time to move on. They climbed onto the road, from where they could see the devastated area around the nearby village of Bouresches, which was still held by the enemy, and then dropped back down into the ravine.

Elements of the 6th Marines, including the 2nd and 3rd Battalions, were charged with taking strategically located Bouresches, but not until their fellow doughboys penetrated Belleau Wood did they attack. Not until 10:45 that night did the 96th Company manage to enter the village; what was left of it anyway. During the assault, whole companies were gunned down; when the 96th finally entered Bouresches, it had but twenty of its original hundred men. They were able to barely hang on until reinforcements arrived an hour later to secure their position.[13]

As the artists pushed around the forest's perimeter to the south end of Belleau Wood, it was relatively quiet because units were being shuffled to protect and strengthen the line. They found Major Sibley's battalion and joined him at his dugout to listen to his recounting of the attack his men had launched against the dug-in Germans. As they listened, shells whistled overhead, snapping off branches and showering them with leaves and wood chips. His men had been forced to wriggle forward on their bellies through the thickets so dense that two men could pass within three feet of each other and not know it, until they were close enough to charge the various machine-gun nests. When the marines smelled blood, and caught sight of the Germans still drunk from their

*Dugouts of the 5th Marines in Bois de Belleau* by Morgan. The shallow dugouts were affectionately referred to as their "graves" by the doughboys.

victory over the French, they couldn't be held back. The marines wanted revenge. Rather than just shooting them, if the opportunity arose, they used the butt end of their rifles to club the Germans over the head. Others bayoneted them. One crazed Irishman chased after a Boche for quite a distance, tripping over logs and underbrush, intent on bayoneting him, until a fellow American kindly yelled, "Shoot him." Only then did the Irishman drop to one knee and put a bullet in the German's back.[14]

As Sibley recounted the prior day's events, Peixotto was struck by how nonchalant he was in his storytelling. The soldiers simply thought of this battle as their first real scrap. Just a scrap. Yet, the Battle of Belleau Wood, weeks from being over, would take on mythic proportions in American military history. While Sibley and many of his boys were nonchalant, some of the soldiers didn't know how they had survived. One junior officer with the 6th Marines wrote his folks in Chicago, "To begin with, I still retain my good health, good looks and happy disposition, though how it happened I am at a loss to understand." In the battle he had lost two schoolmates and witnessed men go mad from the shelling: "Night and day they kept up that constant rain of high explosives and shrapnel. I have seen men go crazy and be taken to the rear, from the shells. Some are raving maniacs and others just follow where they are lead with glassy eyes and expressionless faces."[15] So not all marines were tough leathernecks, unaffected by the carnage.

As Peixotto looked around, he took note of the soldiers scattered among the trees, each soldier buried up to his shoulders in his dugout, like prairie dogs poking their heads out of their burrows. Some were cleaning their guns, some polishing their accoutrements, some brushing their uniforms, and some repacking their kits. To capture the scene, Wally Morgan pulled out a piece of charcoal and sketched quickly with jagged, flamelike strokes; but no black-and-white rendering could do the red-blood day justice. Not with the soldiers now doing their best to melt into the dirt and meld with the trees.

Peixotto suddenly eyed a rather strange scene: a small speckled hen was pecking about with impunity while the occasional hungry eye fell upon her. He turned to Major Sibley for an explanation. "Why, that's Lucy," he replied, the little chicken his men had discovered in the village of Lucy-le-Bocage. While she would have made a tasty meal, the men spared her and adopted her as the battalion mascot. Among the madness, the hen was a symbol of reassurance.

Once evening descended, the Boche bombardment intensified, so the artists decided it was best to retreat to Colonel Neville's farmhouse. During the perilous return, German airplanes seemed to hover overhead as they dropped their deadly bombs, and shell fire fell uncomfortably close, as if the gunners could view them from above. When they hustled into the farmyard, they discovered that a large shell had just burst in the courtyard, flattening the outhouse and killing a man. Their chauffeur was hiding under the car, half dazed, having no idea how he'd gotten there. Other men were busily stacking sandbags in the building's windows. By late evening the action was so hot that Colonel Neville gave the artists a specific order they had no intention of disregarding: "Beat it like hell!"[16] At 11:30 P.M., German troops attacked his marines in Belleau Wood but were repulsed through the splintering and crackling trees. This action was one of many thrusts and parries.

The night of June 7, a Saturday, an exhilarated and introspective Townsend wrote a letter to his wife and daughter, in which he noted that losses weren't too heavy at Belleau Wood, considering the number of men engaged; however, this observation contradicted Major Sibley's

*Soldiers of the Telephone* by Townsend. Townsend was particularly impressed by the composure of the soldiers who refused to withdraw when under merciless artillery barrages, in order to communicate troop movement to HQ.

assessment. The major had said that casualties were indeed heavy. In fact, companies that started 250 men strong were reduced to 50 or 60 men within days, and Sibley's Company D would have just 20 men left by June 15.[17] It would appear, after the first day of battle, that information concerning the tragic loss of life—suffered because the men were forced to cross exposed wheat fields without proper artillery support and to engage machine-gun nests without adequate trench mortars or hand grenades—was being suppressed.

In his letter, Townsend admitted to his wife the fear that had paralyzed him on the hill overlooking Château-Thierry. Clearly he had to talk to someone about the wrenching event, but none of his comrades were going to fill the role of confidant—Townsend could not show weakness to them. He concluded that the experience wasn't worth the risk and told her not too worry about him; he was "playing the game as safely" as he could and he didn't "mean to take any unnecessary chances." In a letter three days later, he again delved into his moment of paralyzing fear—a moment that deeply troubled his conscience. It troubled him all the more when he considered the average soldiers' bravery: "God how I'd hate to dodge anything—or play the coward tho' after seeing what our boys live and do here!" As Townsend ruminated over how short a time he spent in the front lines compared to the soldiers, he realized his chance of falling in harm's way was relatively insignificant. In this epiphany, he realized—acutely now—that as he continued to live his life, while many soldiers "go into the beyond," he must do so with dignity.

The soldiers appeared to sacrifice themselves with righteous courage, Townsend explained to his wife. "It's a fact that they are greatly impressed with the righteousness of our cause." They go into their last struggle "smiling" and, he wrote, if they come out wounded they are still smiling. It was mystical; it was as though God were smiling through them in their time of suffering. Many soldiers displayed a certain fearlessness, too; a quality Townsend desired: "And I find myself thinking and virtually praying aloud that I may think and feel as they do—not that I may fight in the same way—for I have my job to do: but this I may the better accomplish this poor task of mine. . . . There's no reason for foolhardiness or daredevilry—But there's little room for cowardice or chicken heart." He was trying to "fortify" himself. He was trying to "cast out" fear by reasoning through it. He had to adapt or perish spiritually.[18]

On June 8, Townsend and the other artists in his motorcar decided to return to Neufchâteau. It was apparent that there would be a standoff in Belleau Wood for the near future, therefore it was an opportune time to create some finished works for Washington that depicted what they had just witnessed. To escape the war-weary roads, the artists took a shortcut that brought them along "a really beautiful route thro a country that I am sure had seen no American officers that way before. Lovely little towns filled with children and cattle and sheep," Townsend later noted in his diary. "It was night now and they were bringing them in from the grazing."[19] Meanwhile, in the early morning hours—after a meal of corned beef, bread, and lukewarm coffee served in clay vessels called marmites—Noble and his men launched another attack, capturing but two machine-gun nests and little ground while suffering severe losses.[20]

Once back at the Bathoses' home, it was difficult for Townsend to sit down and begin work on refined drawings and finished pieces. For all he had witnessed at Château-Thierry and Belleau Wood, he couldn't put the images to canvas. While in the field, he had made a number of what he called "stenographic sketches" along with notes in a small book, yet, as he reviewed this rough work, it was clear to him that either he or his objects of study were on the move before he had half a chance to note the details—and it was the subtle details that would breathe life into his work. Frustrated by his inability to capture what was an overwhelming experience—to capture the scenes in a way that met his own measures of success—he felt his drive to create dissipating. Also, he simply wasn't in the mood; the notion of painting what he had witnessed was anticlimactic. He blamed it on his studio room under the Bathoses' roof; he claimed it wasn't conducive to painting. While he did have a fine view of the "nice old town," the sun's rays streamed through the large French window and this brightness did not make for good light. Townsend desired a far more subdued atmosphere, to match his subject.

*Vanquished by the Boche Plane* by Harding. It took great courage to go skyward in a balloon, which was defenseless against marauding pilots who relished the target practice.

. . .

In contrast to their fellow artists, Harding and Dunn had little desire to return to their studio billets, felt no responsibility to GHQ or to the General Staff, and remained in the field as much as possible to experience it all. In his June report Dunn wrote, "As a thorough intimacy with the paraphernalia of war is essential in the carrying on of this work I should like to spend as much time with the armies as is possible." That's exactly what he did. In fact, the other artists saw so little of him around Neufchâteau that by mid-June Harding was joking with Townsend that Dunn had gone to Italy.[21]

While with the marines in the Belleau Wood arena, Dunn played his harmonica to soothe their frayed nerves and he slept in makeshift shelters, as opposed to retreating to hotels reserved for officers. On one occasion he was so exhausted that he fell into a deep sleep in a ruined building; when he woke the next morning he found himself suddenly trapped between lines with the Germans laying down a barrage. He beat a hasty retreat. Undaunted by enemy fire, in early June he went up in an observation balloon near Château-Thierry and watched as the observer, using a telephone with a line running to the ground, directed artillery fire.

Dunn's frontline misadventures did not go unnoticed and were captured by the cartoonist H. T. Webster, who, in one widely printed drawing, depicted Dunn with a cigarette dangling casually from his mouth, at his easel as shells explode around him. In the cartoon, an aide to Pershing is saluting the artist and says, "Gen. Pershing p'sents his compliments to Capt. Dunn an' wants t' know if you'll kindly move your easel back a foot or two. We're gonna put over a barrage." Dunn replies, "Present my compliments to Gen. Pershing and tell him I can't move for an hour or two till I finish these composition sketches."[22]

Equally determined as his counterpart, Harding had a reputation for being stubborn and aggressive.[23] Also like Dunn, he did not have much success in his early years as an art student; in fact, Pyle had been reluctant to accept him as a student at his Wilmington school. But Harding persevered and he was forever after driven to make good. So, Dunn and he remained together in the hazardous Château-Thierry zone, and on June 7, they spent part of the day sketching in a village near Belleau Wood. In the afternoon, they hitched a ride on a truck heading toward Château-Thierry but came under shell fire. When a Boche plane spotted them, too, they jumped out of the truck and hid under trees. From there, Dunn and Harding watched as Allied planes soared in, chasing off the enemy, and shot down a Boche observation balloon. Harding proceeded to count more than a hundred Allied bomber planes heading on a mission behind enemy lines.

The two artists continued on to the edge of Château-Thierry, where they watched the action from woods overlooking the town. Near them, three French soldiers were calmly reading a newspaper when shells came whistling in. Both Dunn and Harding dove into a thicket, while the Frenchmen called over calmly, "Es'ce la guerre." In talking to them, the artists learned that the French were expecting the Boche to attack, an assault to be proceeded by gas. It was an unsettling night for the artists, and when a fierce enemy barrage came over at 3:30 A.M., they retreated to Bar-le-Duc, located well behind the lines.

Having come under fire a number of times now—and having experienced many near misses—Harding was quickly becoming a fatalist. "If your name's on the shell," he said, "you get it; if your name's not on the shell, you don't. The shell you heard never got you; it was the shell they didn't hear killed men."[24] He also felt confident that luck was on his side; he had since his youth. Such was the case when as a twenty-four-year-old he was on an expedition to the Arctic, sailing aboard the *Grand Lake*, when the ship became caught in an ice jam. The boat was crushed, but Harding and the crew escaped; they drifted on the ice floe for three days before being rescued. Lucky to be alive then and now, the artist reflected, "They used to say that if I fell down a sewer in a pair of overalls I'd come up wearing a pair of white flannels."[25]

By mid-June, it was certain that the marines were not going to relinquish Belleau Wood and that the American troops had saved Paris, the latter a fact acknowledged by the French and emphasized by Townsend in a June 16 letter to Cory. On the same day, Mary Peixotto wrote to her husband from Samois-sur-Seine, where there was no longer the nagging fear that they may have to evacuate: "Dear—it is as beautiful a day today—the pain and anxiety of the trial of evacuation has passed for the present—and the people are believing strongly that this martyrdom will not be theirs too." With Mary's entire days spent at the hospital, she understood the meaning of martyrdom, as well as the permanent sadness occupying the citizens' lives: "Last night my poor little French neighbor cried her eyes out to me," she wrote, "about the sadness of her life." To survive emotionally, Mary understood that she could not become obsessed by the war, and she hoped that if she involved her neighbor in "a real activity she would feel better." Real activities—gardening, sewing, baking—offered some degree of normalcy to her shattered existence.

As for Mary, she, too, needed a diversion from the war and was greatly relieved when she was summoned to help a young lady in town give birth; the mother-to-be was so poor she couldn't afford a nurse let alone a doctor to help with the delivery. While the birth of the child was a joyous occasion, it was tempered by the fact that the woman's husband was a French officer at the front who could not get permission to come home—a commonplace situation. To fortify herself emotionally at the hospital, Mary Peixotto carried her husband's letters around in her pocket. The pages became scarred and soiled, but she kept them with her, their presence a comfort.[26]

To promote the American success to its fullest, the Signal Corps propaganda moviemakers, who had run for their lives at Château-Thierry, quickly pieced together a film wrought with courage. It was tentatively titled *America's Answer to the Hun*. Before shipping the film to the United States, where the Committee on Public Information would distribute it, they held a screening at GHQ in Chaumont over the weekend of June 21–22, to which Townsend and the other artists were invited. To get the adrenaline flowing, the film opened with the big guns blasting away, but then the moviemakers brought the audience back to the embarkation in Hoboken, New Jersey, from where they followed the troops to their fateful battle in Château-Thierry. At this climactic point, the film naturally included "the undying gratitude and everlasting praise of the French" for the doughboys who saved Paris.[27]

While the likes of Pershing were viewing the propaganda movie, American forces were still mired in Belleau Wood. On June 23—the day after the merry moviemakers had debuted their film—the 3rd Battalion, 5th Marines, launched another assault only to again suffer terrible losses, with more than two hundred ambulances needed to evacuate the wounded. Two days later, the French brought forward enough artillery to flatten the woods. The bitter fighting now reached cruel proportions— no prisoners were to be taken—and on June 26 the marines at last cleared Belleau Wood of the enemy.

On the day the Germans were vanquished, Dunn and Peixotto returned to Belleau Wood to record all that remained of the victory. Where there had once been lush woods, there now were leafless, blackened stumps and scarecrows. After twenty days of fighting over this piece of land, total American casualties were almost ten thousand, with over eighteen hundred losing their lives.[28] One of the survivors of the 5th Marines was Private Malcolm Aitken, who, in a letter home, bluntly described burial detail: "Alas only a few are left of the gang. We buried skads of them this morning, some very badly composed as they had been in the hot sun for two days. They were bluish-black in color and the odor beggars description. It was a job and a half to get their dogtags and personal effects. Took quite a time. After laying them side by side forty or so to a 6ft trench we stood with uncovered heads while the service, short and to the point was recited."[29]

What could be used for propaganda here? Nothing as far as Townsend was concerned; the slaughtering of troops weighed heavily on him. More than a month after the battle for the woods concluded, he was watching a burial detail in the vicinity of Château-Thierry that prompted him to reflect on Belleau Wood, which was still littered with the dead. "One dreads to think of the time when they finally get around to cleaning up Belleau Wood!" he wrote in his diary. "If they ever do. Some say they are not to; others, that they will wait till it's old history then they can go in and get the identification tags. What a thought, tho now one can't approach the place, for we tried the other day."[30] The many ripening corpses patiently waiting to be buried were not the only hindrance to touring the zone: the Germans still held several pivotal villages in the vicinity of Belleau Wood that had to be retaken before Paris could unequivocally be declared safe.

# 7

# THE DESPERATE
# PEACE OFFENSIVE

IF AMERICAN FORCES WERE GOING TO SECURE the front along the Marne River, if they were going to take back vital Château-Thierry, first they had to seize two strategic points located between Château-Thierry and Belleau Wood: the village of Vaux and Hill 204. Vaux was situated on the important Metz-Paris road, a strategic artery, while the adjacent Hill 204 provided an all-too-pleasant view of the area for the enemy's artillery. If these crucial targets could be taken, the Germans in Château-Thierry would be virtually cut off. Of course, Ludendorff was hardly interested in relinquishing his prizes; to the contrary, come mid-July he intended to press home his gains by launching what he would call his Peace Offensive—an offensive so overpowering that it would force the Allies to sue for peace.

So, as was the case at Belleau Wood, the Germans—the 402nd Infantry Regiment and supporting units from the Army Group Crown Prince—would not go quietly into the night. In the stout village of Vaux, the Germans had fire-slotted its many stone walls, their deadly machine guns covering all approaches. But the Americans had one vital weapon: the village's stonemason, who had built or repaired so many of the homes he was able to provide priceless information. He mapped out the village's eighty-two houses, including floor and cellar plans and even the thickness of various walls. In addition, German prisoners were interrogated, and captured documents were examined to determine where the Boche had their defenses. In assaulting the village, elements of the 2nd Division would again lead the charge, while, in concert with this attack, the French would storm Hill 204.

At 5 A.M. on July 1, Allied artillery began to sporadically hit areas in and around Vaux, hoping that this drifting movement of the guns would not alert the Germans to the impending ground assault. Then, at 5 P.M., artillery reached its maximum intensity as the infantry took attack formation, and an hour later the rolling barrage commenced, moving forward a hundred yards every two to three minutes. The doughboys followed closely behind, until finally storming the village, where they discovered that the artillery gunners had achieved their goals with deadly accuracy. Houses were flattened. Machine-gun nests were destroyed. Shell-shocked enemy soldiers had been driven into cellars. Any German combatants still alive were quickly killed in the furor or taken prisoner. On Hill 204, however, success eluded the doughboys' French partners: at the end of the day, the Germans still held the ridge, tenaciously awaiting an encore.

Nestled in a gentle valley, with some two hundred residents living in fortresslike stone houses with lovely gardens, Vaux had been a picturesque village that inspired writers and painters touring the countryside. No longer. When Townsend arrived shortly after its capture, he immediately labeled it the "most wrecked place" he had yet to observe. In fact, one of his pieces resulting from his work at Vaux that was forwarded to Washington was simply titled *Vaux: Shapeless Mass of Masonry*. The climax of the Allied artillery had been so intense, he was told, that it took a mere twenty minutes to level the town. Now a rock pile with its perimeter pockmarked with shell holes, it was beyond repair. It was an amazingly sad sight: "The trees lining the road on both sides of the town are mute witnesses to their sufferings, too, from the shells. Great trees torn off at all heights. Some clean cuts; others sort of torn off, leaving an

*A Village Near Neufchâteau* by Smith. The artists greatly appreciated the beautiful French villages that had yet to be molested by the war.

*Mont St. Pere* by Aylward. If village dwellings were thoroughly devastated by battle, stones were carted off to rebuild roads rather than repair the homes.

effect on the end of the bruised stump not unlike a frayed-out broom."
While Townsend was sentimental in reflecting on the destruction, the
more cynical and perhaps more objective artist André Smith concluded
that the village "was hardly worth considering" in light of the fact that
Paris was at risk. Even so, Smith felt moved enough to sketch the ruins.[1]

Beyond the village, Townsend walked along a railroad bridge that
had been very costly in taking—he had to pick his way through prone
bodies lying awkwardly across the tracks. At a nearby house guarding
the bridge's far side, he discovered a group of dead German machine
gunners who, before meeting their own end, had cut down the many
doughboys scrambling over the bridge in eager pursuit of an enemy in
retreat. At the next crossroads Townsend turned left and came across
more American corpses. And the dead would remain there for as long as
three weeks, until burial details found time in their schedule.

Returning to Vaux proper, Townsend introduced himself to the
French officers—including General Champ of the 52nd Cavalry Division, now in charge of the village—and, displaying his flimsy paper pass,
stated his purpose. He then set up his easel, for the absolute ruins had
caught his attention, as they would all of the artists'. But then, just as he
immersed himself in his drawing, there was a tremendous explosion.
Pieces of rock and shell fragments showered down on the shocked
Townsend, who quickly determined it had come from behind the general's HQ. "I left my easel where it was and made for the house,"
Townsend wrote in his diary, "thinking it had struck there, and wonder-
ing what fate had befallen the general." As Townsend came rushing in,
the French soldiers found a fair amount of humor in his frantic behavior. They had neglected to tell him they were exploding duds, this latest
involving two 75s only fifty yards from where he was working. When he
showed them how the debris had showered down on him, they turned
serious—all the more so when one of their own lieutenants came in with
a piece of shrapnel buried in his cheek. Afterward they invited the artist
to lunch to make amends. There was almost nothing a solid meal failed
to heal, even in wartime.

When Townsend again settled behind his easel, he took stock of the
village: "There are some very stirring pieces of ruin in Vaux . . . and
there isn't the slightest thing to indicate where the church once might
have been that I could discover." A church gone missing—this was
troubling. "There are certainly some tremendous shell holes there in

town," he jotted down. "Most of them are partly filled with dirty, yellow water from mustard gas, and many of the walls that stand are stained a bright canary yellow where they have been hit by mustard shells that were thrown into town." From one shell hole, two legs stood straight up in the air; apparently a German had fallen into it headfirst.[2]

Transfixed by the intense morbidity, Townsend would return to Vaux several times in July as he became increasingly obsessed with and mortified by the devastation. On one trip later in the month, he found a scene of ruined buildings and gardens that inspired him in particular—the way the sun hit it—and started a large sketch in oil. Once behind his easel, however, Townsend could muster no enthusiasm for his subject. Not only had he been suffering from the grippe for almost a week, but the unburied dead were wreaking havoc on his sensibilities: "Then, too, the dead around are beginning to make their presence felt and a number of them are still buried in the debris so that one doesn't quite know what the odor is at first." It shocked Townsend how quickly the bodies began to decompose; in some cases the flesh turned black in forty-eight hours. Particularly disturbing were three rotting doughboys who had been lying in an old house for three weeks—apparently passed over by burial details—until the French assumed the responsibility.

While in Vaux, Townsend met three doughboys burying one of their buddies who had been shot while chasing a Boche up an embankment. As they told the story, he could feel their pain as he heard their voices breaking and watched the tears swelling in their eyes. He watched another American burial detail—"one white in charge of two colored" wearing gas masks to stave off the putrid fumes—dispose of the numerous dead horses lying alongside the roads. Townsend noticed that the French officers were quite amused watching these men pull and push the abused, stiffened beasts. Displaying an acrid sense of black humor, the Frenchmen told him how they had discovered a dead forty-five-year-old woman in the basement of one of the houses. On inspection, the doctor had concluded that she had been dead for only about four days, dead from starvation, which indicated that she had been hiding there for some time, no doubt having sought refuge from the initial Allied shelling. Weeks after she could have emerged into safety, she remained concealed, until her death. It was so absurdly tragic that it did indeed have a comic element.

The next morning Townsend had to impel himself to finish the work he had started in Vaux. Not only was the stench there becoming too much for him, but he was also becoming too immersed in the soldiers' personal stories and accompanying agonies. While working on his oil sketch, he had to vomit several times. "Finally a poilu who is burying as he finds," he wrote, "discovers a Boche about ten feet back of me and pulls him out and leaves him while he digs, so I pack up my things and decide that my sketch is finished!"[3]

As Townsend was struggling to find inspiration among the ruins of Vaux, one of his heroes, John Singer Sargent, had left London and was on his way to the battlefields in northwest France, hoping to find magnificent material with which to work. Later, aware that the revered artist was in the field, Townsend would lament that Sargent was not with them to paint portraits of the high command. But Sargent wasn't interested in portraiture; no, he was on a mission to capture drama, specifically to capture British and American forces fighting in concert.

In the twilight of his career, Sargent had settled into a pleasant routine: the winter, spring, and early summer were dedicated to his London and Boston studios; late summer and early autumn were dedicated to trips abroad, during which he focused on painting landscapes. That routine included a summer 1914 trip to the Tyrol, during which Sargent appeared to be oblivious to the events that had been swirling around him, because when war broke out, he was caught in Austria, which had closed its borders, without a passport. He was briefly detained and his work confiscated. Fortunately, Sargent and five friends managed to make it to the relative safety of Colfuschg, high in the Dolomites. There he settled down while waiting for his emergency application for a passport to go through at the U.S. embassy in Vienna, which it did in November.

Sargent then returned to London, where he made his first political statement concerning the war. Following the German torpedoing of the Lusitania on May 7, 1915, which took 128 American lives, Sargent made a public anti-German statement by returning a decoration conferred upon him by the kaiser. Increasingly distressed by the war, soon he would be selling his artwork and engaging in other projects to benefit the Red Cross, which was frantically aiding war victims. In March 1916, Sargent returned to Boston to continue his mural work—a total of fifteen panels—which the relatively new public library had commissioned, a project initiated in 1890 when he first submitted designs. In stark contrast to the violent situation Europe found itself in, the central theme of the murals was the history of religion—the enlightened side of its history, anyway. The project's name was *The Triumph of Religion*, and Sargent's work—in metal, paper, jewels, and oil—was masterful. However, the artist was drawn ever more to the war.

In 1916, Sargent wrote a friend, "If the accursed is still going on . . . I shall feel tempted to have a look at it. . . . But would I have the nerve to look, not to speak of painting? I have never seen anything in the least horrible—outside my studio."[4] As far as Sargent was concerned, "Rome was burning" and he wished to play witness.[5] Still, while war raged through the next year, Sargent continued with his murals and made portraits of John D. Rockefeller and President Woodrow Wilson, among others. Finally, in the spring of 1918—at the same time the AEF artists were shipping off to France—he decided to return to London. This decision was inspired not only by the death of his niece but also by a letter from Alfred Yockney, the secretary of the War Artists Memorial Committee, of the British Ministry of Information. The ministry was inviting Sargent, among other renowned artists, to venture to France and make commemorative pieces of the war.

At first Sargent hesitated to accept the invitation, but then, on May 16, he received a letter from the British prime minister, D. Lloyd George, encouraging him to do so. Surely, the prime minister had more pressing engagements; however, his influence did carry the day. Sargent accepted and excitedly wrote his friend and patron Isabella Stewart Gardner, "I hope to have the chance of being well scared."[6] The commissioned projects would be housed in the to-be-constructed Hall of Remembrance. Specifically, the Memorial Committee wanted Sargent to record "the fusion of British and American forces." It was to be an epic piece on a twenty-by-eleven-foot canvas. Along with his marching orders, he was given a modest three-month spending allowance, which, of course, would not suffice. The man was accustomed to the finer things and to taking his time. And although Sargent was under contract to—an employee of—the British government, he would largely ignore their orders and do as he pleased. He would travel widely across the front and make many sketches. Like the AEF artists, he wanted to see "the more rugged side of the war . . . the real thing in regard to warfare."[7] If he truly wanted to see the rugged side, however, he was going to have to forsake the posh living—no easy task.

As one Sargent biographer noted, from the moment Sargent started for the front "the whole enterprise was glazed with comedy."[8] To begin, what to wear was one pressing issue. Sargent elected to dress in khakis and boots, and sported a splendid belt buckle—all of which prompted one observer to note that he looked like "a sailor gone wrong." And then there were his big white sketching umbrella, books, camp stool, easel, and extensive painting supplies, all to be lugged around in spacious trunks. Clearly, this celebrity painter would not suffer for proper equipment like the AEF artists. When Sargent departed for France on July 2, 1918, he was accompanied by the British painter and now combat artist Henry Tonks, whose job it was to prepare Sargent for a radical change of circumstances. However, when Tonks attempted to educate him in military ways, Sargent either couldn't grasp the notion of a regimented existence or he simply didn't give a damn. His obliviousness or disregard was apparent when he was in the field sketching and a British guardsman leveled his rifle at the bizarrely dressed artist and demanded identification. Completely ignorant to the names of ranks, Sargent calmly gave his name as though the soldier would recognize who he was. "The Hell you are!" said the guardsman. "I know the sergeant. Come along."[9]

Despite his comical appearance and indifference to military protocol, he was treated with great respect, and, at British headquarters, Major Sir Philip Sassoon, private secretary to Field Marshal Sir Douglas Haig, commander in chief of the British armies, took charge of Sargent.[10] This coddling experience was in stark contrast to Peixotto's encounter with the caustic Colonel Waldo. In part, it was because the Europeans had a much greater appreciation of art than their American counterparts. Like Tonks, Sassoon also attempted to instruct Sargent regarding the ways of war, but he, too, made no progress. Sassoon did arrange for a joy ride in a tank, during which they went up and down slopes, and over trenches, "looping the loop generally," Sargent wrote to a friend. When they passed by a row of obsolete tanks, it reminded him of "the ships before Troy."[11] Troy was once a great Greek city in northwest Asia Minor destroyed by Agamemnon, according to legend, and, in Sargent's mind, the parallel was clear: civilization itself was under attack.

After his visit with headquarters, on July 4, Sargent ventured toward the front, motoring to Bavincourt, some twenty-five miles south of Arras, located in northwestern France. There Sargent was passed onto Major

General Sir Geoffrey Fielding, who quickly found out what he was in for when, in all seriousness, Sargent asked him if the war stopped on Sundays. Fielding assigned Sargent to a billet in a steel tube buried in the ground for protection. On July 13, he and Tonks motored to the forward zone, in hopes of witnessing dramatic action, but the great Sargent now discovered what the AEF artists had already learned: trench warfare offered little in terms of visual grandeur. And to boot, he couldn't find any American troops, let alone any working side by side with the British. "It's hard to see anything really significant in warfare," he wrote with frustration in his diary.[12]

Eventually Sargent would link up with the U.S. 27th Division, one of the few divisions the AEF artists did not follow, and observe them in action; however, he would again be disappointed. And when Sargent did stumble across the epic he was looking for, it would be the antithesis of what the British Ministry of Information desired.

On the heels of saving Paris and their Belleau Wood victory, American soldiers showed little restraint in celebrating July 4 in scorching hot weather. To record the festivities in Paris, which included plenty of warm beer and bare-knuckled brawls, Peixotto traveled to the city. He then snuck off to Samois for a visit with Mary.[13] A few days after her husband left, she traveled to Paris to celebrate July 14, Bastille Day, the French day of independence. While she was there she hunted down cigarettes, a valuable commodity, for her husband, and she enjoyed some real butter with her bread, a newsworthy event that she relayed to Ernest. However, such small pleasures did little to alleviate the collective pain of the war; as a nurse, she was becoming more involved with the soldiers' suffering.

The toll on Mary was evident when while in Paris she became emotionally attached, albeit briefly, to two American soldiers. She and a friend were standing on rue Royale to see the Bastille Day parade when they saw two American soldiers "looking so bewildered" that her friend beckoned them over. The soldiers explained that it was their first time in Paris, having just arrived that morning from the Château-Thierry area. With only a day pass, they would have to return that evening. Feeling sympathy for the boys, who were both volunteers from Sacramento, Mary treated them to lunch. Afterward, she gave them a map of Paris and sent them on their way, but she couldn't let go of the soldiers. "I am fearful—and such blue eyed dear boys!" she wrote her husband. Such innocence thrown into war distressed her. Her concern for the "blue eyed dear boys" would increase incrementally in the coming hours when Ludendorff launched his Peace Offensive.[14]

After having had a good taste of battle in June, Townsend and Morgan, along with their assistant chief, Colonel McCabe, also treated themselves to a sojourn in Paris for Bastille Day. They stayed at the upscale Hôtel Régina, where rooms were a pricey 17 francs a night, but baths and breakfast were included. On the morning of July 14, they went to the Red Cross Headquarters, on the corner of rue Royal and the place de la Concorde, for balcony seating that provided an excellent view of the parade. From the balcony, they sketched the scenes—the crowds lining the streets, the flags fluttering, and the Allied soldiers marching—American, French, English, Italian, Portuguese, Russian, Polish, Slovak, Czech, French colonial, French dragoons, Moorish, African, Scotch, Canadian, Australian, and New Zealanders. "It was thrilling and very touching, this long line of fighting men," Townsend wrote, "all of whom, save the Slavs, had been but recently in the midst of this terrific war." He noted that the American contingent, from the 1st Division, appeared exhausted. Not surprising considering they had been through the scrap at Cantigny and, the day before, had marched some sixteen miles just to be in this "show."

"I can't believe our boys enjoy being pulled into Paris for a mere parade like the continental soldiers who love to be shown off," Townsend wrote to his wife. Still, Townsend was touched by the French girls who gave flowers to each passing soldier. And when they ran out of flowers they gave kisses: "As each soldier passed, there was a girl to grab him around the neck and plant a kiss on his cheek. This made a great hit with everyone, even with the soldiers."[15] After the parade, the troops were immediately pulled out—GHQ was determined to limit any opportunities for brawling or whoring.

That night Townsend, Morgan, and McCabe dined at Voisins—"a fine old place" with "wonderful food"—but as Townsend told his wife ruefully, "Also one of the most expensive it seems." For the three of them it was 135 francs; meanwhile, one meal at the officers' mess was a mere 4 francs. Fortunately dinner was on McCabe, "Mac," who always ate there, a luxury he justified because he lived a Spartan life at Neufchâteau.

While they were eating, Colonel William "Billy" Mitchell entered the restaurant and Townsend, having met him at the airfields, immediately invited him to sit at their table.

Considered the father of the air force, Mitchell had begun his career inauspiciously. He had enlisted during the Spanish-American War, but with his father a senator from Wisconsin, he climbed the ranks quickly. Eventually he attended the School of the Line and Staff College, learned to fly at his own expense, and in 1915 joined the aviation section of the Signal Corps. Appointed commander of all Allied air services in 1918, he would earn a reputation as a flamboyant, daring leader whose blunt views won him few friends. Contrary to popular opinion, Townsend found Mitchell likable and at age thirty-eight "young and very much alive." Shortly after Mitchell joined their table, Morgan and McCabe excused themselves, which gave Townsend a chance to speak earnestly with him about the aviation game. The colonel then "talked freely," his favorite topic the tactical and strategic nature of aviation. As Mitchell preached it, tactical aviation involved observation to aid artillery fire and reconnaissance, while strategic aviation involved attacking all enemy assets. It was this combined threat that made aviation the means for winning the war. Toward the end of their conversation, Mitchell promised to help Townsend in any way he could—even to get him skyborne so he could fully experience the glory of flight.

In a letter home, written after the dinner, Townsend expressed his desire to fly in one of the fighters to see how the light played through the clouds, to see how the colors varied, to see a perspective far different from that on the ground. However, he assured his wife that he would insist the best men in the best machines took him skyward and that Colonel Mitchell would see to his requests being honored. As he explained it, in an attempt to convince himself as much as her, flying would not be nearly so trying or frightening as when he was near the front, in the vicinity of shells, gas, and machine guns. He concluded with a dangerous refrain: "I've got to make good over here—and do it distinctively." So, while he promised caution, he knew risks had to be taken. To pursue his interest—or obsession really—in aviation, Townsend was planning an extended trip to the Meaux airfields in the coming days.[16]

. . .

While Townsend was dining at the posh Voisins and sleeping at the cozy Hôtel Régina, the Germans were in the last stages of preparing for yet another offensive. This was to be their Friedensturm—or Peace Offensive—which was to continue their march toward Paris. Despite losing Belleau Wood, Vaux, and eventually Hill 204, Ludendorff desired desperately to drive a deeper wedge toward Paris; he wanted to split the French forces in two, and he wanted to force the Allies to sue for peace. To do this, he planned a massive assault along the Marne and Vesle rivers, the front running south from Soissons to Château-Thierry, and then eastward before looping northward to Reims. The critical focal point was at Château-Thierry and just east, where the German bulge reached its apex. A massive bombardment would begin at 12:10 A.M. on July 15, and then, at 2 A.M., the ground assault would begin, which included waves of boats ferrying troops across the Marne. On the Allied side of the river, at the most vital point, was the 38th Infantry under the aptly named Colonel Ulysses Grant McAlexander, whose mettle would be sorely tested.

Townsend awoke on July 15 to resounding reports that the Boche had launched an offensive during the night, a punctuation to Bastille Day. He proceeded immediately to the Press Section at the Hôtel Sainte Anne for the latest news, which included a recent communiqué stating that the Boche were driving through the section of Château-Thierry still occupied by Allied troops and that they had also heavily bombed crucial towns—Meaux, La Ferté, Montmirail, and Châlon—behind the lines. The bombing was unsettling; Townsend had made plans to visit Meaux in the coming days. However, he didn't have to go to Meaux to come under fire. That afternoon of July 15, out of the "breathless" silence, a shell exploded in the Paris streets. Five minutes later there was another blast. Big Bertha had returned with a vengeance. "Paris laughed," Townsend noted in his diary, "tho coming as it did with the heavy offensive, I'm sure there was just a bit of apprehension in their minds."

The situation would remain unsettled as Big Bertha continued to lob shells into Paris that evening, with one striking fairly close to Café de la Paix, where Townsend was dining. As he looked around at the smiling patrons he could see that they were not going to let the Germans impose their will on Paris. Still, Townsend could not shake the disconcerting presence of Big Bertha: "What a strange feeling to have things like that dropping out of the quiet sky, onto one never knew just where next, with its death and destruction and that awful mess of ruined building and scattered plaster, and jumbled rubbish slid into exposed cellars. . . . And it is true that a palace looks as mean and sordid and worthless as a peasant's hut after a shell or a bomb."[17]

As the German offensive unfolded, Peixotto soon learned from command in Neufchâteau just what the enemy's plans entailed. The Boche were crossing the Marne in hopes of converging on Crézancy, the town situated at the mouth of the Surmelin Valley, through which they could finish their epic march to Paris.

What Peixotto didn't know was that George Harding was already in the vicinity of Crézancy, having pushed his way there on July 13, even though Pershing had restricted the artists from forward zones during active fighting. Harding knew he had to behave like a soldier: "To know his material, the war artist puts on his steel helmet, his gas mask, his trench boots, his trench coat and laden with only a sketch book, a couple of pencils and some emergency rations in his pockets, like any soldier present, he takes his chances with shell fire, gas, airplane attack, and snipers."[18]

In anticipating where the action would be, Harding perceived that all signs pointed to Crézancy; as he explained:

How do you tell when and where the offensives will be? In various ways. Sometimes, after you have won the confidence of the officers, they will give you tips. But you learn the signs, and you must keep on the alert and use every bit of common sense you have. When you see hospitals being evacuated, headquarters moved, tanks going forward at night and piles of ammunition mysteriously appearing, you surmise something is going to happen. Then you get out your maps and study the region. You know the thick of the fighting will be apt to be in the valleys, and you go there. When it begins, then you know it immediately by the buzz about and whir above you head.[19]

While elements of the 3rd Division diligently prepared for the German assault, in his diary, Harding noted the machine-gun emplacements and anti-aircraft guns set up next to a herd of sheep shepherded by an old man; the lookouts in church towers who would relay signals from the surrounding fields and woods to HQ; "the rush, the anxiety the doubt" as villages just behind the line were deserted; the goats and chickens allowed to run free, only to be slaughtered; and the stench of dead animals. Many times in his diary, Harding, who was feeling "on edge" all the time, mentioned the dead horses and accompanying smell, the poor beasts having just as much affect on him as the dead soldiers.

In the rush to prepare for the imminent attack, accidents happened, and Harding recorded one such tragic mistake:

2 loads of handgrenades in
cart with detonators set
exploded going up to the front
nothing left of men or carts
found one head that was all[20]

In the hours before the enemy's attack, the tension was amplified dramatically, with each side anxious to observe the other. "The Boche often fire rockets in wheat fields on this side of river to light them up," Harding wrote in his diary. "Field grass all ready to cut now and wasting in the region of fire." As he negotiated his way into Crézancy, it was an "awful long hard walk" through craters and muck. In the dark, deserted streets, his thoughts drifted to the comforts of home in Pennsylvania and his wife, Anita: "I never felt so far from all that life means in my travels." Eventually, he found his way into a major's post command, located in a wine cellar, the front and back protected by piles of stone and the ceiling reinforced with wooden beams. While his papers were inspected and as runners came and went, it became apparent to Harding that a night attack was expected.

A lieutenant guided Harding down to the Marne River, where they came to within fifteen yards of the water's edge. They walked along an aqueduct that would be a pivotal defensive line, and worked their way around shell holes big enough to drop a horse in. It was dark, no moon, but then flares in the valley lighted their faces and artillery batteries opened up. "The spit of artillery the flashes continually lighted up the hill," he later jotted in his diary when under cover. "The Boche burned a house so they could see—the whole valley suddenly lighted up and we were plain to each other miles away."[21]

As German artillery zeroed in with cruel patience on the roads and the houses in and around Crézancy and Fossoy, Harding took cover in basements; he made sketches of the 30th and 38th Regiments as they moved into position, and then of their wounded soldiers struggling to first-aid stations. He would remain in the front line for five days; once again he had no interest in returning to his studio billet in Neufchâteau, his studio actually in the kitchen of a family's home. There would be no finished pieces to turn in at the end of the month, a situation he didn't hesitate to communicate to his superiors in his July report: "At the front I make as many as sixty sketches or notes during a trip, besides constant observation. At this time it is impossible because of conditions such as shell fire and quick movement to complete the sketches to a condition suitable for handing in to the Department."[22]

With the German assault now launched, the perilous situation in Crézancy quickly became hotter than Harding expected. Indeed, at GHQ in Neufchâteau, there was a pervasive feeling that Germany was a desperate animal, feeling cornered, which was to be feared. In fact, later in the morning, the news was not promising for the Allies. "The French, sorely pressed," Peixotto wrote, "yielded along the Marne from Jaulgonne to Chatillon, and the Germans, crossing the river, threatened to pour up the Surmelin Valley and continue their march toward Montmirail and Paris."[23] There was only one impediment: McAlexander's 38th Infantry Regiment.

Four regiments from the 3rd Division—the 4th, 7th, 30th, and 38th—were strung along the Marne, from Château-Thierry and eastward to Crézancy. In describing the 38th's position and the action in his official report, Colonel Ulysses Grant McAlexander's language was as colorful as his name: "Dividing our sector longitudinally wound the little Surmeline River, almost due north and south through a valley rich in ripening grain, and from behind each knoll, peeped the spire and clustered groves where dwelt the tillers. Flanking the valley, as if guarding its peacefulness, rose heavily wooded hills. And when at midnight, July 14–15, 1918, the Hun made of our little valley a veritable inferno, he thought to penetrate it unmolested at dawn to a great depth." A savvy tactician, McAlexander was well prepared.

Running parallel to the Marne River were two natural lines of defense: a railroad and behind it an aqueduct, which Harding had

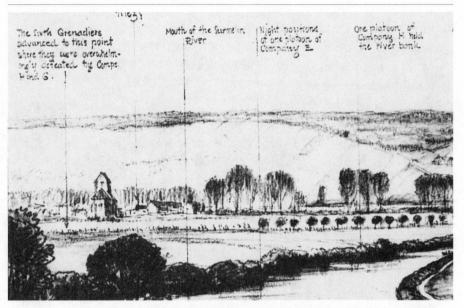

The fourth Grenadiers advanced to this point where they were overwhelmingly defeated by Comps. H and G.

Mouth of the Surmelin River

Night positions of one platoon of Company E

One platoon of Company H held the river bank.

*Battle of the Marne* by Smith. Typically quite cynical, an impressed Smith sketched the layout of the battlefield where the 38th made their heroic stand.

walked along the prior day. Still farther back were the woods. But as McAlexander surveyed the situation, he comprehended that he didn't want the Germans even getting a toehold on the river bank, so he placed men in front of the railroad—down at water's edge—in rifle pits among the reeds. He then checked with the French to make sure they were similarly dug in because they would be protecting his right flank. They assured him they were perfectly ready. Still, McAlexander had an uneasy feeling and decided to take no chances, so, as he later told Peixotto, he ordered his men to dig trenches in echelon along a hill on his right flank that "commanded a wide field of fire *toward the French*." The French couldn't have been too happy about American guns bearing down on them; as McAlexander said, "I don't know what they thought of me, but I never asked."[24]

Then came the terrific blow: shortly after 3:45 A.M., the German bombardment that had "descended like a sheath of steel" lifted and organized into a creeping barrage, behind which the German troops stormed the Marne. As the first wave attempted to cross by pontoon bridges thrown down by their engineers and by boat, many of the boats capsized as the dead and wounded tumbled overboard. Scores upon scores of soldiers started to swim across. Other boats managed to stay afloat. Hand grenades flew. Doughboys jumped from rifle pits. Smoke burned nostrils. Men and boys screamed. Even though a fusillade of bullets met the Germans now scrambling up the river embankment, they nevertheless succeeded in "exterminating" the first two of McAlexander's platoons positioned to his left side on the riverbank. Without hesitation a third and then a fourth platoon joined the fray in desperate hand-to-hand fighting. By this time the thinned German ranks were easy prey; however, losses were heavy, with the 38th's G Company losing 150 men.

The center of McAlexander's line also held, while fifty-eight men were killed, wounded, or missing. But then his right flank suddenly came under "severe enfilade fire" from the rear right, from where the French were supposedly dug in. At first, on seeing troops approach in the gray dawn light, the Americans had hesitated, assuming they were French soldiers. "My troops were not aware that they were Germans as the French had occupied those positions and had evidently retreated without a word of warning," Captain T. C. Reid later reported. "Upon discovering they were enemy troops, we immediately opened fire and seeing that they were hesitating, the command to charge with bayonet was given and they were repulsed in disorder and forced back over the road."[25] Despite the French failure, McAlexander's men held; in part because the colonel had wisely dug those trenches in echelon along his right flank. However, the situation on both of his flanks continued to deteriorate.

As of noon, on McAlexander's left side, the 30th Infantry had been driven back about two miles to Crézancy, which left him the remaining wedge in the enemy's line; so, to protect himself, he partially withdrew his exposed flanks. At 2 P.M. he sent a runner to report on the dire conditions, and, at the same time, he ordered the F Company to "stop that infiltration" on his right and rear. "Fight them hard—you can do it. Your companies are strong and willing and our troops better than theirs. If they are in the woods east of you—face them."[26] All the while, overhead the air was thick with German airplanes that strafed them with machine-gun fire. With the enemy eventually three miles deep on either side of him, by late afternoon, McAlexander was throwing cooks, clerks, signal operators—every available man—into the line.[27] Toward the day's end, having suffered 40 percent casualties, the 38th finally pulled back to the aqueduct to straighten the line.

On the German side, even with their gains, line officers acknowledged that they had suffered a severe defeat, as the riverbanks were literally carpeted with German dead. Ludendorff concurred with the dour assessment and, withdrawing some troops back across the Marne, reorganized into a defensive position. "To continue," said Ludendorff, "will cost us too much."[28] His Peace Offensive was a bloody mess.

McAlexander and his regiment were immediately anointed the Rock of the Marne. Even the usually sarcastic André Smith was duly impressed, declaring with earnest that their defense "stands unrivaled in the records of American fighting."[29] To record the achievement, he sketched the smoky panorama and even labeled the disposition of troops. With their valiant stand an overnight legend, Peixotto knew he, too, must visit the battlefield without delay. On his way there he drove up the Surmelin Valley, the very valley the Germans had planned to march down. When he pulled into Crézancy—in bright July sunlight reflecting off bayonets and the muzzles of 155s—he discovered a town "smashed to bits. Shells had ploughed through its houses like knives through cheese. Disembowelled, their walls stood tottering. Their red tiles, shaken by terrific concussions, had slid from the roofs and lay in heaps, littering the streets, leaving the bare beams and rafters, skeleton-like, against the sky." In a "hopelessly shattered" church the men "were eating their 'slum' in its battered pews."[30]

Peixotto stopped for lunch at the 38th's headquarters—a large house dubbed the Château—where he found himself seated next to Colonel McAlexander and seized on the chance to ask him about the battle. "I was, I think, the first outsider he had talked to since those stirring days," Peixotto wrote, "and he became quite excited—as excited indeed as I was, for it was a thrilling story to listen to this at first hand." In recounting the German push, McAlexander brought out maps and aerial photos captured from the Germans to illustrate his story. After lunch, he offered Peixotto a tour of the battlefield, which, of course, the artist accepted. So the colonel called his orderly and grabbed his stout cane, a handsome war souvenir with a Prussian officer's black-and-silver saber-knot twisted around it.

They drove down to the wheat fields and then proceeded quickly by foot to the trenches along the railroad tracks. The artist soaked in the details:

Khaki caps and coats and heaps of empty cartridges lay in them. Their field of fire toward the river was wide and open. Some of the dead had already been buried but many had not, and all sorts of things lay in the tall ripe wheat. The July sun was ardent and there was a sickening odor in the air.

As we walked about, the colonel, with his cane, raised the fallen wheat enough to show the direction in which it lay, trampled one way as the Boches advanced and in the opposite direction as they fell back before his murderous fire.[31]

Peixotto followed McAlexander across the railroad embankment and down to the Marne, to the slit trenches that offered the soldiers no escape once the Germans were upon them. The river was running quiet now, all the blood washed away. Here, too, grenades and other American equipment lay scattered among the rifle pits. Careful to walk around the fresh graves, the colonel stopped before one and saluted. After lowering his hand, he turned to Peixotto. "Do you know who lies here? No? Corporal O'Connor. Corporal O'Connor hid himself here in the reeds and waited until the first boatload of Germans—men in the famous Sixth Grenadiers—had almost succeeded in getting across, and the man in the bow was just reaching with his grappling-hook to catch the shore. Then he rose from his hiding-place and gave them his grenades full in the face, sinking the boat and killing all its occupants. He also was killed where he stood."

Later, as Peixotto reflected on McAlexander's unbreakable defense, he concluded, "This spot upon the Marne where the Germans never crossed should be hallowed forever by every good American, for here, to my mind, was marked the turning-point of the war."[32]

Peixotto and McAlexander continued west along the river to a point between Mézy and Chartèves, where the Germans had crossed to face the 30th Infantry. "To our left, Mézy's beautiful old Norman church-tower still reared itself sadly against the sky," Peixotto wrote, "surrounded by the shattered remnants of its parishioners' homes. Across the river Chartèves' church lay in ruins, only a fragment of its tower pointing like a thin finger toward heaven, calling for vengeance." The scenes of destruction were all the more vivid against the backdrop of gardens, golden wheat fields, and hillside orchards. And just to the north there was the constant, ominous rumble of cannon fire—the unceasing drumbeat—the drumbeat to which men marched as new battle lines were etched into the dry dirt.

Now turning back from the river, they traipsed through fields littered with Boche equipment and ditches filled with unidentifiable objects stinking of clotted blood. Thinking he would collect a souvenir or two for himself, Peixotto reached for a helmet, but when he turned it over, to his horror he discovered it to be filled with matted dark hair: "After that I didn't care to investigate nor look for souvenirs."[33]

They climbed into the colonel's car for the return drive to Crézancy, which took them through what had been the beautiful village of Fossoy. In the center square, McAlexander caught sight of an enormous unexploded air-torpedo lying under a cart. "Don't you want to take it along as a souvenir?" he asked Peixotto with wry smile. Smiling right back, Peixotto respectfully declined. The artist turned his attention to a graveyard next to the village's Romanesque church: the graveyard had been skinned, the earth peeled back, the innards exposed. "Its graves gaped wide open," he wrote, "its crosses lay prone upon the ground, and in its midst, cause of most of the wreckage, a huge air-bomb had exploded, smashing in the side of the church and digging a vast crater, thirty feet deep, upon whose edge lay poised a fragment of a marble headstone showing only these two ironic words printed upon it: 'Regrets Eternels.'"[34]

# 8

# VISITING THE WILD COWBOY SPIRITS

ON THE SECOND DAY OF THE GERMANS' great Peace Offensive, Townsend made his way to Gare de l'Est, the Paris train station that was in the neighborhood bearing the brunt of Big Bertha's shells. From there he traveled to Neufchâteau, then to press headquarters in Meaux, located halfway between Paris and Château-Thierry, from where he could visit the nearby airfields that were home to the 1st Pursuit Group. This group was comprised of seven squadrons, the members of which had begun shipping over in January 1918 to train at French and Italian facilities that were likened to prisoner-of-war camps. They were armed with secondhand planes, such as the outdated Nieuport 28, which the United States actually had to buy from the Allies. In these first months, those American pilots who had been serving with the RFC and then the Royal Air Force (RAF) were integrated into the U.S. squadrons and expected to take on leadership roles. By April, the first American squads were patrolling the skies and engaged in dogfights.

While history was being made on the Marne battlefields, Townsend chose this time to visit the airfield because Mitchell had told him Air Services would be heavily involved in supporting the ground troops. And so the American pilots were, holding their own against sixteen German squadrons in superior Fokker planes. Townsend also eschewed the front because he had promised to dedicate himself to aviation in memory of his brother. However, it wasn't until now—mid-July, almost three months after his arrival in France—that he was finally making an extensive trip to the airfields. It had been one thing to envision dedicating his war art to his brother Henri; it was quite another to follow through, to contend with the emotions involved.

Townsend's apprehension was only made more acute by the Germans, who were currently bombing the hell out of towns behind the lines, such as Meaux, a historic town with a magnificent cathedral and charming mills built on stone bridges arching over the river. He had no expectations of what conditions might be like: "I dug up a gas mask and helmet in Paris, for they were necessary in Meaux, no doubt, and out I went with a bit of trepidation, for no one knew in Paris just what was in store for one's arrival there. So little news gets into the city, and so much speculation and rumor is always in the air there." As he approached Meaux, the precaution of having acquired a helmet and gas mask did little to ease his anxiety: "I shall never forget my feelings as we approached the danger zone."[1] That helpless feeling that death was awaiting had again grabbed hold. All of this on what was his wife's birthday.

Once in Meaux, he still had to hitch a ride to the 1st Pursuit Group's airfield; however, any journalist in town with access to a motorcar was packing up for an adventure on the Marne River. Not a confounded soul was venturing to the airfield. Frustrated and under the constant threat of an aerial attack, Townsend was forced to kick around town for the remainder of the day. Later that evening, as a consolation, the dreary scene was spiced up with the appearance of the newspaper reporter Floyd Gibbons—sporting a black eye patch and with his arm in a sling—his first outing since suffering the grave wounds at Belleau Wood. In the fading light, Townsend and Gibbons, among others, went for a stroll, but it was hardly pleasant as they recognized it was going to be a beautiful moonlit night—a perfect night for air raids. Under the rising half-moon, Townsend watched as frantic families evacuated the town to seek shelter in the surrounding hills. While he would not be spending the night nestled in the countryside, the artist took comfort in the fact that he was billeted on the edge of Meaux, away from primary targets, in a new villa with lovely gardens, no less.

At ten o'clock that night he sat down and penned a letter to his wife. He told her of the anticipated air raid, and, in exploring his feelings, wrote that he had "no sense of fear, after all, one's chances of safety—even if it should be raided—are always pretty high. . . . And I know I'll be protected." As his daughter, Barbara, had said in a prior letter, love was taking care of him. As Christian Scientists, they devoutly believed love and prayer protected and healed, but such beliefs did little to comfort Townsend in wartime; he comprehended that there was an enemy out there who killed indiscriminately. When he finally climbed into bed, sleep was difficult; he lay there just waiting for the Germans' air assault, waiting for those indiscriminant bombs to start falling from the sky. The next morning, Wednesday, he continued his letter: "Your birthday finished perfectly. Not a raid—nor a big shell arrived last night!" There was only the distant rumble of artillery at the front.[2]

Wednesday was cloudy, raining, the weather miserable, so there was little interest in going to an airfield where the pilots would be grounded. Then, later in the morning, Townsend heard a rumor that Henri's old unit—what had become the 147th, also part of 1st Pursuit Group—had moved to a nearby airfield in Saints to be closer to the front and, therefore, in a better position to support the ground troops. Here was a chance to visit with Henri's old mates, to find out more about not only his death but his life in the squadron, and to achieve some kind of closure. It was a frustrating morning as he doubled his efforts to secure transportation to the Saints airfield; his being a captain apparently had little pull at Press HQ. Finally, that afternoon Townsend caught a ride with a *New York Sun* correspondent.

At the Saints airfield he met the very man who had recruited his brother to join the RFC: Major Geoffrey Bonnell, commander of the 147th Squadron. While Townsend could hardly blame Henri's death on Bonnell, his emotions were in turmoil. As for Bonnell, well, he offered his regrets, but by now he had seen many a pilot go down in flames; the high risk was part of the game. You had to steel yourself against it. Still, he catered to the artist by giving Townsend the freedom to explore anywhere and by personally taking care of his billet assignment.

That night Townsend would retire to a bed that belonged to Daniel W. Cassard, a man just lost to the war. Cassard had been shot down on July 16, while engaged in a dogfight against a superior force. His father, with whom Daniel had lived before enlisting, would receive the Croix de Guerre awarded his son.[3] The billet was with a French family, the father a university professor who taught science and had an extensive mounted insect, butterfly, and moth collection, which he showed Townsend with loving attention. His daughter and her two children lived with him; his son-in-law was off at the war. Seeing how this family was mourning Cassard as though he were their son, Townsend, not yet knowing the pilot's fate, attempted to allay their grief by suggesting that he may yet make his way home or had been taken prisoner, but they all sensed the truth: he was dead. For Townsend, sleeping in a dead man's bed would have its discomforts.

After dinner at the hangars—cavernous and camouflaged makeshift structures of wood and canvas—Townsend soaked up the pilots' conversation: "It is most interesting to listen to their 'hangar flying'; the gossip and experiences told and recounted; the badinage or persiflage that flies like a shuttlecock from one to another. They radiate wit and humor and fellow-feeling and sympathy."[4] As he listened to their chatter, Townsend realized that the boys worshipped Bonnell, who had 29 officers and 196 enlisted men in his ranks.[5] The higher-ups, however, were not so fond of him. Townsend's conversations with Colonel Mitchell made it clear he was not partial to Bonnell. There was a feeling that he embodied too much independent RFC spirit, that he didn't exercise enough discipline over his men, that he catered to them. One time, believing his men needed more sleep and rest, he had refused to send them out; yes, he had declined to act on a flight order, which tended to upset one's superiors. On the other hand, Bonnell's protectiveness reassured Townsend that Henri had not been merely thrown to the wolves.

The 147th pilots flew the Nieuport 28, a French plane that caught Townsend's eye; he considered it "the most beautiful and graceful perhaps of all the machines in the air," and in his sketches he would capture the craft's supple lines. While the Nieuport was appealing esthetically— a very sleek biplane—it was known to lose wing fabric during steep dives, which tended to be hazardous to flying. Even the legendary Rickenbacker, with the 94th Squadron, limited his aggressiveness in maneuvers for fear his Nieuport's wings would give way. Yet, one of the 94th's

*Lame Ducks* by Smith. The makeshift hangars offered no protection against enemy raids.

more brazen pilots, Lieutenant James Meissner, had managed to survive the loss of wing fabric several times while engaged in combat.[6] Meissner's reckless abandon typified the attitude of many pilots: if they didn't have a death wish, they certainly had a flair for the dramatic.

The entire 1st Pursuit Group—these men who were outfitted in fur-lined flight suits called Teddy bears—had a reputation for being cowboys; in fact, by mid-June so many of them had gone AWOL on drinking binges that a threatening memorandum was issued: "The next soldier of this command reported absent without leave will be sent for trial by a General Courts-Martial, recommending that he be sentenced to six months hard labor and then transferred to the infantry." And by July they were barred from patronizing the Hôtel du Saints du Progrès in Saints because they kept getting into drunken fistfights with other units. They were just boys looking to blow off steam. Indeed, when members of the RAF came over for an evening of cards and drinking, their commander, Major Freeman, and Bonnell—old flying buddies—were "like a couple of small boys," Townsend noted in his diary.[7] Later

*Alert* by Townsend. Once the alert was sounded, crews rushed the aeroplanes into position.

that July, Bonnell would be relieved of his command and Freemen would be dead.

While at the airfield, Townsend felt a chilling thrill when he witnessed the pilots answering an alert: the enemy had been spotted crossing the lines on a bombing run. The Nieuports were rushed into position, lined up on the field, with a mechanic at the propeller and other crew members holding the struts. Then the pilots rushed out and jumped in with the same intensity as a marine going over top. When ready, they yelled, "Contact," and the motor was swung over. Once "caught," it began to rev and then roar. The machine "strains to get away," Townsend noted. "It's for all the world like a frantic horse straining at the bit and held in leash. Here's a long line of them roaring and chafing to be off, like anxious runners. The chock blocks are drawn from the wheels at the pilot's command; the men let go or run along directing it out onto the field, and they are off and instantly in the air, one after the other like a flock of birds."

As the ground crew awaited the return of their planes, they placed bets on who would arrive first. Before seeing the number on the plane, some of the crew knew a pilot by the way he flew or how he landed. One character they enjoyed joking about was Jim Healy: "a fine pilot they say," Townsend wrote in his diary, "but watch him land, they ask you, and they wager that, as he comes down on the field, he will lose his own hangar and go, likely as not, taxiing straight over to a Spad hangar before he discovers his mistake. And true enough he does."[8] Healy had established his reputation as being somewhat careless when he crashed a plane back in May while the squad was relocating to a base at Toul; however, in combat, it was a different story as his skills came to the fore and he had his share of kills. In fact, on July 24, Healy and several mates would destroy four Fokkers.

If a pilot did down an enemy plane, on flying into home base he would tip his wings from side to side rapidly or cut off his engine only to bring it back to life with full force to signal victory. Once the pilots landed, everyone rushed out to hear their adventures, and of course, when they scored a kill, they never tired of telling the story. A recent tale involved Quentin Roosevelt, former president Theodore Roosevelt's son, who was shot down on July 14 and whose grave site the artists would later visit. Only a few days before his death, he had gone behind enemy lines with the 95th Squadron, but then, taking a chance, he peeled off to investigate an enemy formation in the distance. On approaching, he discovered that they numbered twenty to his one so he prudently turned back. Flying alone for a while, he finally caught up to what he thought was his own formation and fell in behind. After following quietly along for about fifteen minutes, he noticed the plane in front of him raise its nose, and, to his horror, Roosevelt, who had poor eyesight, saw the Maltese cross emblazoned on its wing and tail. He had been blindly following an enemy squadron. Before pointing his nose down and streaking for home, he fired a long burst and blasted one enemy from the sky. It was another example of the audacious behavior that typified the wild cowboy spirit reputation of the American pilots.

Another big story circulating while Townsend was at the airfield involved Lieutenant Walter L. Avery, 95th Squadron, shooting down his first Boche and then capturing him. The victim was the German ace Captain Karl Menckhoff—with twenty-six kills to his credit—who survived his forced landing. With great dash and pomp, Avery retrieved him in a motorcar. According to the story, the German was all smiles until he learned that he was Avery's first kill—ah, such humiliation. Avery would turn up missing, presumed dead, before war's end.

On July 20, Townsend was still with the aviators when the RAF boys visited for a night of drinking and poker. It had been a tough day for the aviators; the 27th had lost several men over enemy territory. Even so, Townsend was once again struck by the esprit de corps of the RAF boys as they sang their songs late into the night: "They show a spirit, these songs, that must be worth considerable in the flying corps." He found his days with these air combat men so wonderful that he began to regret his age, that he was too old for the flying service: "I have always loved the aeroplane as a spectacle too, the wonder and the mystery of its conquest of the air, and then its own beauty of form, a beauty built, too, on necessity, which, making its aesthetic appeal even higher, has always fascinated me."[9]

Yet, in the midst of this invaluable camaraderie, Townsend felt very much alone; it was his twentieth wedding anniversary. In a letter to Cory, he reflected, "How strange it seems to be here in this secluded spot so many miles away on this day." He missed his wife and his daughter terribly.[10] His emotions had also been stirred by news that some of Henri's belongings had arrived home. Missing, however, were his brother's poems, which Townsend so desperately wanted to read, the poems that would bring his brother back to life, if just for a moment.[11]

The artist was preoccupied by his family, particularly because Cory and Barbara had recently moved to Chicago to be closer to family for support, which brought its own set of concerns. He worried about how Barbara would get to school. He worried whether she would make new friends. He worried about her needing a heavier coat for the colder Chicago winter.[12] To occupy his mind, Townsend bought a copy of Baudelaire's verse in French—*Les Fleurs du Mal*—but the magisterial work moved him little. To soothe his soul, he read his *Christian Science Monitor*, but only half of the issues were reaching him, another cause for frustration. In truth, the *Monitor* provided little comfort or distraction; for Harry Townsend, religion was beginning to lose its purpose. At this time, while war raged in the Château-Thierry–Marne sector, Harry Townsend's faith in God and Jesus was seriously challenged.

Christian Science had taught Townsend that God was all good; that

God's infinite goodness, realized in prayer, would heal; that sin and death were either mortal error or merely illusion. Well, the war was no illusion. And neither was the death he was witnessing. It had to be mortal error then, as physical power wrongly destroyed spiritual power. Or was there no philosophy that could explain the madness? Cory sensed her husband's growing ambivalence and despair in his letters and asked him to talk with Harvey Dunn, also of the Christian Science faith, but so far Townsend found little to like of his blustery fellow artist. Instead, he assured her he was not taking any "careless or reckless" chances. With perfect logic he reasoned that he wouldn't be able to do what he had been sent to France to do if deceased.[13] Regardless of what he told Cory, he was still very much obsessed with his brother's death. While he should have been in the field capturing the war, or in Neufchâteau finishing his pieces for the month, the end of July found Townsend back at the Saints airfield tracking down his brother's old friend Pat Maloney, who had been assigned to the 147th Squadron.

On July 31, at the airfield's firing range, Townsend watched as Maloney realigned the guns on his new Spad, for tomorrow he would be going out after the Boche. The artist noted that the guns spit "long tongues of flame like some fiery dragon"—every third bullet a tracer that even in daylight left a trail of fire and smoke. The planes could also be equipped with a special gun that fired incendiary bullets for use against petrol tanks and observation balloons. Unfortunately, Maloney had no new information for Townsend regarding Henri's death. There was no closure.

As it turned out, Maloney was missing what was a bad day, for the 94th, 95th, and 147th squadrons each lost a man, while only one Fokker was downed. Offsetting the bad news, aviators on morning patrol returned to describe how Allied artillery shells were bursting below them in the dim morning light as lines of troops moved forward against the enemy. The French general Ferdinand Foch had ordered a brash counterattack.

# 9

# MARSHAL FOCH'S COUNTEROFFENSIVE

WHEN LUDENDORFF ATTACKED ON JULY 15, the French general Ferdinand Foch had been in the final stages of preparing a counter-offensive to reclaim the Soissons–Château-Thierry–Reims pocket the enemy had carved for itself. He had mustered enough reserves to mount a sledgehammer blow along the entire western face of this salient, as well as to push hard from the east in a pincer movement. While the AEF's 1st and 2nd Divisions would play an integral role in the main thrust to the northwest, the 26th Division, under Major General Clarence R. Edwards, was now positioned at the toe of the salient, a position of honor as they stood between the enemy and Paris. This latter division would attack just northwest of Château-Thierry in hopes of cutting off the Germans defending the city. Because the 26th was at a pivotal point easily accessed by and familiar to the artists, once the counteroffensive was launched, they would immediately follow the 26th into battle.

A mere three days after Ludendorff had launched his Peace Offensive, on July 18, Marshal Foch delivered what Peixotto called "his smashing counter-stroke."[1] For the 26th Division, which had been encamped in the vicinity of Belleau Wood, H hour was 4:35 A.M., and one of their first objectives was the village of Torcy. They rushed from the shelter of woods, shouting, yipping, and war whooping, and swept down the hill across open land. Covering their advance was a battery of three 37mm guns under the command of First Lieutenant D. F. McGrew, whose men concentrated their fire on machine-gun nests. The Germans quickly abandoned their positions and, with the 3rd Battalion leading the charge, the village of Torcy was taken a half hour later and the village of Belleau shortly thereafter. While the German defense appeared to be

*His Bunkie* by Aylward. In this stark rendering, Bill Aylward captured the consequences of war.

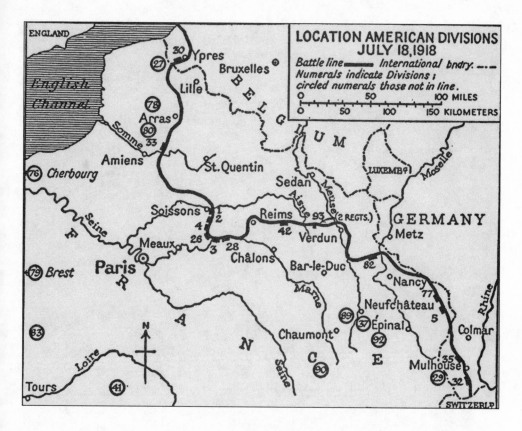

collapsing, they would mount a well-coordinated rearguard action and their machine gunners would be ordered to fight to the death.

As Peixotto, along with Wally Morgan and André Smith, now followed the advance, it was obvious to him that he was behind the New Englanders of the 26th Division: left behind in their encampment were copies of the *Boston Transcript* and the *Springfield Republican*. From there it was easy enough to follow their charge, Peixotto noted, as the fields "were dotted with lonely graves—sometimes one, sometimes three together, sometimes a group of six. A rude wooden cross marked each grave, with a musket stuck into the ground beside it and a flat khaki-colored helmet hung upon it."[2] The lonely, crude grave sites inspired another AEF artist, William James Aylward, to compose a watercolor simply titled *His Bunkie* (see previous page), a stark rendering of a soldier looking down at a helmet and shallow grave, as if his buddy had simply melted into the earth.

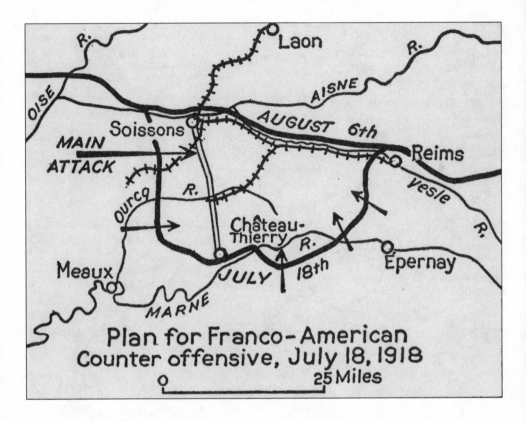

When Peixotto entered Torcy, it was apparent that the village had recently changed hands—it was nothing but ruins. Before pushing forward, the artists decided to investigate nearby Bouresches, which they had seen from the culvert in Belleau Wood and which had been taken with severe casualties. As Peixotto and Smith walked through Bouresches, their boots crunching across crushed rock, both men were struck by the gaunt skeleton of an oak tree—a tree of the centuries—whose leafy arms had once shaded the village square. Now it was shot to pieces, limbs partially amputated but reaching out with despair. The artists paused and pulled out their sketchbooks and pencils to capture this humanlike casualty. As Peixotto finished his rendering, he was suddenly overcome by hunger and realized that for breakfast he had consumed but a scrap of bread and a cup of coffee. It was now noon.

A group of French officers invited Peixotto to join them for a meal in a house that actually had all four walls standing but a large hole in the roof, courtesy of an artillery shell. Amid the destruction, the meal was surreal: the Frenchmen had spread out a red-and-white-checked oilcloth and carefully arranged dishes on the table in a symmetrical pattern, along with two vases filled with wildflowers. While it may have appeared bizarre to Peixotto, the meticulously set table gave the officers a respite from the distant clatter of machine guns and thunder of howitzers. As Peixotto listened to the Frenchmen's conversation and studied their leisurely consumption of the food, he compared this civilized scene to that of an American soldier's meal. The doughboys would line up with a mess kit in one hand for the slum of vegetable and meat, and a cup in the other hand for their ration of a half pint of coffee, after which they "went off like healthy young animals into a corner to devour their food in silence, growling if any one came near to disturb them!"[3]

In the afternoon Peixotto wandered through the onetime bastion of German defense, Hill 204, which had fallen back into Allied hands only after a horrific bombardment: "Rifle-pits and shelters, dugouts and P.C.'s, excavated deep into the sand under gigantic boulders, honeycombed the ground under its rounded brow, which was ravaged and torn by shell-holes and completely denuded of its woods, only a few blackened stumps standing like the last few hairs on a bald head."[4] Littering the area was bedding stolen from local villages, uniforms and overcoats, Mauser rifles, hand grenades—or potato mashers as the doughboys called them—cigarette boxes, scraps of food, and even a German 77mm gun. The shelters were carved into the hillside, perfectly tiered by the German engineers; and on one side were the graves of German officers, decorated with elaborate crosses and flowers.

Very early in the counteroffensive, General Hunter Liggett, commander of the I Corps, which included the 26th, had visions of trapping the German garrison in the Château-Thierry zone and was pleading for bridge-building engineers to support a river crossing. But not until the night of July 20 were the 26th and 3rd Divisions finally in position to enter Château-Thierry and was Liggett able to give the order for all divisions to "push forward at all cost."[5] When elements from both divisions entered the embattled city the next day, they discovered it abandoned. Comprehending that they had overextended themselves, the Germans were now carrying out a well-orchestrated rearguard action to straighten their line between Soissons and Reims.

Also entering Château-Thierry was George Harding, who took

fragmented notes in recording the havoc the enemy's rearguard action was wreaking: "the Boche planes dropping bombs, the machine gun sprayed the road . . . the confusion, ambulances, motorcycles, the dead lying by the road side . . . the observation balloons thick behind us. Men shooting with rifles at Boche planes. The army sergeant who holds me for investigation." Yes, once again, the artist was suspected of being a spy, for who in his right mind would immerse himself in such violence with only a pencil and a sketch pad.

Harding passed by German dead in lanes cutting through wheat fields, the dead floating in the river, a dead sniper being pulled out of a tree. As the doughboys inspected their victims, from the enemy's packs they pulled letters from loved ones and pads of paper with which to write back. In the city, Harding watched as a French soldier arrived at his own home and immediately set to work on cleaning it up for his mother; the artist could only imagine what the Frenchman thought about the "2 dead Boche buried in his garden."[6]

A day after the German retirement, as Peixotto gazed down upon Château-Thierry from the southern heights, he ruminated over its history, for this was not the first time the city had witnessed war. It had been captured by the English in the thirteenth century and recaptured by Charles V a century later. In 1814, Napoléon's troops fought both the Prussians and the Russians here, the enemy leaving behind twelve hundred dead and eighteen hundred prisoners. And then came the kaiser. Peixotto wondered who could have prophesized that it would be the Americans vanquishing Germans from the city, which was now unnervingly silent even though long columns of khaki-colored troops marched ceaselessly along the river and swarmed like ants over two pontoon bridges built by American engineers.

Peixotto could see that sections of the city were gutted and blackened by fire. "Beyond the river, the soft green slopes of the Marne hills," he observed, "covered with woods and wheat-fields and orchards, seemed, by contrast, a mockery to the tragedy of the shattered city." Once in the streets, he noted that the town was "not hopelessly ruined" and had "only suffered in spots."[7] Always piqued by the country's glorious religious edifices, Peixotto entered the Church of Sainte Crépin, which was not so astonishingly filled with booty collected by the Germans, who had been intent on bringing it back to the fatherland but then forced to abandon it in their hasty departure. He also visited the site of the old château built in the eighth century for King Thierry, after whom the city was named. All around him soldiers clattered along the stone-paved streets, heading north to bolster the advance.

To the northwest of Château-Thierry, the Allied goal was to secure the strategic road running northward to Soissons, but the situation was a bit dicey as the Germans, initially surprised by Foch's counterattack, had now dug in and positioned their machine guns to strafe the approaches. Holed up in the Bois Bouresches—lying beyond the villages of Torcy, Belleau, and Bouresches—the enemy commanded a complete field of fire across the wheat fields through which the 26th had to advance. And they were absolutely merciless. "German machine gunners and snipers were shooting, not only at moving men, but at wounded men who involuntarily threw up their arms above the wheat," artilleryman Lieutenant McGrew wrote in his report. "They were even shooting at prone wounded men who lay in bald spots in plain view in the edge of the woods, and with white bandages upon their mutilated arms or legs." On a number of occasions, a member of McGrew's battery, which had an excellent view of the battlefield, ran into the wheat field to pull out or treat the wounded.[8]

*The Harvest Moon* by Dunn. With a bloated harvest moon rising, German snipers picked off American soldiers, including the wounded lying in the wheat fields.

The Americans' left flank began to suffer such severe casualties that they were forced to withdraw from their position under the cover of darkness; on July 20th casualties for the 103rd's 1st Battalion were already at 30 percent with complete companies wiped out.[9] The only way men could advance was by crawling and taking shelter in shell holes, until men like McGrew were able to bring up their batteries—dragging their guns themselves because they couldn't establish contact with their caissons—and pick off the machine-gun nests. Then, as the doughboys approached the strategic Soissons–Château-Thierry Road, the German fire became even more murderous. Groups of dead horses, as well as human arms, legs, and heads—German and American side by side—lay scattered across the fields harvested by farmers.

While the 26th was entangled, on the morning of July 22, Harry Townsend hitched a ride with two newspaper correspondents from the airfields to Château-Thierry to tour the battle zone. The countryside behind the lines was beautiful, of course, but it was slow going as they neared the Marne River. In addition to the roads, the river itself was full of American troops, Townsend noted in his diary: "They seemed to relish the chance to not only get a bath, but to have a real swim as well, and every fancy diver in the AEF seemed to be on the job that morning. What a contrast was . . . this young, enthusiastic American youth enjoying himself in what seemed his element, to the Marne a little farther down filled with the dead Boche killed along its banks and even on its bosom."[10] Not far from the frolicking swimmers, they passed by the clamoring 155s lobbing shells at the retreating Germans.

Taking a roundabout path over churned-up roads, Townsend and his companions reached 26th Division HQ at a farm in Grand-Ru, where it had been established on July 21 and would remain for the rest of the month. After hiding the car along a ruined wall, he took in his surroundings: "What a bustle and air of importance this old farm had, but also what a feeling of a sort of suppressed presence the whole place manifested. . . . Soldiers lay around on the grass on the edges. Never a word they seemed to speak. Officers walked rapidly from building to building with a glance upward at a passing aeroplane . . . and with never a word to another passing officer." A spacious cow stable served as the HQ's nerve center.

When Townsend entered the stable, he discovered that the stalls had been converted into offices, each filled with various staff members performing their duties: "A couple of the stalls had groups of boyish-looking German prisoners in them who were being questioned by intelligence officers. They all seemed more or less composed and satisfied, as do practically all the prisoners one sees. . . . Always tho, there are some among them who wear strange faces, long, distant, wistful looks, a bit of fear, perhaps, or anxious wonder maybe at what his fate may be." While Townsend understood their fears—especially considering the German propaganda that portrayed the Allies as bloodthirsty animals intent on slaughtering them—he didn't "waste much sentiment on them."

General Edwards strode into the barn "smiling as usual"; Townsend noted, "he always seems to wear a smile, tho I'll wager he can be a stern master to his officers and men at times. A few words with him. He expresses satisfaction with the way our boys are keeping contact with the Germans as they run, and that they will likely have to move HQ, they go so fast." Edwards's enthusiasm, however, did not accurately reflect the situation. Contrary to a rapid advance, his HQ would remain in Grand-Ru for nine more days; his soldiers would suffer at the hands of German machine gunners; and his total casualties from July 18 to July 25 would be 4,108, killed, wounded, gassed, or missing. Eventually, the 42nd Division would come in to relieve them.[11]

After the brief interview with Edwards, Townsend and the correspondents returned to the rear, their route taking them alongside Belleau Wood. "A long artillery train passes us here on its way forward," Townsend wrote, "the boys singing, astride the great guns. One of the boys wore a silk hat he had picked up somewhere, another a ladies hat, and another carried a broken parasol over his head. What fun they seemed to be snatching out of their running fight! They carry the spirit of eternal youth it seems, and the French remark about this often."[12] In the Wood just beyond the artillery train, burial details wore gas masks to protect themselves from the stench of slain bodies that had been there a month and were still being found; in the heavily shelled upper end of the Wood, fragments of bodies remained strung through the trees like ornaments. The artists would not be permitted in Belleau Wood to make further studies.

In the afternoon of July 22, Townsend, again with the two correspondents, motored toward Château-Thierry, intent on visiting the headquarters of the 3rd Division, the division driving forward along a line that ran east of the ravaged city. As they entered its outskirts, Townsend was relieved to hear that the Germans had retreated northward under withering Allied artillery; however, he soon discovered that 3rd Division HQ was in Gland, half a mile farther north of Château-Thierry, where fighting was hot.

While the motorcar was sitting in the snarled traffic, waiting to cross one of the pontoon bridges over the Marne, Townsend was approached by a lieutenant who had seen his captain's bars and was in desperate need of some advice. The lieutenant had been ordered to bring his guns to the bridge, where he was to meet his captain at 4 P.M.; it was now 4:30 and his captain was nowhere to be found. The lieutenant knew his guns were needed in forward positions, so he asked Townsend what he should do. Townsend's first inclination was to explain that he was merely an artist with no knowledge when it came to military matters, but he could see the young man was genuinely perplexed. "What should I say?" Townsend wrote. "I thought a minute, said he might wait a few minutes more, then if he knew where they were to go, to proceed, at least on into Gland, where there would certainly be an artillery operations HQ." The lieutenant mulled over the advice, then concluded it made sense.

While pleased he had managed to issue an order he had no real authority to give, Townsend immediately began to second-guess himself. As they passed over the pontoon bridge, he could see Boche artillery firing on Gland, where he had directed the boy. Then, as he looked around at the congested road and milling troops, he came to the uncomfortable conclusion that their very location appeared to be an ideal spot for the Boche to bomb: "You can bet that everyone watched the air and every motor that hummed by overhead was a possible Hun. There was very noticeable, in the whole atmosphere of the region there, a certain nervous tension lest the inevitable happen earlier than they wanted it to, for that bridge and road were bound to be shelled soon."

As the car pushed closer to Gland, Townsend's anxiety level rose incrementally: "This didn't look very good to me, for the noise from the bursting shells over the town was both annoying and extremely menacing. . . . The streets were crowded—traffic going forward at an excited speed, for the Germans were on the run a few kilometers ahead, and they were after them as close behind our contact as it was possible to get." Once in town, Townsend and his companions proceeded on foot to locate the 3rd Division HQ. As the shells burst around him—spewing shrapnel, stone, and acrid smoke—Townsend did his best to remain calm, to discreetly watch the sky from under his tin hat. It was some comfort to notice that the French soldiers were equally nervous even though they had had four years to steel themselves. "I kept my mouth shut tight to keep my heart somewhere near its right place," Townsend wrote with self-deprecating wryness.[13]

Surprisingly, and courageously, perhaps, HQ was effectively in the open, near the large gate of an old home, whereas the zone's French HQ was in a cellar, a veritable dugout. As shells and bombs exploded around them, HQ staff members went about their business unperturbed, a scene Townsend would not forget. The division commander, Major General Joseph T. Dickman, who had a bulldog personality and a thick neck to match, with his chief of staff, Colonel Robert H. C. Kelton, at his shoulder, was looking rather sharp with his helmet on as he calmly studied a map spread across his lap. "But, from the extreme concentration the General was giving a large map spread over his knees, following

*Street Fighting* by Dunn. Street fighting in the villages along the Marne River was vicious.

the finger of a captain who was tracing locations for him which he would immediately spot with his thumb, to the nonchalance with which Colonel Kelton received me, listened to my demand and granted his permission to work anywhere in their sector, one would never have guessed there was reason for the slightest anxiety, tho the air was full of it."[14] The setting made for a very dramatic painting, Townsend noted, but there was no time to linger; the 3rd Division was battle weary and not yet finished with its violent work.

While at HQ, Townsend learned that only the day before, the 3rd's heroic 38th Infantry, under McAlexander, had crossed the Marne on a makeshift footbridge at Mézy, even though the Germans were shelling them heavily to cover their retreat. This rearguard action was so intense that a brief delay during this crossing had cost McAlexander twenty men. Once over the river, their mission was to push northeast of Château-Thierry and secure first Chartèves and then Jaulgonne, both picturesque villages that would be reduced to ruins; however, as soon as they pushed uphill past Chartèves their left flank encountered strong resistance. All of McAlexander's men were subjected to severe shelling, constant machine-gun fire, and enemy aeroplanes continually swooping down to rake them with machine guns.

Over the next few days, the 38th would lack food and they would lack sleep. Even so, they would press the attack on Jaulgonne and beyond. During the advance on the village, Captain Jesse Woolridge took the point and was crawling through a drainage ditch when he encountered an American soldier ahead of him. It was Colonel Ulysses Grant McAlexander—the Rock—intent on some personal reconnaissance. This encounter, discovering his colonel scrambling about on hands and knees, was Woolridge's favorite five minutes of the entire conflict.[15] After seizing Jaulgonne midmorning of July 22, they chased the Germans northward to Le Charmel, keeping such close contact that they came under friendly artillery fire. A flare sent skyward signaled their presence and the shelling ceased, but not before three men were killed and five wounded. Fighting would remain vicious as the 3rd cleared out woods along the right flank of the 26th.[16]

The daring George Harding was there to witness the events, in the advance lines, splitting time between a machine-gun company belonging to the 3rd Division and an artillery battery. He moved with them

*Morning on the Marne* by Dunn. Resolute in their pursuit of the enemy, the doughboys marched through fields littered with the dead.

through Jaulgonne and Le Charmel; he was with them through the blistering fire of the enemy; and he continued to make dozens of quick studies. The images came quick and vivid: shot-up houses, shot-up roads, dead horses, dead doughboys, dead Boche. "Boche in colvert. The stench," was all Harding jotted down at one point. Some of the dead were already being buried—some in the very trenches and shell holes in which they had sought cover. If the boys couldn't be identified, they were buried by platoon, the platoons identified by position. Harding was passing by one burial detail that was successful in identifying a ravaged corpse—Ed Hunter of Kansas—because he had "his girls letters" in "his bloody pack."

Harding passed by destroyed camions, burned clothes, dugouts built into every hill, and blown-up graveyards alongside churches, the skeletons exposed; he watched as a French balloon was shot down and a French plane was driven into the ground. "The airplanes always," he jotted in his diary, for the sky was filled with swooping fighters and bombers. Just outside of Jaulgonne, he noted, "the shell fire either side of us and behind and ahead." And yet, there on the road, was a field kitchen. And ambulances were attempting to evacuate the wounded from Jaulgonne; however, in this village, 40 of the 120 men in the ambulance corps would be killed or wounded. In spite of the mounting casualties, the spirit of the doughboys was undaunted; as Harding noted, the slogan of the day was, "Heaven, hell or Hoboken in 6 mos."[17]

In evaluating his experiences during the defense along the Marne and the subsequent counterattack, Harding wrote, "one really saw the villages, the woods, the fields destroyed." There was no doubt in his mind that he was absorbing "the greatest pictorial material" a wartime artist could ever desire.[18] When he was in Jaulgonne, he elaborated, the "enemy was on overlooking hill. The material gathered was to my mind wonderful." One of his crude sketches in pastel—titled *In Pursuit of the Enemy: American Troops Entering Village during Advance across the Marne*—depicted a doughboy staring angrily at a fallen enemy soldier, with a ruined village in the background. From his posture and expression, it was evident that the doughboy was outraged that this man had wanted to kill him and that the doughboy, in turn, had no choice but to shoot him. That was the anger Harding conveyed; it was flavored with not exultant gloating, but more of an outraged offended annoyance.[19]

While Harding was in the line, Townsend was visiting 3rd Division HQ in shell-torn Gland, but he and the newspaper correspondents quickly decided to return southward to 26th Division HQ, where it was a bit quieter. Just a bit. The return trip took them along the crest of a hill running parallel to the "utterly used up and abandoned" Hill 204. It was nerve-racking as they passed the staggered batteries of 155s firing on the Germans, who had, in turn, located the Allied batteries and were reciprocating in kind. Among the thunderous explosions, Townsend tried in vain not to dwell on the haunting fear sitting in the back of his mind that the "dreadful one" would find him, that it took only one shell. He spent the night in Meaux, billeted in the Press chalet, on a cot with no sheets and one blanket. It was a cold, sleepless night as great columns of French troops rumbled through, bringing up armored cars and moving into reserve positions to help in the pursuit.[20]

Over the next several days, Townsend sketched the battlefields that were now behind the front lines, so he could later reconstruct aspects of the fighting accurately. Once again in Vaux, Townsend watched the ravaged refugees filtering in, returning home even though the town was so hopelessly wrecked little could be salvaged. What else could they do? Over in Lucy-le-Bocage, André Smith encountered similar sights: "One could have no more impressive revelation of the fullness and bitterness of all this than the sight of refugees returning to their homes, to find their houses not only hopelessly smashed but more often entirely vanished in a pile of stone and timbers. I have seen old men and women, standing before the crumpled fragments of their homes, speechless and dazed, in an attitude of utter despair. It was a sight that was pathetic beyond words." Smith feared that "the thousands of pictures of this vast destruction" would disguise the "supreme pitifulness" of the war—the suffering innocent—and would dull "our true appreciation of its awfulness."[21]

While walking through Vaux, Townsend also encountered two young, psychologically scarred soldiers from the 26th Division who had been left behind to guard a cache of trench mortars. They moved around "like ghosts," he noted. "They had been thro hell . . . and you could read it in their eyes, too. They looked like creatures of another world with a strange, wild, hunted look."[22] Officers had a habit of telling Townsend that their boys take the war as if it was all in a day's work, but he didn't believe it. Not when he saw soldiers like these, wandering about aimlessly and murmuring to themselves. In a moment of lucidity, they explained to Townsend that they were supposed to have been relieved already, but had apparently been forgotten and were without food. They had to scrounge, forage like animals. Conditions now were not much different than just after they had captured Vaux from the enemy; lacking food then, too, they had had to sneak out at night to dig up potatoes in village gardens not already uprooted by the shelling.

Several days later, Townsend met another pair of doughboys who left him equally unsettled. In a wheat field not far from Bouresches, he discovered them stumbling about in search of their buddy, wounded and suffering from shell shock, who had run from an evacuation hospital. They were desperate to find him before he died from blood loss, or an accident, or enemy fire. The whole situation was "pathetic" to Townsend as he listened to "how fine a pal" their friend was. "What an incident!" he wrote. "Yet it's only a mildly pathetic one as compared to some of them."[23] It was one such incident after another, which followed one fierce battle after another.

. . .

To reconstruct McAlexander's heroic stand of July 15, Peixotto and Morgan returned to Fossoy on July 23 to sketch the battlefield and the remains. In the village, their driver happened to park the car near the cart under which the massive unexploded missile had been—the dud McAlexander had jokingly offered to Peixotto as a souvenir. To their relief, someone had removed the monstrous thing; however, the very moment they climbed from the auto, a French engineer rushed toward them waving his arms wildly. "Allez-vous en; allez-vous en!" Not quite sure what the Frenchman intended, they hesitated. Now flinging his arms in the air like a madman, he shouted, "Boum, boum, boum!" Well, *boum*—an international word that required no further explanation—set them in motion. They jumped in the motorcar and the driver tore up the ground as he careened into a ruined hangar for cover. "No sooner had we done so than a terrific explosion rent the air and fairly shook the earth," wrote Peixotto. "Broken walls tottered and fell in and a great mass of dirt shot upward as if vomited from the crater of some hidden volcano, falling again mingled with a rain of shell fragments and shrapnel." The engineers had exploded the dud.[24]

After a day of sketching the historic battlefield and before chasing after the advancing troops, Peixotto and Morgan decided they desperately needed a good night's rest, so they motored farther rearward to La Ferté-sous-Jouarre, where they knew there was a decent hotel. They took the last room available, located up under the mansard, and after dinner they retired. While undressing they heard someone from the street shout, "There's a light up there." Peixotto went to the window to see who the foolish culprit was—lights were to be extinguished or windows covered at night—and to his great dismay realized it was Morgan and him; their light was a beacon for any raiding Boche planes. As if on cue, the distant drone of an aeroplane wavered through the night, strengthening in sound when it was abruptly punctuated by the explosion of a bomb. The explosion brought the artists to their senses and they blew out their candles. But then they were paralyzed by the sound of more planes, the engine noise rising toward what would be a crescendo of explosions.

Peixotto was gripped with the same helpless feeling that had enveloped him on the train to Paris months before, when it came under attack and the women in his compartment were in hysterics. "Nearer and nearer came the buzzing motors," he wrote, "so near indeed that, even in the darkness, we felt we could see big black objects moving against the stars, and bang, bang, bang went the bombs as they began to land in the town about us. Should we retreat ignominiously to the cellar?" The only issue was that the hotel was dark, blacked out, and they didn't know where to access the cellar. "Again and again the great black bombing planes circled over the city," his recounting continued. "Again and again the bombs fell and their explosions rent the air, mingled with the sound of broken glass and the crash of crumbling walls."[25] And then the droning engines grew distant. A deep feeling of relief and thankfulness settled in with the silence. So much for their restful night, but they were alive. Meanwhile, American troops in town suffered nineteen casualties.

Peixotto and Morgan spent several more days sketching along both sides of the Marne, crossing to the north bank over a pontoon bridge that American engineers had constructed from captured material and labeled cleverly "Made in Germany." They passed through a string of destroyed villages—any within the range of the artillery paid the price—the buildings now formless. It struck Peixotto that in the dazzling sunlight "they resembled only the reefs of some coral islands." One decrepit old peasant came up to him and remarked bitterly, "Joli pays." Pretty countryside, yes. Like Townsend and Smith, they witnessed the returning peasants, who, having evacuated quickly, had been unable to take much of their possessions. Lamenting their losses, the villagers pointed out blood-soaked mattresses used by the wounded and visibly shuddered, which prompted a saddened Peixotto to observe, "All was chaos and confusion where only a few days before had been order and content."[26]

While closely tailing the troops, Peixotto wrote to his wife, Mary, to update her on his activities, but regulations prohibited him from disclosing precisely where he was and what divisions he was visiting with. For her, it was strange and discomforting to know he was somewhere among the carnage but not to know exactly where; however, as she wrote him, "I do not want to know." To occupy herself, Mary continued her work at the French auxiliary hospital, and, in addition, was now visiting a nearby American hospital, whose number of patients, some of them "terribly torn up," had suddenly swollen to about a thousand during the Marne battle.[27]

. . .

During the night of July 29, elements of the 32nd filtered forward to relieve the 3rd Division, which, moving north of Le Charmel, had become bogged down due to strong German resistance in the Bois des Grimpettes. With no time to clean the battlefield, the soldiers of the 32nd witnessed the consequences: "Dead men and horses littered the fields and putrefaction, aided by warm weather, was well along," wrote First Lieutenant Charles Donnelly. "Of all the odors I have experienced, none is as repulsive as the sweetish, nauseating smell of rotting flesh, especially in hot weather." To cope with the smell, he helped himself to some cigars being handed out by a Knights of Columbus representative; Donnelly was a cigar smoker the rest of his life.[28] George Harding also traveled over this battlefield and the carnage began to take its toll on him as the scale of it was beyond expression. While considered a man's artist, lithe and muscular, resilient and determined, he began to retreat into himself emotionally, so much so that Townsend would comment on how difficult it was to connect with Harding, how Harding preferred to be alone.

Because many boys from the 32nd, made up of Wisconsin and Michigan National Guard units, were of German ancestry and could speak German, they thoroughly looked forward to haranguing the enemy in their own tongue. As one doughboy jested, "When Boche goes after Boche, there'll be plenty of hell to pay."[29] They didn't have to wait long. At 2:30 A.M. on July 30, the 127th Infantry Regiment of the 32nd went over top behind a rolling barrage. There to witness the Allied firepower was George Harding, who recorded his impressions in his diary:

> A rain of fire from both sides of the road. One minute the gun in front was silhouetted by the fire from the other side of the road. Next moment it barked and lighted up the road and showed troops moving up. Back and forth the effect plays. A rain of fire from all sides and rear. A full half circle, the moon overhead suddenly pales to the insignificance of a star. The horizon is a dawn of red sky, lighted with flashes of a thousand thunderstorms rolled into one, with each gunfire a burst of thunder. The screech of 75's; the camouflage over a 155 catches fire, still the whine of its shells continues as they go over you. There are 210 split tails—and away off that must be the roar of the twelve-inch naval railway guns.[30]

The dramatic manner in which the guns' flashes lit up ruined buildings, crawling troops, and tattered countryside—the stage effect—tantalized his artistic mind.

The 127th was soon stopped by machine-gun fire on their right flank, from where the Germans remained well entrenched in the Bois de Cierges. Despite the sheath of bullets, the doughboys were able to establish a foothold in the edge of the woods, and then, through the night of July 30, there was a bayonet melee that raged for hours in the dark, thick, entangled forest. The next morning the 32nd's two infantry brigades, the 63rd and 64th, attacked side by side to completely secure the woods, but they were still short of their ultimate goal, Fismes, about twenty miles north of Château-Thierry, on the Vesle River. To get there they now had to surmount some of the Germans' most formidable defenses south of the Vesle River, which included the daunting Hill 230. In the first days of August, the 32nd finally overran the heavily defended enemy enclaves in the village of Cierges, on Hill 230, and at Bellevue

*Mopping Up Cierges* by Morgan. Chasing after the advance, Morgan witnessed the mopping-up operation in Cierges.

Farm, all strategic targets. As the Allied grip on the salient tightened, the Germans were forced to retreat, and, on the evening of August 3, forward units of the 32nd Division stood triumphantly on the hills overlooking the scenic Vesle River. Their goal of the counteroffensive, Fismes, was just a little over a mile away.

Now on the heels of the 32nd, Peixotto and Morgan passed by large piles of abandoned German ammunition cased in wickerwork; they passed by German cantonments for man and beast; and they passed by rotting bodies with their sickly sweet smell. On reaching the crossroads at Courmont, they overtook American columns moving north to where the Germans were regrouping. To Peixotto, the doughboys presented a magnificent scene: "Here were the guns, the artillerymen bestriding their horses like centaurs, draped in their slickers and casqued with the flat helmet of the soldiers of Cyrus—giving a wonderful impression of youthful calm and manly vigor. Here were the 'doughboys' plodding doggedly along."[31] And why not exude vigor? The Boche were on the run.

As darkness descended, the two artists groped their way into war-torn Cierges, which was still being mopped up—enemy soldiers had gone so far as to hide themselves down in water wells, perched on ladders. Seizing an opportunity to render the patrols at work, Morgan took out his sketch pad and a piece of charcoal. Crouched behind four doughboys moving warily through an utterly shattered street as they looked for any remaining enemy, he captured the tension by portraying the soldiers' hesitancy—their hunched posture and tentative steps—and the deep, ominous shadows melding with the growing darkness.

Morgan and Peixotto proceeded to division HQ in a "less ruined" villa on the outskirts of town, where they checked in and were assigned billets in the remnants of a shell-torn house. "There they gave us an empty room," Peixotto wrote, "windowless, doorless, with a shattered ceiling that, every time a big truck went rumbling by, shook down upon our heads. We placed a door or two on the stone floor to sleep upon and were fixed for the next few days."[32] Harding would also spend a night in Cierges, in a house so rickety that when a truck rumbled by the roof collapsed on him. While the room was indeed a disaster, another captain, looking desperately for the silver lining, jokingly reassured Harding that in the dark the room looked like any other room. The upbeat officer was also good enough to tell Harding about a lieutenant who had been in this very room, had a light on in the evening, and was getting "all dolled up" when shot dead by a sniper. A sergeant and three other men in his company located the sniper in a tree and captured him; subsequently, and without remorse, they hammered him with the butt end of their pistols until he fell to his knees, praying for mercy. His pleading had no effect as the soldiers reached for their bayonets and "gutted him."[33]

On August 4, 32nd Division commander Major General William G. Haan himself gave Peixotto a tour of the surrounding battlefield. As they stood in on the edge of Cierges, Haan pointed southward to Grimpette Woods, where his troops had concealed themselves in preparing for the assault on the town, which lay in a hollow, its dominant and only land-mark the church tower. At dawn his men had charged across the open fields and captured Cierges; however, the Germans proceeded to lob gas at them, the gas sitting so thick in the hollow that the Americans were forced to withdraw. As Peixotto surveyed the town, he noticed a Red Cross flag hanging from the church steeple, the flag used to signify a hospital, but in this instance it was a dirty German trick, for in the tower was a machine-gun emplacement. He took the time to sketch this incriminating image.

The 32nd's more critical target had been the high ground to the north of the village: Hill 230, which was capped by a fortresslike farm. "On top of this eminence," Peixotto wrote, "the general pointed out a farm called Bellevue and a long line of trees that, he told me, screened some quarries that had been made into veritable fortresses studded thick with machine-gun nests." Snaking up the hill were several paths cut through the brambles, scrub, and shrubbery. These were the only routes—obvious to all, including the enemy defenders. Before dawn the men crawled partway up these trails, then the whistle blew—the damned trench whistle—and the men bolted upward through thistle and stiletto limbs. "Hand-to-hand fights in the quarries," Peixotto recounted, "fierce combats round the farm. The machine-guns had to be taken one by one, but finally the last of these hornets' nests was silenced." Later in the day Peixotto toured Bellevue farm and the quarries: "The farm was shot to pieces; the quarries filled with kits and knapsacks, with coats and rifles and strings of empty cartridges. The dead still lay unburied in the fierce August sunlight."

Once the Boche had been cleared from Hill 230, Peixotto learned, the next target was Reddy Farm, an important German headquarters that the enemy had also transformed into a stronghold. As Peixotto toured Reddy Farm, he noted that "its walls were peppered with shrapnel and breached with shell-holes, and it had now been converted into a field hospital." Inside there were operating rooms with their menacing surgical instruments. Outside, the view northward was spectacular, without limit, hill after hill with patchwork woods giving shape and texture to the rolling countryside.

The artists pushed northward; near the village of Chamery they encountered the grave of the aviator Quentin Roosevelt. "He was buried by the Germans where he fell," wrote Peixotto, "in a lonely spot marked from afar by a single tall poplar, a conspicuous landmark. Parts of his aeroplane lay upon his grave and a few flowers gathered from the field had also been placed upon it by our soldiers."[34] As Peixotto closed in on the front line he noticed that the villages were more intact than those behind; the Germans were retreating so rapidly that they had little time to plunder them and the Allied troops had little need to bombard them. But then, along the Vesle River, the situation changed quickly: German resistance became more anxious and stubborn as the rearguard protected their retirement to the northern side of the river.

At a location not far behind the lines, just north of Dravegny, Peixotto took shelter in an old monastery to observe the American artillery harassing the entrenched enemy: the batteries were supporting the 32nd's assault on Fismes, which had been launched the morning of August 4, in the hours before Haan gave Peixotto his private tour. Replying with murderous artillery and machine-gun fire, the Germans managed to hold onto the town and the surrounding railroad yards into the afternoon, and they so decimated the 127th Infantry Regiment that late in the day U.S. command had to organize a provisional battalion to launch yet another assault on the town. (Harding later learned that fifty-five of eighty-three officers in the 127th were casualties.) Finally, at nightfall, the town was in American hands and the next two days were spent mopping up any pockets of resistance and collecting prisoners.

Patrols were sent across the river to test the enemy's defenses, but no toehold could be established, so the men dug in along the southern embankment. Major General Haan was damn proud of his men, but with quiet modesty he later admitted to Peixotto, "At the time of the battles on the Marne, I told General Pershing that, while my division was not, perhaps, all that I might wish it to be, I felt sure that, if he would give it a chance, it would give a good account of itself and could take its place in line for combat work."[35] Certainly the 32nd had proven its mettle—it was anointed "Les Terribles," the only American division upon which the French bestowed a nom de guerre. But for Peixotto what glory was there to render? The death still lying in the farmyards and quarries? The 3,547 casualties suffered by the 32nd Division over seven days and a twelve-mile advance?[36]

Off to the west, the 42nd Division—having relieved the 26th, which had been depleted by severe fighting—was also making notable gains against the enemy. The 42nd was charged with taking both the Ourcq Valley, which ran east-west, and the heights to the north. "The Orxois (or country of Ourcq) is a great plateau," Peixotto wrote, "cut by numerous deep little valleys, drained by tiny water-courses, locally called rus, swift-flowing rivulets that, in rainy weather, quickly swell the more placid Ourcq. A few patches of woods, sometimes quite extensive, alternate with great open fields that afford no shelter whatever to attacking troops."[37] Of course, it was across those exposed fields that the 42nd Division would have to advance if they wished to secure the heights of the Ourcq.

It would indeed be no easy task taking the Ourcq Valley, considering, just as the 32nd was encountering at the time, that every farm housed machine-gun nests and every village was a virtual fortress. Each would have to be taken through bitter hand-to-hand combat. The village of Sergy changed hands four times before it was taken; and Seringes was taken, held for a mere forty-eight hours, then lost, and then retaken the next morning. On July 27, the 42nd captured the Croix Rouge Farm, a vital strategic point for supporting a crossing of the river Ourcq, which would be a bloody affair as the Germans had been ordered to hold their positions on the other side of the river at all costs. Two days later the Ourcq was finally crossed; on this day alone it took several waves and the 42nd Division suffered heavy casualties. Elements of the 42nd continued their relentless pursuit of the enemy until August 2, when they were relieved by the 4th Division, but not before suffering

184 officers and 5,469 enlisted men killed, wounded, or missing in eight days of fighting.[38]

Having followed the 32nd Division, Peixotto did not witness these battles in the Ourcq Valley; however, he toured the area a short time later. What remained was graphic evidence of the battles: "Their [the villages'] streets had not as yet been cleared of debris nor had the shell-holes been filled up. Their houses were gutted; their churches disemboweled by high explosives. A sickening stench of rotting horse-flesh, of unburied dead, was in the air, augmented by the heat of early August. Flies that bred by the million infested the air and stung like poisoned needles; the clouds of dust strangled you on the roads."[39] In Fère-en-Tardenois, he discovered that some of the more courageous, or foolish, inhabitants had remained in their cellars during the bombardment. Slowly they emerged like bewildered rabbits and began to repair their destroyed homes and to recover what possessions they could.

The field hospitals were overflowing with casualties, Peixotto observed; the doctors and nurses working feverishly without rest to save a life here and there. Yes, the soldiers were making sacrifices, but the German Château-Thierry pocket no longer existed and Paris was no longer remotely threatened. Exhausted from Ludendorff's offensive and Foch's counteroffensive, in August both sides would again dig in and settle into a war of grinding attrition, as they caught their breath and surveyed the field for the next point of attack. It would come soon enough—in the Toul Sector currently held by the Americans. Once again individual artists would be in the heat of the combat. But first there was a battle with the General Staff in Washington to fight.

# 10

# THE FIRST CASUALTY OF WAR IS TRUTH

AFTER THE HEATED BATTLE FOR BELLEAU Wood, the heroic defense on the Marne, and Foch's brazen counteroffensive, the General Staff in Washington was anticipating a plethora of action drawings and paintings to use in propaganda to bolster the country's morale in the face of mounting casualties. More so, because another draft registration drive was under way, scheduled for September 12, with the eligible age now extended to a grizzled forty-five. Yes, fresh, inspirational propaganda pieces that would dazzle the newspaper and magazine editors and the public were in high demand—apparently expected before these glorious battles ended, but of course that was an impossibility.

It simply wasn't so easy to churn out war art. As Harding explained, what they witnessed in the field was overwhelming, worthy of "years of museum study afterward." It took time to understand their subject matter. It took time to absorb both the massive scale of things and the intricate details. "One crosses terrain held by the enemy for years," Harding explained. "You are actually in places the enemy was an hour ago, places you have contemplated through powerful glasses and that are still smoking and burning, pounded to a shapeless mass by the barrage you gloried in at midnight. But it is the loneliest place in the world just behind an attack with 77's and H. E. coming in from the enemy, and not conducive to the production of exhibition pictures, such as critics seem to expect can be produced, by a sketching easel and arranging a palette after careful selection of the arrangement of material in front of one."

Even if well positioned to view the action safely, the artists faced a host of other challenges: "These difficulties overcome," Harding continued, "there still confronts the artist the problems of his craft, to be solved perhaps in a cold drenching rain, with a sketchbook held under one's trench coat making each pencil mark mean something. The sketch secured, one is unable to rush to the studio to record it while the impression is fresh, one tramps on adding notes, not for a day, but for a week, during which time one is fortunate to average a meal a day or three hours sleep. . . . There were months when one only had ten days to straighten out sketches. So you scraped together what was intelligible and turned them in. From the time of making a drawing to turning it in never more than two or three weeks elapsed, often only a day or two." Once the drawings or paintings were submitted to GHQ in France, they entered a bureaucracy that invariably resulted in delays in shipping the work to Washington; as Harding pointed out, some drawings they made during the Marne defense and counteroffensive did not reach stateside until the war was over.[1]

Naturally, the General Staff wasn't interested in such difficulties. The General Staff also wasn't particularly interested in the grim realities of war. Gutted cathedrals and soldiers lying filleted in wheat fields—which were what had impressed the artists so far—were not exactly conducive to propaganda. Such scenes were certainly not in concert with the mission of the Committee on Public Information (CPI), which had been created to bolster the morale and the resolve of the American public, as well as to publicize the United States' efforts overseas. The CPI was busy fusing sophisticated advertising with blunt messages to create a propaganda machine on a scale never known before—even though the United States was the last ally to enter the war, it would produce more propaganda posters than any other individual nation. Comprised of nineteen subdivisions for national work alone, the CPI was the kind of intense propaganda machine normally associated with a totalitarian regime, but this was war. The key for the propagandists was to influence individuals so that they would behave in a certain manner while thinking they were behaving as individualists. To accomplish this goal, Chairman Creel's people had several tools at their disposal: emotional appeals, demonization of the enemy, and outright lies. In addition, there was one other persuasive argument at their disposal: that this war was the war to end all wars; if we sacrificed valiantly now, our children would enjoy everlasting peace. Demonization of the enemy was a particularly effective route in appealing to the masses, and, with creative aplomb, the CPI didn't hesitate to depict the Germans as depraved killers and to fan rumors of atrocities. In graphic detail, the Allies perpetuated the story, among many other stories, of how the German soldiers would throw Belgian babies into the air and then catch them on their bayonets. And the Germans accused the French of gouging out the eyes of prisoners and the Americans of slitting prisoners' throats. All was fair; after all, when the war ended there would then be time to sift through the destruction for truth. As California senator Hiram Johnson proclaimed, "The first casualty when war comes is truth."[2]

The drawings of soldiers charging forward heroically was what the General Staff wanted but had yet to receive, so by mid-July, the General Staff was expressing impatience. In a letter to his wife, Townsend confirmed that there were "rumblings from Washington about the fellows drawings not being sufficiently interesting and please get more life in them and all that and where are the work of the rest of us." A particularly harsh critic was Major Kendall Banning, chief of the Pictorial Section of the Historical Branch, and he penned complaining notes to Smith, Peixotto, and Morgan, the last artist taking the criticism particularly hard.[3]

Meanwhile, Peixotto wrote a letter to his friend Gibson, who served under Creel, in which he admitted that only after seeing all the fronts did the artists realize "how big a Proposition" they were up against "and how different the whole thing is from what people imagined." Peixotto voiced his fear that their work would be judged too quickly and they didn't want to disappoint anyone.[4] Having anticipated trouble in Washington, Gibson had already written to Townsend to say that the General

Staff expected instantaneous results, but once they understood the conditions under which the artists had to work they would be more understanding. In a conciliatory tone, Gibson said that the committee and he had complete confidence in them.[5] So did the artists' superiors in France, including McCabe, who wrote, "During the past ten days, the artists have done considerable work in the rear of the Marne battle front, drawing sketches of the French refugees, which it is believed will prove of considerable value for use as propaganda at home and abroad."[6] At GHQ, the artists' July exhibition was well received, too. Of course, Banning and his cohorts would not see this work for over a month.

Also coming to the artists' defense was Brigadier General Dennis Nolan, head of G.2. Intelligence, who, on July 17, wrote directly to General Peyton March, chief of staff in the War Department. Nolan acknowledged that Washington's disappointment with the work received up to July 15 was "justified by the facts then at their disposal" but their fears would soon be allayed. Except for one or two exceptions, he believed the artists were doing "reasonable good work" and there was no need for change at the moment. Years later, when Nolan was dictating his memoirs of World War I (never to be published), he declared, "We had a group of official artists who were sent over and who drew the AEF as it was, and they did an awfully good job. . . . Their work didn't appeal to their [superiors] over here in the U.S. however because the stuff was sort of drab, nothing like the French. . . . They would show artillery in the rain and mud and the soldiers all covered with mud and the staff as it was at the front. It was good but wasn't enough like what they wanted here. The man in charge [Banning or Gibson] had no idea about war, being an artist, but these fellows were doing a good job."[7] And the seasoned Nolan knew war.

Peixotto summed up the situation most succinctly: "At first our work was criticized by the General Staff at Washington as not being sufficiently lurid for their publicity campaign. After a barrage of such criticism, General Headquarters at Chaumont explained that the artists were making pictures of things as they really were and not as the General Staff in Washington thought they should be, and they were advised, if they wanted inspirational pictures, to have them made at home and not trouble to send artists to France as the grim actuality might warp their imagination."[8]

. . .

Pershing himself weighed in on July 18, writing to March that he felt the artists' work had been "fairly satisfactory" to date, taking into account that they did not have adequate supplies and optimal working conditions. He also reiterated that there was the learning curve to consider: they needed time with the troops considering that all but Smith had no military training. Demonstrating broad-mindedness, Pershing noted that the quality of the artists' work could not be judged as "would be possible in [a] purely military endeavor."[9]

Evidently, an obstinate Banning failed to understand the difficult conditions noted by Gibson, McCabe, and Pershing, as well as by the artists, because in August he would unleash what was playfully labeled by Peixotto as the "Banning Barrage." Beginning on August 5, Banning fired off a barrage of criticism in a series of letters to Smith, the senior officer among the artists, a position that would now be more of an annoyance than a privilege. "You men have opportunities for portraying American participation in this war on a scale that is unprecedented and with advantages that have never before been accorded to American artists," he wrote. "You are occupying a front seat at the greatest drama the world has ever known. The human drama of which you are now a part; the vast events which are taking place within a few miles of you, ought to and I believe will, put an inspirational quality into your work, which is quite lacking in the first pictures that have arrived. Generally speaking your pictures are lacking in human interest and they are also lacking in importance." Yes, Banning pulled no punches.

Banning went on to explain that Creel and Gibson were so disappointed that they were holding the first pictures for release to publications until others arrived with more action. (Interestingly, in a September 9 letter to Peixotto, Creel would express no negative criticism of their work.) That's what Banning wanted: action. Action pictures more suited for propaganda and more valuable to the periodical press. One letter on August 5 was not enough; in a second letter that day he clarified, "What the magazines want particularly are pictures showing battle line activities of the U.S. troops and pictures of inspirational nature."[10] That desire was all fine and good except that, as Smith pointed out, all of France was not "a seething battlefield," especially not for the Americans in the months before Belleau Wood and the defense of the Marne. Contrary to Washington's romantic visions of "over-the-top" action, much of the front was relatively quiet, especially in the American-held zones. This situation would change as additional divisions of the AEF became ever more involved, but the future couldn't help resolve the current conflict with Banning.

Another impediment to witnessing the action in the trenches was Pershing's standing order expressly forbidding the artists from being in the front lines during active engagements. Disregarding their commander in chief, Dunn and Harding had managed to enter the hot trenches at Château-Thierry, but even then their ability to witness any real action was severely limited by the nature of what had been predominantly trench warfare to date. It also took time for the artists to comprehend the ebb and flow of battle, to anticipate where they should position themselves. "We found ourselves going through a process of schooling which, I think, came to us all as a surprise," Smith would write in an August letter to Colonel James G. Steese in Washington. "I don't think it occurred to any of us that like our brother officers in the various branches of the Army we too would have to pass through a period of training. But it has been exactly that and it is only recently that there has grown up a feeling of confidence in our group in regard to our work and our ability to handle it in the way we feel that it should be handled."[11] In a letter home Townsend echoed similar sentiments, and it wouldn't be until the end of August that he finally became comfortable enough to be truly productive. Meanwhile, in his barrage, Banning noted with irritation that they had yet to receive any works from not only Dunn and Harding, but Aylward and Townsend, prompting him to write, "What has become of these men?"[12] Well, Harvey Dunn, whose whereabouts were unknown to GHQ most of the time, would turn in some of his best work at the end of August.

Dunn's work was based on his observations in the field, impressions that he allowed to percolate in his mind before committing them to canvas. In his September 1 report, he explained, "The pictures which I am delivering are of no specific place or organization and while, consequently, may be lacking in fact, are not, however, barren of truth in so far as I have succeeded in expressing in them the character of the struggle and the men engaged." Among them were some of his most memorable works, which would enjoy critical and popular success; these paintings and drawings captured "the shock and loss and bitterness and blood of it"; they were powerful images of physical and emotional destruction.

During his time in the trenches, he sought to identify himself with his subject; then, as the vibrant impressions swirled in both Dunn's conscious and subconscious, what came to the surface was the "universal man" at war, which he "dug out of himself." Because his audience could identify with these characters, it made his work especially gripping.[13] Ultimately, his resolute soldiers were not much different than his family's fellow pioneers who settled Dakota country: some were stalwart, some fragile; all wanted to survive. The finished pieces involved far more emotion than illustration, for as he explained, "If you paint what you see

*The Looter* by Dunn. This ignoble soldier was fighting for more than just his country; he was seeking booty for himself and his family.

you won't have a good looking thing. Paint a little less of the facts and a little more of the spirit. Let it be expression rather than description. Everything is dramatic if we can only see it so. Those who paint dramatically get a lot more out of life. Paint more with feeling than with thought."[14]

The soldiers that emerged were stark, at times grotesque and silent, at other times brutal and relentless. Two of Dunn's works turned in on September 1 were indeed diametrically opposed.[15] There was *The Engineer* (see page 57), a caricature of the typical doughboy hunched under the absurd weight of his pack—the weight pressing upon his fragile life—plodding methodically along, his eyes focused straight ahead. In glaring contrast, there was *The Machine Gunner* (see page 56), a muscular, square-jawed, archetype of the fearless marine, an ideal propaganda piece. As for characterizing the enemy, Dunn turned in *The Looter* (see previous page), a charcoal-and-oil drawing of a German soldier who, weighed down with stolen goods, has a look of both indifference and annoyance. At his feet is a broken umbrella, a piece of the more refined world he no longer has a need for. While Dunn depicts him with his back turned to the war, there is a bloody bayonet pointing forward, suggesting he is still fighting but for something other than country. Hardly a noble enemy, he is just a man trying to survive and to feed his family any way he can. Although there was little subtlety in these character sketches, there was the dramatic expression Dunn desired.

Dunn illustrated more complex emotions associated with the consequences of war in several action-oriented pieces finished that August. In his *Morning on the Marne* (see page 153), the soldiers appear to have a purposeful stride as they move toward the front line; however, with these young men's determination come resigned, worn-out expressions. There is the barbed wire imprisoning them, which Dunn inserted into the work, and on the other side of the wire is their fate: a hunched figure who may be wounded or dead. The tension in the partly featureless soldiers Dunn created is accentuated in *Combat Patrol* (not pictured), which depicts the boys clustered together in wary positions in dark shadows, their profiles conveying an expectancy that they are about to be fired upon, while the contrasting dark and light patches give the work a vibrant energy.

The fleeting glimpses of facial expressions Dunn provided made his studies of the dead and wounded all the more disquieting and indefinite.

His ambiguous attitude toward war is apparent in *The Hand Grenade* (see page 98)—the title explaining what has occurred—which shows two soldiers carrying a stretcher. The lead soldier gazes blankly toward the horizon, uncomprehending of how far he must go but marching anyway; the second soldier gazes down at the wounded man, his expression hidden but his posture suggesting he knows all too well that it could be he on the stretcher; and the wounded soldier appears mummylike, wrapped and prepared for the burial ceremony as waist-level smoke begins to envelop him. It resonates a barren feeling; there is no life in the blurred landscape.

These soldiers were extolled for their bravery in carrying themselves and their fellow wounded soldiers rearward, but they have also been defeated as individuals, and the spirit of youth has been taken from them. As for the dead, Dunn provided an unsettling image in *The Harvest Moon* (see page 147), the title suggesting a time to celebrate the bringing in of the harvest, a time to pay tribute to nature and the cycle of life; yet, lying in the wake of the reaper among the golden wheat are dead soldiers in unnatural positions, dead young men who should not have been harvested. They are illuminated by an engorged moon low on the horizon, the light eerie and subdued. So, of Dunn's pieces, only one was worthy of propaganda—*The Machine Gunner*—but the others were powerful and laudatory pieces of art. Without a doubt these pieces were infused with personality and human interest, infused with pathos and loneliness evoking emotions everyone could identify with, just not the kind the General Staff desired, which was blunt heroics.

Clearly, Banning could not conceive that the artists were working under arduous conditions, that they were not ensconced in cozy Paris studios churning out fabricated, colorful work, because, further demonstrating his ignorance, eight days after his first stinging indictment, on August 13, Banning again wrote to Smith, his opening comment blunt: visitors to his office were not moved by the artists' work he had displayed. "Neither the magazine editors for whom the pictures are largely intended," he wrote, "nor the officers of the General Staff appear to express very much interest in the pictures. They do not serve either a military purpose nor propaganda purposes." Twisting the knife, Banning called Smith's attention to the "splendid color reproductions" in the French magazine *L'Illustration* by the artist François Flameng. In particular,

Banning complimented the Frenchman's depiction of attacks and bombardments—day and night scenes—trench life and human interest. Banning found them "splendidly alive," examples of precisely what he desired.[16]

In drawing such comparisons and contrasts with other artists, Banning did not have the opportunity to view the work the renowned Sargent was only just beginning to create. However, if the major had seen Sargent's sketches to date, there is no doubt the propagandist would have been severely disappointed. So, what war material did attract the eye of the acknowledged leading painter in the English-speaking world, a man born in Florence, Italy, who trained in Europe, a man adept at painting portraits, landscapes, and epic murals? The ruins of a cathedral. In August, Sargent moved forward to the city of Arras, just behind the front line, where he would spend several weeks. There he encountered a bombed-out cathedral, its bleached white columns rising out of the rubble, a thin arch remaining, and sunshine streaming into the blown open cavity. Symbolic of man's fall, the surreal scenery captured Sargent's imagination and he set to work on a piece simply titled *Cathedral of Arras* (not pictured). Such striking images and symbolism had also attracted the AEF artists, and Smith would execute a piece titled *Pathways to Peace* (see page 282) that depicted soldiers clamoring over debris in a bombed-out church but with Christ on the cross still standing, looking over them.

Sargent also found himself fascinated by war's victims, not heroics. While touring near Arras, on the evening of August 21, Sargent heard of British soldiers who had survived a gas attack and were being treated at a dressing station on the Doullens road. Morbidly intrigued, he and his friend Tonks, the latter charged with making a medical picture for the ministry, motored to the dressing station. There Sargent witnessed what he described as a "harrowing sight, a field full of gassed and blindfolded men." He encountered soldiers—leaning on each other, guiding each other, slumped prone across the grass—blinded by mustard gas and awaiting treatment. The line of blinded men—the tragic scene having nothing to do with his assignment—immediately struck him as a natural subject for a frieze, for a mural. To capture the moment, Sargent made notes and sketches in pencil and charcoal.

As he continued to tour this zone immediately behind the frontline trenches, like the AEF artists, Sargent also made many sketches and paintings of the men and military equipment he encountered—soldiers marching, soldiers bathing, gun carriages, mules hauling ammunition— and he didn't alter details; the work was matter-of-fact, at times businesslike, as Smith had discovered war to be. While hoping to encounter British and U.S. troops operating in unison in the Arras area, Sargent actually found less inspirational material. He wrote that "the further forward one goes the more scattered and meager everything is. The nearer to the danger the fewer and more hidden the men—the more dramatic the situation the more it becomes an empty landscape. The Ministry of Information expects an epic—and how can one do an epic without masses of men?" To his friend Mary Hunter, he wrote, "I have wasted lots of time going to the front trenches. There is nothing to paint there—it is ugly, and meager & cramped, & one only sees one or two men." He went on to conclude, "In this Somme country I have seen what I wanted, roads crammed with troops on the march. It is the finest spectacle the war affords, as far as I can make out."[17] The finest spectacle he had witnessed so far was the roads crammed with troops on the march—thankfully, Banning was spared this assessment.

One of Banning's colleagues, Colonel J. R. M. Taylor of the General Staff, War College, was also moved to add his bit in appraising the AEF artists' mission. On August 19, he issued a memorandum in which he suggested what subjects should be treated by the artists; in particular, subjects they should capture in color and subjects they could better portray than the camera. His well-meaning list included:

- Tanks in attack formation moving through the mist of dawn. They look like monsters of the ancient world.

- A tank coming down a dusty road at sunset. . . . Men are seated on it, cheering as they pass by an outpost they have blown up and taken.

- Airplanes fighting in the clouds.

- A battle at night. Under a moon great spears of headlights cross each other and shells like rockets fall from the air.

- Sturdy soldiers in full uniform.

- A group of German prisoners being herded by a young American soldier, handling them like he would a herd of cattle back in Kansas.[18]

No self-respecting artist could be dictated to, however, especially when it came to subject matter or medium. Art is too personal for that, so very subjective, and the AEF artists could only greet such advice with incredulous retorts shared among themselves.

Because Smith did not report to Banning or Taylor, there was no formal channel through which he could reply or defend their work. In a letter to Banning, Smith explained, "In regard to your criticism of our work I must confess that my position renders me powerless to reply to you as I would if the matter were a purely personal one." While powerless, Smith felt compelled to tell Banning that despite his misgivings their work was being well received in France and that he was reporting the relentless criticism to GHQ: "The nature of your criticism and your very evident disappointment in our drawings in the face of a general expression of approval that our work has received here is to me such a serious thing that I have felt it necessary to bring your letters to the immediate attention to our chief."[19] The thorny Banning was a matter for the higher-ups to contend with as far as Smith was concerned.

After this latest barrage, coming to the artists' defense with a few choice words of his own was Major Robert M. Johnston, who was head of the Historical Sub-Section, GHQ, and favorably impressed by the artists' work. Johnston wrote to Banning's superior, Colonel C. W. Weeks, chief of the Historical Branch, declaring "a considerable injustice is done to Capt. Smith and his colleagues by Major Banning. . . . Major Banning's point of view seems to be of an extremely simple character; namely, that if the artists are not sending what the magazines particularly want, the result is 'disappointing.'" He believed that Banning had a "fundamental lack of appreciation of the nature of the artists' work."

Hammering away, Johnston's counteroffensive continued, "The two exhibitions held here at Headquarters, which have been very successful, have given us a group of pictures of the battle zone that are marked not only by conspicuous talent but by artistic conscience, an artistic conscience striving hard to produce faithfully as seen by an artist's eye the scenes and action in which the American Army is taking part. The demand for 'inspirational' pictures seems to me nothing less than fool-ish, and it utterly fails to get at the grim reality under which the Ameri-can Army is struggling in Europe." In wrapping up his letter, Johnston wondered why Washington had bothered sending real artists to the front if merely inspirational pictures were desired; after all, those kind of pieces could be turned out by the bushel full right in the United States by propagandists. Johnston also noted that the artists were taking their work very seriously, while constantly risking their lives.[20]

By early September, the artists' actual superior, Major A. L. James, the recently appointed chief of G.2.D., had had enough of the controversy and fired off a letter, along with Banning's correspondence, to his supe-rior, General Nolan. James stated emphatically that it was "hardly fair" for Banning to criticize their work directly considering the artists had no military procedure for "answering him direct in their own defense." He opined that Banning's concerns had already been addressed adequately, and, as far as James understood, action pieces were not necessarily the priority. "Major Banning would seem to be under the delusion that the official artists are constantly in the front line trenches," James further charged, "and he seems to fail totally to understand that there are limita-tions to their circulation."[21] As the war of words continued, Townsend noted, the officers at GHQ "would stand back of us to the end."[22]

To bolster his defense of the artists, James asked Smith to file a writ-ten report on the entire situation, from their own expectations as artists, to the conflict with Banning. Eagerly responding, Smith spoke frankly as he once again summarized the situation, and, unafraid to lambaste Ban-ning, he wrote, "It is my personal opinion, and I am very certain that I am expressing the opinion of the other artists as well, that Major Ban-ning's attitude toward our work is an extremely narrow one in that it is, or seems to be, limited to only one phase of the work which we have been asked to do, namely, to supply drawings for current publications." A broad viewpoint that related to the historical nature of their work didn't appear to "enter at all into his consideration." Smith was quite upset with Banning's language, too, with his declaration that they had failed "to make good." To top it off, Banning's forceful intrusion into the chain of command had once again left the artists in doubt as to whom they were primarily responsible, as to who should be governing their work.[23]

Understanding to whom they were responsible was inextricably tied to the artists' overarching duty as artists. As artists, as war correspondents, as recorders of history, they had serious moral issues to contend with: was their first duty to humanity or to the Allied cause? To their country or to truth? What if they exposed the destruction, the hardship, the death and suffering at the front, while eschewing individual heroics—would they be behaving unpatriotically?[24] There was no doubt in Harvey Dunn's mind concerning his position on their duty: as he said, he went to France "with a fervent desire to picture the war as it really was—the shock and loss and bitterness and blood if it." And Wally Morgan said, "We have the duty of showing up fraud and pomposity and to get across human frailty." And Smith, too, was emphatic in stating he wanted to be truthful and honest in his work, "without resorting to sensational tricks and fakes."[25] Clearly, they didn't believe their duty was to the propagandists in Washington.

It remained to be seen if their more recent work covering the battles of Belleau Wood and along the Marne would reverse Washington's negative opinion and take some pressure off not only the artists but even the likes of Pershing, who had more pressing matters to contend with than defending artwork. Yet, in September, Pershing would buckle somewhat to Washington's demands by modifying the artists' orders: in a letter to Chief of Staff March, he wrote, "I have issued instructions that hereafter these artists work will be confined to advance areas." However, Pershing again insisted he didn't want the artists in frontline trenches during "active engagement."[26] On the heels of Pershing's new order and continued pressure from Washington, all of the artists would have no choice but to seek "active engagement." Beginning in mid-September, Peixotto, Townsend, and the others would have ample opportunity to witness the American military machine grind its way across battlefields, and Dunn would decide to go "over top"—which was expressly against Pershing's orders.

# 11

# RAMPING UP
# IN AUGUST

WHILE THE ARTISTS' SPAT WITH WASHINGTON escalated, the Allied counteroffensive along the Western Front was stalled against stiffened German resistance. And while the Germans had relinquished all ground gained from their Marne offensive, there remained one other enemy bulge ribbing the Allies: it was the Saint-Mihiel Salient, located twenty miles southeast of the legendary Verdun. To cut off railroad service between Paris and Nancy and to disrupt supply lines, in 1914, Bavarian troops had stormed forward to seize Saint-Mihiel, a strategic city along both the rail line and the Meuse River. The French had endeavored to wrest it from the Germans in February 1915, only to suffer tragic losses. They did not bother with another attempt. Now Pershing assumed the responsibility of vanquishing the enemy, and, under the watchful eyes of the French, the doughboys would feel the pressure to make good.

To assault this zone, Pershing was permitted to create what he had longed for: an autonomous American army, the U.S. 1st Army. It came

*The Artillery Train* by Harding. The horses were literally driven into the ground as the
beasts of burden hauled artillery, caissons, and mess wagons.

into existence officially on August 10, a victory against his own French
and English peers, who continued to clamor for AEF units to be inter-
spersed among their own. Even though there was this egotistical conflict
between high commands, in recognition of Pershing's accomplishments to
date, the French command awarded him the Grand Croix de la Légion
d'Honneur. To record the regal event, Townsend was at GHQ on a day
when it rained continuously except for a merciful pause during the
impressive ceremony. Admiring how the AEF commander carried himself,
the artist observed, "Gen. Pershing certainly looks fine—he's every inch
the soldier—and looks much more military and masterful than the
French generals—truly!"[1] Townsend may have been biased because, in
contrast, French president Raymond Poincaré was a paunchy, balding
man; also, he placed the scarlet sash over Pershing's shoulder upside down
and one of the French generals had to flip it around. The French president
did speak excellent English in extolling Pershing and resoundingly con-
cluding, "You arrived on the battlefield at the decisive hour."[2]

As Pershing now planned for the Saint-Mihiel Offensive, Townsend
wrote to Cory, "We have to strike a mighty blow—with all the resources
at our command to finish the thing as it must be finished—to bring
Germany really to her knees and that's the only way it can be settled

right. It seems she really must be crushed—not allowed to quit the
minute she feels she had had enough." Desiring a measure of revenge for
his brother's death, Townsend feared the Allies would quit too soon, that
they would say "Done" if the Germans cried "Enough." As far as he
was concerned, having seen so much of war's brutal reality, Germany's
venomous military leaders had to be "completely wiped off the map."
Townsend lamented that Allied artillery couldn't reach the Boche leaders; of course, the cowards were most likely hiding in bunkers anyway.
For now it didn't appear the French had any interest in anything but
total victory, he noted with satisfaction, and American troops were
rolling through France in large numbers to achieve that objective.

The marching doughboys continued to appear happy and self-assured
to Townsend, who noted that their buoyant attitude had injected fresh
enthusiasm into the British, who broke through German lines on
August 8 in the Battle of Amiens. Confidence soared and at the
Neufchâteau officers club there was wild gossip of being home for
Christmas. "When we are ready for a real concentrated American
drive—it will be interesting for the Boche I am sure," Townsend wrote
enthusiastically. "I should think we would be ready before long!"[3] On
that account he was correct.

While sounding martial, Townsend did not entirely bask in the
doughboys' glorious victories, nor was he wholly convinced that the end
was imminent. To the contrary, almost six months in France found him
less settled and more homesick—not a healthy mental framework for a
man now expected to confine his activities to the front. Complicating
matters, his marriage to Cory had become strained; in her letters she was
beginning to make comments, "little remarks," about Townsend being
out dancing, perhaps dancing too much, and flirting. To reassure her
that was not the case, he explained how he was keeping a diary, writing
at night so his hours weren't entirely wasted on sitting in cafés and dancing. Also, when in Neufchâteau working he didn't socialize at all until
supper at 7:15 P.M. at the officers' mess, and, if he did go to the café to
shake dice for drinks, it was for either coffee or citronade. He and his
fellow artists and officers might talk until around nine, or listen to a
musician playing the piano, the violin, or the cello, but then it was
home for a little reading, writing, and bed. In his letter, Townsend playfully noted that he had yet to learn how to curse like a soldier, so all in
all he was living a moral life.

The truth was that Townsend missed Cory and his daughter, Barbara, greatly and he dreamed of dropping in for a visit almost daily. When the Bathoses entertained a family with an eight-year-old daughter, it only exacerbated the artist's emotional despair. He admitted to Cory that he dwelled on his homesickness too much for it did him little good. The utter loneliness of his studio work was also preying on his health; in fact, he was thinking that it was almost better for him to be in the field, where it was more dangerous but he was interacting and socializing with soldiers. This latest letter to Cory was rambling, disorganized, and clearly reflected a troubled, lonely man.[4]

And then came an emotionally roiling letter from Dwight, Henri's widow, her first communication with Townsend. Full of disbelief and waning faith in God—full of doubts about life and death—she wrote,

> I don't know Harry, I have been thro every stage of doubt and dis-believing and now I don't know where I stand. If only we could know where he is—whether he is—I try to reason it out and think and I am only just baffled. I thought once I really did hear from him—shortly afterward—in the night I was feeling very miserable and I simply begged him to let me know where he was and to send some message just to let me know he was near the babe and me, and immediately just like an answer I thought of the message he sent me when the babe came—"although he couldn't be with me in person, he would be close to me, all the good in him would be right there, keeping watch with me and the unworthy would stay away." I haven't told anyone this but I think you must be going thro much the same struggle that I am.

Townsend did share the struggle and the letter opened deep wounds that had hardly begun to heal as he once again grieved for his brother as if his death had only just occurred.

In her mournful letter, Dwight dealt with practical issues, too, such as Henri's personal effects; she wanted to know what Harry might like to inherit. While he wanted to take nothing that would further rob little Stephanie, his infant niece, of her father's existence, he did desire Henri's uniform for sentimental reasons. What he coveted even more were the poems Henri had supposedly written while serving; those, more than a uniform or anything else, would keep his brother alive. Dwight also raised the issue of whether Henri should remain interred in France. There was "the romance" of being buried where you fell, she acknowledged, but perhaps Henri would have preferred to be returned home. Townsend wanted him to remain in French soil, among the honored fallen, in the very ground he had chosen to defend, but he knew it had to be his mother's decision.

All this while, Townsend had been keeping secret the searing letter that Henri had welcomed him to France with, but after receiving Dwight's forthright letter, he was finally prompted to confess its existence to Cory. "I never told you about all this before dear," he wrote to her, "knowing a time would come, and it seems to have come now when I must tell you and mother." He wasn't sure why he had destroyed the letter, he explained, except that it was "too full, too intimate" to chance anyone seeing if he was killed, too. Also, he knew that every time he would reread the letter it would tear open the wounds of grief as Dwight's letter had just done. Even so, he took comfort in the fact that Henri's song and smile were still with him.[5]

The moment had also come to finally communicate with Dwight, so, as difficult as it was, on August 20, Harry Townsend sat down and wrote to his younger brother's widow, the sister-in-law he had yet to meet. Clinging to every shred of his brother's memory, he thanked her for her long letter because "every little scrap of information seems to mean so much to me. . . . I think now that I have really conquered the old sorrow of that it has been overcome with a new faith in Henri's continual presence," he wrote, "for I've come to feel even as you say he wrote to you that his spirit, the good in him, is with us always and will be as much an influence in our lives as tho he were here in the old way. I say this and yet there are some times when my faith of course wavers. But that's my weakness." The two brothers had felt they needed each others' support, Townsend expounded, much more so once "we were here in this awful conflict," to sustain their ideals. Now a pillar in his life was simply gone.

Just as he had confessed to his wife, Townsend divulged the letter from Henri that had awaited him in France, as well as its contents, and how he had felt compelled to destroy it. At the end of Harry's own breathless letter, he said he was counting on Dwight for emotional support, and felt "much better now that I really have unburdened myself to you all." He apologized for his long letter and hoped it didn't force emotions to the surface that she had "stilled." Nevertheless, Townsend had felt emotionally coerced to write it—driven internally to purge himself for his own sake.[6]

In stark contrast to Harry and Cory, Ernest Peixotto and his wife, Mary, had discovered a youthful zest in their marriage, inspired by the dangers of war and their occasional but intense encounters. In early August he was again able to slip away to visit with her—a clandestine meeting of lovers—for only a few hours. The day after he departed, she wrote to him, "I feel like purring! Yet I am past kitten age!" It was good for her to see him so calm and "full of happiness," the antithesis of Townsend's emotional state of mind. On this latest visit Peixotto had brought one of his recent drawings, which Mary thought to be excellent. You are "in full power," she wrote. "The power of the man I have always known." In this letter, Mary also explained that she had been planning to go to Paris; however, a man under her charge was to have his leg amputated and she intended to "see him through. He counts on me." While both Ernest and Mary faced travails, being together in France made it far more sufferable than for those separated.

In spite of the war's hardships, Mary was relatively optimistic. In another letter to her husband, she wrote:

You are back at your billet, I know by your letter, and perhaps enjoying the intimate pleasure of a large arm chair—for a few short moments—which because lacking any other, has become your very own. And how often, this adaptable brain of ours takes pleasure, and how kindly, in creating real luxuries for us out of mere nothings.

Of late, I have vainly attempted to find out what this pleasant faculty of mine is. . . . Decidedly, I am created to see more good in men than bad despite my attentiveness to gather what other people say is bad. Again and again it is the same old story—a sympathy goes to them—and all excuse.

This optimism came from a woman who had not seen a loaf of white bread since May 14; that is, until Ernest actually sent her one in mid-August.[7] It was astounding to them that bread and butter were now luxury items, but such was the case as the armies seemingly had an insatiable appetite.

While tension was mounting quickly in Neufchâteau as gossip and activity surrounding the next major U.S. action intensified, the evening of September 4 started off pleasant enough for Townsend, with a dinner at the Officers' Club and a shake of the dice to see who would buy the coffee afterward. Later, he and the entire Bathos family sat on their porch to watch the searchlights near Toul play across the sky, and then they retired to the dining room to look at some new magazines Townsend had received. Suddenly, at precisely 8:30 P.M.—in a complete surprise—three successive explosions rocked the house. As the walls shuddered and they braced for another blast, they could hear particles falling on the roof and terrace. "There was no alarm on the part of the Bathoses," Townsend noted in his diary, "having been thro it all many times before. Thro their calmness, there was no nervousness on my part, I am glad to say." Although not panicked, he simply couldn't become accustomed to the artillery fire, the shelling, the bombs—the notion that some unseen object falling from the sky could kill him instantaneously.

The next day Townsend learned that a Boche aviator had dropped eight bombs in a straight line, the closest one to the Bathos house falling a mere 150 yards away; in fact, Henri Bathos spent the day picking shell fragments from the garden. Reflecting on the bombing run, Townsend concluded that it had been a rather ridiculous caper. "One is at a loss to understand how any pilot could risk a trip so far back of the lines as this is," he wrote in his diary, "having a perfectly clear field with no defenses here, have a whole, closely settled town for a mark with large railroad yards with their lights lit, and too, at the particular moment he was here, to have a trainload of troops on the track at the station and then to display such a poor ability as a marksman. One wonders what sort of glowing report he will turn in to his CO on his return."[8] For the artist it was another piece of evidence for condemning the madness of war.

A week before the Saint-Mihiel Offensive was to be launched, Townsend noticed a sudden increase in traffic—trains and cavalry, troops and artillery—moving through Neufchâteau toward the front. "And they were all hurrying thro madly, as tho things were at stake," he noted in his diary on September 5. "This all goes to confirm the suspicions that . . . we are getting ready . . . now to pull off a big offensive of our own." It rained throughout the day, but the sky cleared that night, making it a good night for a raid. However, no Boche airplane was heard. Instead, the military traffic continued to rumble by unabated; at 3 A.M., Townsend was awakened by soldiers marching and whistling "Yankee Doodle." He went to the window to watch, but it was too dark to distinguish much of anything.[9]

A few days later a stream of trucks carrying the 78th Division roared through town; Townsend could hear them singing and laughing, the soldiers excited to be part of something, even if they didn't know what it was yet; and he could sense a thrill pass through the large crowd that had gathered in the streets to watch them. "There has been a spirit in the air," he noted on September 10, "a subtle something like a premonition of impending events; of course, we are all keyed up and have been for some time waiting for it."[10] Peixotto noticed it, too: "Then, suddenly, a feverish activity developed. Something certainly was in the air, a great military secret, but every one was talking about it. New divisions kept arriving until eight had been gathered in the salient—two hundred thousand men."[11] Meanwhile, the artists made preparations to rush to the point of attack pursuant to their new orders even though no one at headquarters would tell them where that point would be.

To prepare for the offensive, American troops had been descending on the Toul sector, located between Neufchâteau and Saint-Mihiel to the north, the sector easily accessed from Neufchâteau via two roads, the more attractive route through Domremy and Vaucouleurs. Domremy, a secluded village just six miles north of Neufchâteau, is the birthplace of the heroic Jeanne d'Arc, who lived in the fifteenth century and was canonized a saint in 1920. Her family's house—with cross-shaped windows and a Gothic niche above the doorway—is just off the road that winds along the valley floor. Nestled among fir trees, preserved and protected, it presented a romantic picture for Peixotto, who visited there on a number of occasions. The locals gave him a tour, which naturally included pointing out the window through which Jeanne heard God's voice commanding her to save France, then partly occupied by the English during the Hundred Years War. While there, Peixotto noticed that a constant stream of soldiers, both French and American, paid tribute to this woman king. It was emotionally moving, and a lump formed in his throat as he witnessed one French regiment march by at a salute, the officers raising their swords to their chins and then sweeping them outward as they passed the sacred site.

To further orient himself to the sector Peixotto journeyed to Toul, a sizable walled city with a majestic cathedral lying west of Nancy and just south of the front, its suburbs effectively a massive barracks for the troops. It was a strategic gateway as the strip of land between it and Verdun guarded France's eastern flank. "All the way from Toul to Verdun stretch the Côtes or Hauts de Meuse," wrote Peixotto, "a regular succession of truncated hills resembling the mesas of our southwest, their gentle slopes rising to flat, platform-like tops that form admirable positions for defense."[12] Along these hills, the French had built a string of fortresses; unfortunately the Germans now controlled many of them. Yes, the Germans dominated the heights, including the formidable Montsec, a hill overlooking the Meuse valley and the Woëvre lowlands. The lowlands were a great marshlike plain extending north of Toul, the land thick with ponds and mud, not fit for an army. However, an army was indeed required to dislodge the Germans from atop Montsec, their main stronghold.

*Forced Landing* by Smith. The rough airfields, which flipped many an airplane, were an insult to pilots facing enemy guns firing at them from all directions.

. . .

The 1st Pursuit Group was also ramping up for what would be a historic role—Colonel Mitchell was assembling a formidable and unparalleled force of fifteen hundred planes to support the attack. However, the big news in Neufchâteau was that the French ace Paul-René Fonck, along with the eighty other French aviators, was to be quartered in town. Brash, egotistical, and a consummate boaster—all perfect qualities for an ace— Fonck would end the war with seventy-five kills, the highest among the Allies.[13] To accommodate their aeroplanes, a great *chasse* field was under construction on the outskirts of town, which was greeted with mixed feelings. "It gives promise of putting our town on the map, both in Allied circles and with the Huns, I fear," Townsend wrote with a wry wit.[14]

While anxiously awaiting the alleged offensive, Townsend and Morgan motored to the nearby air depot at Colombey-les-Belles to make studies of the aeroplanes. Just as they arrived, an RAF pilot landed a D. H. 4—a delicate but substantial machine, according to Townsend—the same plane Henri had piloted. "It seemed somehow as tho I were looking at the very machine he had and loved so much," Townsend jotted down. His attention, mercifully, was quickly diverted. As Morgan and he stood there admiring the planes, another D. H. 4 came in for a landing, only the plane hit a rough spot in the field that smashed its undercarriage and spun it around before the plane flipped forward onto its nose. This position caught Townsend's imagination: "He poised there for all the world like a big dragonfly with his nose searching the ground for sweets."[15]

After visiting several airfields—including the pilots of the 147th, who had lost only Lieutenant John H. Stevens since July 20—the artists returned home. Just outside of Nancy, they stopped at Evacuation Hospital 114 so Morgan could visit with a nurse, a Miss Barclay, an old friend. In a few days' time the hospital would be overrun with casualties. More than fifteen hundred soldiers would be admitted in the second half of September, but only seventeen would die there—the low mortality due to the fact that many of those soldiers with severe wounds were either left to die in the field or never made it rearward alive.[16] When Townsend and Morgan departed the hospital at nine that night, the roads were filled with men moving forward in absolute darkness, which resulted in much last-second swerving and braking and generally haz-

ardous driving conditions. When the artists put on their headlights as a
last resort, they received an immediate remonstration from the marching
soldiers, who were fearful of attracting the enemy's attention.

Just two days before the offensive was to be launched, Peixotto and Morgan were the first of the artists to acquire some solid information on
where the doughboys would make their glorious strike. On September
10, they were at the Lafayette Club in Neufchâteau dining with their
friend Frank Sibley, a correspondent for the *Boston Globe* who was
accredited with the 26th Division. Throughout dinner, the journalist
was most anxious to return to the division, which was located near
Verdun, the HQ in Rupt-en-Woëvre, and he *strongly* suggested they
accompany him. Sibley knew the 26th would be involved at the point of
attack.

While rumors continued to swirl, there was a comical element associated with the imminent Saint-Mihiel Offensive: the Germans knew
more about it than the doughboys who were to participate in it. Spies
and traitors had given them detailed information, and a newspaper in
Switzerland went so far as to publish the date, time, and planned duration of the opening artillery barrage. Seeing as Peixotto and Morgan
didn't subscribe to the Swiss newspaper, they took Sibley up on his offer
and journeyed to 26th HQ, positioned on the west side of the salient, in
hopes of exacting some precise information from the division's commander, General Clarence R. Edwards.

On September 11, Peixotto and Morgan pulled into 26th Division
HQ, located in a "vulgar dwelling" in a "squalid village," the farming
village of Rupt-en-Woëvre; yet, General Edwards appeared quite comfortable in the rustic surroundings, with his two-starred cap poised
jauntily to one side. "I suppose you'd like to see what we're going to do,"
he said cheerily to Peixotto and Morgan. "Come over and have a look at
the map." Standing over a large relief map of the area, all physical fea-
tures modeled carefully to scale, he pointed to rough country around Les
Eparges and explained that his men were to clear this zone of Germans.
"It's a bad country to operate in and we've got a tough job to push down
through it, but we'll do it." He looked out at the rain falling in sheets.
"Is it raining down in Toul?"

"Yes," said Peixotto.

"That's bad." He knew the lowlands in the Toul sector would quickly become soft and the roads thick with mud—yet another impediment.

Peixotto ventured coyly, "I don't suppose you can give us any idea when this operation is to take place, general."

"No. All I can say is, 'you are warm.' And I can add, for your information, that the best place to be is up in the Grande Tranchée, near O.P. No. 2. To-night, however, you'd better sleep a mile or two back in Genicourt, and," Edwards added with a chuckle, "get up when the big guns wake you." Edwards continued to play the secrecy game, no doubt following orders with uncompromising allegiance; meanwhile the Germans knew precisely at what hour the opening barrage would wake the two artists.

Peixotto and Morgan took his advice to heart, but before beating it back to Genicourt, they surveyed the area for a suitable observation post for when the battle commenced. As they retreated down the valley, Peixotto noticed that the road under their feet was already "the consistency and color of potato soup." It was the potential quagmire that Edwards feared would impede his troop movements. As Peixotto took in their surroundings, he also perceived an eerie quiet, an unsettling stillness—until the artists took a closer look into the woods. Under the cover of trees he could make out the silhouettes of big guns and dense crowds of soldiers huddled together.

On the road to Genicourt, they also encountered a forewarning of what was to come: "A pair of horses that lay in the road still hitched to a wagon that had been smashed to bits by a shell. The poor beasts," Peixotto wrote, "in their death struggle, had rolled over and over, and lay white as clay statues, livid, coated with this sticky mud, through which great pools of blood welled forth."[17] Peixotto and Morgan spent the night of September 11 in a ruined house, Peixotto with his head on his haversack, the rats beneath gnawing on its straps.

On September 11, Townsend, along with Duncan and Smith, decided to motor to 1st Army HQ at Ligny, to see what information they could obtain. Clearly, the artists were now under pressure to witness combat from a much closer proximity than ever before, and it appeared they were competing against one another to be best positioned for the pending offensive.

While in Ligny, Townsend tracked down Colonel Mitchell to discuss aviation's role in the coming offensive, but Mitchell was tied up in a conference concerning that very subject. Afterward, Mitchell gave the artist only a minute of his time and made it clear that for the next couple of days—during the early stages of the battle—there would be no chance of Townsend's visiting the forward airfields. There were positive orders against it, which, of course, Townsend found absolutely outrageous because they had just been so roundly criticized for not capturing enough action. "So that this coming from Colonel Mitchell, who is more or less of a friend of mine, and is particularly interested in my devoting myself to picturing aviation, was something of a blow to me," Townsend noted in his diary.[18] The very next day the artist would face a much greater aggravation.

"Woke this morning to find that the big offensive was begun by us in the night," Townsend wrote in his diary on September 12, "heavy artillery beginning at 1 o'clock and infantry at 5 on a sector to the north of St.-Mihiel, and on the sector between there and Pont-à-Mousson."[19] Initially there were few battlefield details to report because it was too windy for balloon observation; indeed, Townsend watched horrified as several raised Allied balloons broke from the moorings and floated away. Only one observer was seen jumping with parachute while one balloon was last seen at "about 10,000 feet sailing toward Germany." The wind also took its toll on the aviators; at least two came down over the Neufchâteau airfield.[20] Eager to catch the action at the front, Townsend looked hurriedly for his fellow artists so they could motor forward together. It was not to be.

# 12

# THE SAINT-MIHIEL SALIENT: A BLOODLESS OFFENSIVE

INSTEAD OF BEING ABLE TO SEIZE A fantastic opportunity for themselves and give Washington what it wanted, Townsend, Duncan, and Smith had been abandoned by their fellow artists, who had commandeered the one motorcar currently at their disposal. Severely disappointed and chagrined, Townsend returned to his billet in the Bathoses' home to write Cory:

Dearie:

You are reading in the morning about the big American Push—and the names you will follow on the map. Peixotto and Morgan were up the line and ran by accident into the northern part of the fight at its commencement. Dunn, Harding and Aylward somehow got a tip, and with out letting any of us know—slipped away about 2 o'clock last night—or this morning early.

And I'm mad—why they never let me know—I don't understand—
for they took the only car of ours—and there was room in it for
another, so Smith, Duncan and I were left here to gnash our
teeth—and realize that we weren't there to see the commencement
of this big and glorious affair. But tomorrow morning we have
arranged for a car and will make the trip.

Townsend was particularly incensed because it was another in a series
of callous incidents involving the motorcars. While sharing two motorcars among eight men made transportation logistics difficult, he still felt
that some of his fellow artists behaved selfishly, at times simply com-
mandeering a vehicle with no word to anyone. Townsend's evaluation of
his peers was blunt: "Queer crowd that was sent over here when it comes
to human sympathy. Good artists and good fellows but all for self, it
seems. This doesn't apply to all but it does to most all." Specifically,
Townsend found Dunn to have "a terribly keen sense of self—and it
always comes to the surface somehow—and I'm conscious of it—so I
decided to talk no more with him particularly—not that I won't
occasionally of course—but I mean not systematically."[1]

Apparently, Dunn had been lecturing Townsend on Christian Science, attempting to aid him with lessons in a time of tested faith. However, as Townsend explained to Cory, "Now don't mistake me, we are as
friendly as ever—but I don't believe his help in science is what I want—
truly." Distinct fissures were developing between some of the artists. In
this latest episode, either the trio of Dunn, Harding, and Aylward was
negligently self-absorbed—which artists tend to be—or they felt the
pressure to so impress Washington that they had now acted in a cut-
throat manner.

Knowing he would join the offensive the next day, in his September
12 letter to Cory, Townsend alluded to the danger he would face at the
front now that they had been ordered to confine their activities to the
forward areas, and he wanted to make sure she understood where they
stood financially: "You must not worry about my writing this—and the
reason which I will explain. I don't anticipate great danger tomorrow—
there shouldn't be—but its merely to say should anything happen I
haven't had my pay yet for the month of August. I haven't put in my
voucher cause I only got last months—or rather July check—cashed
today. When I get back I'll write you—then I'll put in my voucher. But

as it stands now I haven't had August pay."[2] His monthly base pay was just over 200 francs, which included commutation to pay for utilities, minus the monthly deductions for such expenses as life insurance. He was writing this down as a record for her, Townsend stated, and had no desire to discuss it further. He reassured her that we "know in whom we live and move"—inferring God would take care of him. This letter would be quite a shock to Cory; in his letter written the day before, Townsend had given no intimation of what was to come and even reiterated that "you need have no fear of my doing a little joy-riding."[3] Twenty-four hours later he was putting his financial matters in order.

Harding for one expressed no regret that he had slipped out of Neufchâteau for a front-row seat at the Saint-Mihiel Offensive. As he pointed out, "It is essential that the artist be at the point of real attack, where artillery will be blanked, where tanks will wallow over, where masses of men will follow moving barrages, where transport will surge forward to supply the advancing divisions." The point of attack was

*American Gun Fire Early Morning* by Harding. George Harding captured the intense noise of the big guns, the morning fog, and the confusion that preceded the attack.

where the war was truly persecuted, where the plan was executed, and where every participant suffered immediate consequences. "The man who missed the Marne offensive, St.-Mihiel, and the Argonne-Meuse," Harding wrote, "even though he saw all of France afterward, missed the greatest pictorial material that occurred in our participation in the war. The man who never saw those events can scarcely conceive of them."[4] However, when Dunn and he left their warm Neufchâteau beds at 3 A.M. on September 12, Harding's outlook was hardly sanguine. It was cold, raining hard, and going forward "looked like a fools errand."

Halfway to the Saint-Mihiel front, they saw the "first flash of guns," an indication that perhaps they weren't fools after all. Near Beaumont, about two miles behind the lines, they pulled the automobile into a field and then walked forward to a position where they witnessed the first tanks moving out in support of the infantry. Frantic to capture the scene, shortly thereafter Harding jotted notes in his diary:

> behind road were thousands of men
> spread in valley between German trenches
> thousands more lying down the
> barrage ahead smoke bombs making
> queer Chinese shapes in the air
> the gas shells drifting ahead of
> us the tanks attracting machine
> guns in woods first butting in then
> backing out.[5]

The artists attached themselves to the 42nd Division, which would be jumping off at 5 A.M., with the wire cutters taking the lead to punch holes through any barbed-wire barriers. Obsessively intent on witnessing the action, Harding joined the first detachment pushing forward into no-man's-land—the 1st Battalion, 167th Infantry—slogging, slipping, and cursing through the mud. Throwing caution to the wind, Dunn attached himself to Company A, 1st Battalion, and charged forward, a rolling barrage sweeping ahead of them. His wife and children were far removed from his mind; he harbored fears he would leave nothing for posterity and this attack was his opportunity for artistic heroics.[6] Both men were lucky to be with the 1st Battalion because, by the time the 2nd Battalion followed over the same ground, German gunners had

*The Tanks at Seicheprey* by Dunn. Dunn and Harding followed the tanks through Seicheprey and beyond, the vivid images unrelenting.

emerged from behind the rolling barrage, taken their posts, and proceeded to pour fire into their line.[7]

Across treacherous mud and trenches filled with barbed wire, the artists clamored forward, from Seicheprey to Essey, almost three miles into enemy-held territory. For Harding, the images swirled around him with a fury:

5 Amer dead high
explosive ones brain entirely out
the dead horses just on road the
boche—the machine guns etc.
the wet rain—the mud—the dugouts
at Essey—the first aid station there . . .
mud on horses. 42 div going 4 miles
the horses heads standing against
weather in road the men in blankets
boche coats the shell holes in

> road truck overturned, the carts
> overturning in road dead horses,
> the cavalry—the tanks stuck
> other out of gas . . .
> abandoned villages shell and pieces
> slept in car No food—36 hours
> started at 5.30 am
> went on and on . . .

Villages were burning; ammunition dumps were being exploded; planes were shot down; and all the while "masses of men" moved up the valley in single file, in continuous streams.[8]

The advance was so rapid over the next few days that Harding and Dunn had no time to eat and little time to sleep, and they made few if

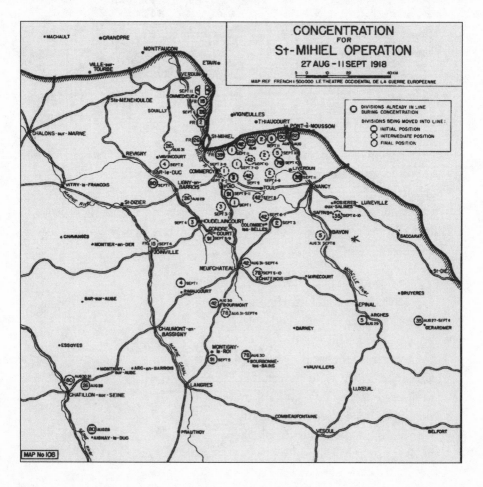

any sketches; as Dunn reported, "Owing to the conditions of the weather and the extremely rapid advance, I was unable to make sketches, but as mental impressions are of more value to the nature of my particular work, I did not come away empty handed (or should I say headed), and shall, when opportunity offers, render those impressions in pictorial form."[9] Those pieces would include *Kamerad—The Sniper* (see the next page), *The Machine Gun Nest* (see below), and *The Tanks at Seicheprey* (see page 197). In the latter piece, a watercolor, Dunn depicted tanks leading the charge in the misty gray morning light, shadowy infantry following, crumpled bodies in the field, the landscape barren.

As Edwards had promised, the big guns that entranced Harding awakened Peixotto and Morgan in these early hours of September 12, the morning enveloped in fog and a drizzle falling. "The howitzers and naval guns that had been silent were now splitting the air with the clamor of their voices and fairly shaking the earth with their concussions," wrote Peixotto.[10] Because there was little return fire, Morgan and he decided to risk taking their motorcar along the road and pushed forward until they

*The Machine Gun Nest* by Dunn. No ground was sacred when it came to strategically positioning an artillery battery or a machine-gun nest.

*Kamerad—The Sniper* by Dunn. During the Saint-
Mihiel Offensive, German soldiers surrendered in
droves by calling out "Kamerad."

hit a traffic jam of ambulances and ammunition trains. They hid their
motorcar in the woods and proceeded on foot until they reached the
American trenches, where they learned that the troops were already in the
Germans' first-line defenses.

Peixotto scanned the battlefield for action—the action Washington
pined for—but observed with disappointment, "Out in the blasted
wastes of No-man's-land, however, where hill succeeded hill, once
covered with dense forests, now but shell-torn barrens spotted with a few
blackened stumps, nothing was visible but the shell-bursts that kicked up
clouds of dirt or broke in dense balls of smoke. The 'doughboys,' as had
always been the case up to this time, were practically invisible, hidden in
shell-holes, in trenches, or under any cover that they could find."[11]

As the 26th assaulted the northwest face of the salient and seven divisions assaulted the southern face, the latter including the 42nd Division, it became clear to the artists that the overall strategy involved a pincer action—as it had at Château-Thierry—to snip off the bulge. Failure being out of the question, Pershing used overwhelming force that pitted some 550,000 American soldiers supplemented by 110,000 French against a mere 75,000 Germans, the enemy aided somewhat by superlative defensive positions anchored by machine-gun nests.[12] Supporting the ground attack were over 3,000 artillery guns, along with 3.3 million rounds, and nearly 1,500 planes—the greatest concentration yet of air power. Although they did have a superlative defensive posture, the Germans had fully comprehended that the massive concentration of power across the line would overwhelm them, so, on September 10, they had already begun a retreat toward the Hindenburg Line, which naturally permitted a swift and relatively bloodless American advance.

As Peixotto and Morgan stood frustrated by what little they could see, the wounded began to filter back through the trenches. Some were "walking quite erect with head or hand bound up;" Peixotto observed, "others stooping, doubled up with pain and fear, their khaki coats spotted with great brownish stains, their faces and hands bloody. Then came the litter-bearers, staggering through the slippery mud up the hill, steadying themselves by a hand pressed against the trench walls as they bore their heavy burdens—still forms stretched flat, immobile, covered with an O.D. blanket from which protruded a pair of spiked shoes with the toes turned up."

To acquire some information of the battle's progress, Peixotto and Morgan moved back to the 103rd regimental PC, where a first-aid dressing station had just been established and the number of wounded increased noticeably. "The stretchers lay upon the ground with the doctors stooping over them," wrote Peixotto. "The ambulances came up one by one, were filled as fast as the wounds were dressed, and dispatched to the rear." As the artist mingled with the troops, he learned that the 103rd had marched into position on September 8, with regimental headquarters set up at Guilmont, after which battalion and company commanders made reconnaissance of the front lines. Then, at 10 P.M. on September 11, the order for attack was issued and outposts were withdrawn. While other elements of the 26th Division would meet enough resistance to stop them from reaching the first day's

*On the Trail of the Hun* by Aylward. A snaking stream of troops miles long chased after the
Germans over open country.

objectives, the 103rd's 1st Battalion found itself behind the Germans'
first position at 5:40 P.M. and had yet to encounter any opposition. That
day the 1st Battalion lost but four men, along with nine wounded, and
one missing, all to artillery fire. Much of the battalion's effort went into
simply escorting prisoners to the rear, the enemy surrendering with
shouts of "Kamerad."

Peixotto observed that prisoners were indeed being brought back in
droves; he counted more than 140 in the first group. "Most of them
were serious-looking men of middle age," he wrote, "who certainly
seemed glad to be through with it, flinging down their helmets with gestures that plainly said, 'Thank God, that's over.' A few were slightly
wounded, but the great proportion wore new uniforms, clean, unspot-
ted with mud, showing clearly that they had given up without a struggle; in fact, had dressed to go into captivity." That evening, Peixotto and
Morgan passed through Rarécourt, where hundreds of prisoners had
been herded, forced to stay the night under a drizzling rain and huddled
together behind barbed wire.[13]

. . .

While trapped in Neufchâteau, on September 12, Townsend read the incoming communiqués eagerly. He learned that the whole front, with light tanks in the lead, had made great strides. Some sectors had moved forward six miles, the average being five. "When the last communiqué came at 10 tonight, Montsec, that has always been thought almost impregnable, was in our hands, taken without resistance, and the French, who were advancing in the middle sector directly against St.-Mihiel, had their patrols there at the end of the day." Townsend noted that there had been "practically no resistance. No artillery reply to speak of, and no Hun air activity."[14] The only serious impediments reported were the mud, resulting from five days of rain, and the confounding trenches; after all, the Germans had had four years to dig an intricate maze rigged with traps and strung with barbed wire. There was nothing the doughboys could do to combat the mud except curse at the mire. As for overcoming the walls of barbed wire, they brought with them two innovations: giant, two-handed clippers and rolls of chicken wire to be thrown down and rolled out as pathways.

Meanwhile, at the front, the observations of Major Raymond Austin, 6th Field Artillery, 1st Division, who was operating to the left of where Harding and Dunn were moving forward, confirmed the reports Townsend was receiving. "Not a shell landed anywhere near my batteries and during the whole fight not more than four shells fell near me to be dangerous," Austin wrote his family on September 17. "The Boche evidently left in great haste as our advance was extremely rapid. In one place an excellent dinner, ready to be cooked, was left—steaks, potatoes, cheese, etc. One of my batteries got two cows and several had pigs, chickens and a great number of rabbits. . . . The whole thing was a walkover for us." Two weeks later Austin would be dead.[15]

Finally supplied a motorcar, on September 13, Townsend, accompanied by Duncan and Smith, drove forward to Seicheprey, now several miles to the rear of the 1st and 42nd Divisions, where they spent the afternoon touring by foot because traffic was so congested. "Such activity," Townsend noted in his diary. "As one looked across the country forward or back, as far as the eye could reach, and not only on every available road but on many new ones built by our engineers, were the same long, toiling lines of troops coming out for relief, having driven way beyond their objectives." In fact, by early morning on day two, the 1st Division had linked up with the 26th, the pincer clamped shut. The doughboys had liberated a sector that had been a virtual no-man's-land for four years. As for the French civilians who had survived the German occupation here, most were either whiskered old men or young women with war babies.[16]

Subsequently, the Germans did launch several counterattacks, but their attempts were halfhearted. Some enemy battalions even refused orders to advance against the Americans, a situation Townsend learned of from a young refugee: "A French girl has come into our lines saying that on the evening of the attack, the 12th, the Germans officers were at her home, Souleuvre Farm, and that when the battle reached some headway, two battalions were ordered to take Bois Gerard. After repeated attempts and failing, they absolutely refused to advance again."[17]

Prisoners were put to good use and Townsend now watched a large number of them take off their coats as they prepared to work on road repair: "They were a healthy-looking crowd too, and seemed in no way depressed." Of course not; they had survived.

The artists also encountered a number of light Renault tanks— 6-ton, 2-man vehicles—stuck in the mud and shell holes, the machines listing and the treads frozen. A Captain Baldwin, whom Townsend had met at the U.S. Tank Center and who was now salvaging the tanks, explained that they had 144 tanks employed in the operation. Of those, about thirty had been knocked out of commission by mud and hole— not one had been shot. The next day Townsend would meet the liaison officer between the American and French tank corps, Lieutenant Sewall, who painted a rosy picture concerning the tanks and couldn't say enough about what had been accomplished under Colonel George S. Patton, the prodigal tank commander and strategist. According to one story, in a brazen and impatient action outside the village of Jonville, on September 13, Patton used unsupported tank platoons in a cavalry-style attack that pushed back the Germans some six miles even though the Americans were outnumbered.[18]

Townsend, Smith, and Duncan decided to spend the night at the Yale Mobile Hospital #39, where they hoped to find available beds. Just as the artists arrived, so did a Bréguet—a two-seater French plane—that had been in a scrap with a squadron of Germans. With his gunner shot, the pilot managed to escape and flew straight to the hospital, where he hoped the doctors could save his comrade. Hit in the leg and hips and bleeding profusely, the gunner died later that night. The pilot had not a scratch.

After a late supper, the artists spent the evening touring the hospital. The "mobile" hospitals had been developed during the war; and, as suggested by the name, they could be completely taken down and loaded into trucks in an hour's time. The Yale outfit had a shock room, a preparation room, two X-ray rooms, three operating rooms—manned by eight teams—and a sterilization area. The unit also had a transportable laboratory for undertaking clinical and bacteriological work such as examining urine and blood counts. One of the impediments to their work was frequent contamination, such as mold growth; it would be another ten years before such molds revealed their secrets to Alexander Fleming, who would discover penicillin. For now, in an attempt to prevent infections, a bacteriologist would make a bacteria count from a patient's wound or incision, and not until the count was low would the surgeon close the wound with sutures. Even in death, some of the soldiers served a purpose, as the hospital's lab also conducted autopsies from which the doctors learned about the human body; thus the practice of medicine advanced.

In preparation for the Saint-Mihiel Offensive, the hospital had constructed six new barracks to have a total of 500 beds available, and the number of personnel was increased to about 220. Over the first twenty-four hours of the drive, they received just over 200 cases and operated on 170, even though, according to the French, this unit had the capacity for only 144 daily operations. To maximize its facility, however, the hospital had "arranged a new operating room and triage on the principle of the Ford factory."[19] If Henry Ford, a pioneer in assembly-line production and a peace activist who had tried to stop the war, only knew.

In addition to the wounded, the doctors also had to contend with more run-of-the-mill illnesses such as measles, meningitis, scarlet fever, dysentery, and diphtheria, as well as treating those sexually active soldiers who came in with gonorrhea and other venereal diseases—in war, pleasures also had their price. And then there were the ubiquitous lice. To combat this enemy, the hospital used an improvised delouser machine, which they built by piping the steam exhaust from a sterilization truck to a wine cask that served as a steam chamber for sterilizing clothing. The hospital was so proud of its improvisation that commanding officer Major Joseph Flint forwarded its design to the AEF's chief surgeon.[20]

During his visit, Townsend watched as YMCA officers handed out cigarettes to the grateful wounded and the hospital's staff prepped soldiers for surgery. He then mustered enough courage to spend time in the operating rooms: "I managed better than I thought that I would, tho I had to go out into the fresh air a couple of times." That night he found himself in a situation he never dreamed of being in: he slept with the enemy, next to a wounded Boche lieutenant in one of the wards. Meanwhile, Smith had three Boche next to him. A smile played on Townsend's lips when he heard the surprise and subsequent cursing by the orderlies who had just discovered they had Boche under their care. The orderlies, all soldiers, had themselves been wounded, therefore, they were just slightly biased against any enemy visitors. When it came to catering to their fellow doughboys, on the other hand, the orderlies were exceptionally compassionate; it touched Townsend to see their humanity among the madness.

In the early morning hours, as Townsend roused himself from sleep, he overheard two nurses discussing Duncan's apparent ailment. Because of a peculiar rattle and murmur Duncan made as he slept, the one nurse was convinced he was one of the wounded who'd been operated on, while the other nurse was arguing he was an officer simply there for the night. Townsend chuckled to himself: "Too bad they couldn't find some reason for waking him to give him some medicine or attention. Would have been a good joke on him."[21]

After breakfast Townsend went to have a close look at the Bréguet aircraft that had come screaming in the day before. It was beautiful as it sat there in the low sun "like some insect that had alighted for a fleeting moment on the grass." But its image evoked tragedy, too, considering the gunner's fate. As he surveyed the damage done by the German aviators, Townsend wondered at how the pilot had managed to escape. There was a bullet hole right into his pit and the machine's body was badly scarred, so much so that Townsend "shuddered to think of the veritable inferno they must have been in for a time. There would have been a perfect rain of fire around them . . . all the while."[22]

Townsend, Smith, and Duncan motored westward to Xivray and Apremont, among other towns that had been in no-man's-land for years, and, at every opportunity, made vivid sketches of the ruins and desolation. Once-cultivated fields were overgrown; once meticulously cobbled streets were filled with rusty barbed wire; and in towns formerly occupied by the enemy, the public signs had been changed to German, a slanderous insult to the French. Between these towns, the shelling that had preceded the American advance had been so effective that traffic could only crawl along the shattered roads, while the 57th Engineers frantically repaired them. Once in the relentless flow of vehicles, Townsend's motorcar proceeded forward with everyone else—there was no turning off, there was no stopping, regardless of which direction the front shifted.

Slowly, they made their way several miles north to Essey, which the 42nd had taken with such speed on September 12 that German officers had abandoned their saddled horses and a regimental band had fled without its instruments. While Dunn and Harding had continued forward with the 42nd, Townsend's car of artists paused in the village to sketch the aftermath. Using just a pencil, Duncan captured a war-torn building now serving as both a barber shop and a first-aid station staffed by the Red Cross; certainly not a sight he'd ever see in New York. Smith positioned himself on a street corner to render "a small fragment of the of the endless procession of wagons, motors and men that swarmed the roads on the heels of the Hun-hunting doughboys." As for Townsend, the battered remains of the church impressed him: "The church is a very beautiful ruin for, after all, a ruin can have all the elements that make for beauty even though it may not be consciously created." For protection, the Germans had built their PC on the far side of a church, in the shadow of the spire, where the thick, impenetrable stone walls of the edifice allowed their generals to work and sleep in peace.

Having arrived in Essey at the same time as the 42nd's artillery batteries, Townsend watched as the men set their guns up with expedience: "Here and there were balloons in different stages of inflation getting ready to get into the air for observation, and here were batteries of 155s getting into new positions along the roadside to strafe the retreating Huns."[23] Just as Townsend was absorbing the activity, a round of Boche artillery shells came whistling in, landing on the town's edge. He quickly comprehended that the advance had to continue hastily so the Germans had no time to set their own artillery pieces and find their range; otherwise, a few well-placed

*No Man's Land* by Dunn. As Dunn witnessed more of wars' devastating consequences, his work became more subdued; his no-man's-land is brutally desolate.

enemy shells would wreak havoc on the congested roads.

Continuing toward the front line, on the road north of Essey, Townsend stopped to pick some wildflowers that had managed to survive the battle, which he later mailed to his daughter, Barbara. "I am sending in this a little flower or two that I picked up on the battle field one just after the Huns had gone," he wrote. "I picked it up in a country that has been No Man's Land for four years where the ground was all torn up with big shell holes, old and new, and it was on just a little farther than where I saw the kitties that I wrote you about."[24] The artist André Smith determined this no-man's-land to be the ugliest piece of France he had ever seen; yet, he concluded that it was also "a setting of solemn magnificence . . . a true background of war."[25]

As Townsend's motorcar now pushed on to Flirey, he noticed that the German trenches had been torn asunder and large groups of "colored troops" were busy rebuilding roads, under the watchful eyes of engineers. It took the artists seemingly hours to travel no more than a few miles. "Finally, the delicate skeleton of the church at Flirey was in view," he wrote. "What a lovely but sad wreck has been made of it." It was a grim silhouette, observed Smith, as the artists made studies of what was in their minds a monument to modern warfare.[26] Further degradations to the edifice were still very possible, for next to it U.S. soldiers were setting up a battery of 155 cannons. Although it had remained in Allied hands throughout the war, Flirey was another village bordering no-man's-land that had been hammered. The village's houses and farms were demolished, the scattered trees were leafless and scorched black—if still standing—and the roads were scarred by a network of trenches. Purely from an artistic standpoint, Townsend delighted in the scale of it all: the houses had once been relatively spacious, so the crazed geometry of their substantial ruins was extremely interesting to explore in terms of composition. It was as if a cubist mason had rearranged the village.

Although Smith also appreciated the artistic merits of the savage scenery, it prompted him to ruminate over the arbitrary nature of death and destruction. "It was interesting at times to contemplate the discrimination exercised by an exploding shell," he wrote, "and this, too, in spite of the indiscrimination of German artillerymen. The same chance that would, for example, kill two men in a group of three would demolish a row of houses and leave one in their midst untouched."[27] Certainly, while Flirey was in American hands, doughboys there died at the hands of an indiscriminate enemy. There was Private Charles H. "The Kid" Lynch of Woburn, Massachusetts, who was returning from a routine patrol when killed by a German sniper's bullet that caught him behind the ear. Apparently, the Germans had sent out a raiding party, and had Lynch returned to his dugout only a minute sooner he would have been safe. The company's chaplain, the empathetic Reverend Boucher, wrote to Lynch's mother that her boy "was well prepared, for before going to the firing line, he went to confession and communion."[28]

During the offensive, one of the primary goals was to wrest the strategically important Saint-Mihiel, on the nose of the Salient, from German control by surgically snipping it off with the pincer movement. Because there were symbolic implications of national importance to the French in freeing this town long held by the enemy—of being the first to march through its streets—the French were given the privilege to do so even though the Americans were shedding most of the blood. Eager to view the town and its inhabitants after four years of occupation, on the morning of September 13, Peixotto and Morgan left for Saint-Mihiel despite not knowing whether there were still pockets of resistance. This particular day would indeed prove to be one of historic importance; little did the artists know they would be active participants.

The only passable approach into town was from the west, following "an abandoned road in a desert landscape: tall dead grass where once had been rich fields; acres of barbed wire where yellow wheat had sprouted— a country that had been a no-man's-land for four long years." When they reached the Saint-Mihiel suburb of Chauvoncourt, traffic came to a halt; a mine had exploded in the road the night before, leaving a twenty-foot crater. To Peixotto, Chauvoncourt presented an eerie scene: vines turning autumnal blood red had strangled the few buildings left standing; grass and weeds carpeted the road's paving stones; and it was so silent that "a strange feeling came over one, as if walking in the streets of some plague-stricken city, of some town in a fairy-tale, cursed and enchanted by the wave of a Merlin's wand."

Still a little over a mile from Saint-Mihiel, the artists were forced to continue on foot to the Meuse River, where a group of French engineers had just completed a flimsy footbridge. Some of the inhabitants trapped in town for four years tentatively negotiated their way across and Peixotto engaged them in quiet conversation. It was heartbreaking to hear them describe how for four years they could see the French lines and were convinced on many an occasion that they would be liberated, but were not—until now. As the artists entered Saint-Mihiel, a small group of children waved French flags and held strips of tricolored ribbon tightly in their tiny hands. They were accompanied by a few women and a couple of old men, the children's fathers either fighting or dead. More curious citizens, many in their Sunday clothes, noticed the American uniforms. These were the first Americans they had ever seen. "At first the people did not know who we were," Peixotto wrote to his wife of the momentous occasion, "but some of the few French soldiers told them and word went round, 'Ce sont les Americains.' I don't dare describe my feelings as these poor people pressed about us. Oh, but I was proud of my country and of our brave boys who had made this deliverance possible!"[29]

Peixotto approached one group of eager inhabitants, and, looking over the children, he remarked that they appeared healthy.

"Yes, they were good to the children," said one citizen. "The soldiers were not so bad, many of them fathers themselves—but the officers! If ever you get hold of a Prussian officer . . . " The sentence was concluded with "a savage gesture of hatred and murder." The stories these people told were not lurid tales of torture and atrocity; no, just the simple tale of mental and physical anguish—along with the privations of food and heat and warm clothes—as they waited four interminably long years to be liberated.

"Four years, monsieur; think of it!" said one elderly woman to Peixotto. She had not forgotten the day the Prussians came: September 24, 1914. "I was one of the first to see them coming and I cried out, 'Mon Dieu, here they are, the Prussians,' and I almost went crazy. . . . They were proud in those days—proud and arrogant. Ah, if I had known that it was going to last four years, I should have died on the spot!"

One of the men recounted to Peixotto how the Prussians had hated to be told that the entire world, black and white, was against them. And when residents needled their captors about the Americans joining the fight, the Prussians laughed at the notion. "Our submarines will sink them all," they chortled haughtily. Their tune soon changed. By late summer, with hundreds of thousands of doughboys pouring through France, the Prussians refused to discuss the American matter.[30] It was a small measure of revenge for the Saint-Mihiel residents to finally watch the Germans slink out of their city with their tails between their legs, with no rearguard action, no harassing machine-gun nests. Yes, the city had been taken without a fight. At sundown the prior evening, the townspeople explained to Peixotto, the Prussians had ordered them into their homes until dawn. During the night they heard orders shouted and troops clattering across cobblestone streets. Come morning there was nary a Boche.

As Peixotto and Morgan strolled through the town, they came upon the place de Halles, the entrance square to the town, where they encountered a well-dressed, animated crowd gathered around a platoon of French cavalry and a platoon of infantry. Meanwhile, standing to the side were two young women "with powdered cheeks and painted lips" who apparently were not so happy to see the Germans go; these women would not feel welcomed among their own, especially while the other citizens regaled the artists with stories of suffering and pain.

"Ah, monsieur," said one wizened woman, "at the beginning of the war, I had three sons in the French army, and never a word of them have I heard since. I dread to have tidings of them now."

From day one, the townspeople said, the Prussians had confiscated all of their provisions, so for years they had not had a drop of wine or beer; they survived on black bread and canned meat. One woman, tugging at the clothes draped loosely over her shrunken body, said, "Look at me; my own daughter won't know me."

Continuing through the town, the artists were quite surprised to run into a lone American aviator adorned in his Teddy bear flight suit wandering in front of the Hôtel de Ville. Without missing a beat, he simply explained that he was looking for a telephone. Well, Peixotto replied glibly, that would take some time because there aren't any. As they all now strolled along, the aviator described how he had been merrily machine-gunning the retreating Germans when engine trouble forced him down.

Returning to the place de Halles, Peixotto was amazed by the number of French flags "resurrected from heaven knows what hiding places" now gracing the streets.[31] Deciding it was time to move on, Peixotto and Morgan started to walk back to their motorcar, only to encounter an illustrious group of approaching soldiers. It took them but a moment to identify two unmistakable figures: General Henri Philippe Pétain, the French commander in chief, and General Pershing, standing erect yet relaxed. They saluted. Somewhat surprised that two captains had beaten him to Saint-Mihiel, Pershing returned their salute with a bemused look and a pleasant, "Good morning, gentlemen."[32] There was no mention of this encounter in Pershing's memoirs, although the general did recall in detail how enthusiastically the citizens had greeted the soldiers' arrival at this historic moment of liberation. Indeed, as the artists followed this group back to the center square, the locals cheered, "Vive la France! Vive l'Amérique. Vive Pétain!" Cut off from the world, they had no idea who Pershing was, thus no "Vive Pershing!" In his speech, Pétain explained graciously that while the French had marched into Saint-Mihiel, all credit was due the Americans, who had crushed the Germans on the south and west side of the salient.[33] In response, a bent, elderly woman shuffled forward with a bouquet of wildflowers and presented them to Pershing, who accepted them with great dignity. The simplistic beauty of the scene so impressed Peixotto that he could find no words to express the emotions of the historic moment, and the sketch he subsequently made did not do it justice.

If the arrival of Pétain and Pershing wasn't enough to signify what a

symbolic victory this was for the Americans and French, then the subsequent arrival of the U.S. secretary of war, Newton Baker, who looked
"strangely out of place" in his civilian clothes, and France's premier,
Georges Clemenceau, certainly did. All wanted to bask in the glory of
liberating a major French town after four years of captivity.[34]

Peixotto and Morgan were eager to journey northeastward, where the
doughboys were still engaged in securing the salient. Yet again they had
to pass through a ghostly no-man's-land, where the long-abandoned
houses were crumbling into the earth. Near the French outpost of Saint-
Aignant, they encountered engineers already repairing the ravaged front
by filling in the French trenches; as their motorcar now bounced over
this healing land, the artists joked that they went "over the top in a
Dodge." Not until Bouconville did Peixotto and Morgan catch the
advancing army, its relentless tidal march impressing Peixotto: it simply
"flowed on, never-ceasing, slow-moving but endless, sometimes congested and dammed for a while, then pushing on again; eating, resting,
sleeping, joking, swearing, grumbling as it went, but ceaselessly and
stubbornly advancing, oozing up every road it could find, as it followed
the 'doughboys' that blazed the trail, pushing the Hun back to his main
defenses on the Hindenburg line."[35] Turning southeastward and then
northward, they entered Essey, now home to a brigade headquarters of
the 42nd Division, which advanced twelve miles over two days. Eager to
catch the forward units, Peixotto and Morgan continued northward to
Pannes, a village that the Alabamians of the 167th Infantry Regiment—
the regiment Dunn had attached himself to—had liberated with support
from U.S. tanks the prior day, in the late afternoon of September 12.
The proud tank officers told Peixotto how "their steel beasts had
devoured the machine-gun nests in the houses." According to reports,
Patton had led the charge into town, literally astride a Renault tank
with Germans unleashing a sheath of bullets at him. Not until he
noticed the bullets dinging off the steel did he jump down and take
cover behind the metal beast.[36] Climbing a hill, Peixotto could see
artillery shells falling on the beaten Boche, who were still retreating.
Clouds of smoke from fire and shell bursts hung lazily in the air, a stark
contrast to the feverish activity on the ground as infantrymen fought to
save themselves.

From Pannes, Peixotto and Morgan pushed hard to Bouconville,

immediately behind the front lines. On the road they passed German
dead, whom the doughboys were in no rush to bury, and on a hilltop
they came upon a quarry housing a German machine-gun nest that had
been neutralized with one shell. Climbing out of their car, they investi-
gated: "Its four gunners had been caught eating when the shell came
over and lay in a heap just where they had been sitting with their black
bread and sausage still clasped in their stiff hands."[37]

As the road took the artists northeastward, they encountered elements
of the 89th Division, which was positioned to the right of the 42nd and
now earning a reputation for its combativeness. At the moment, trucks
belonging to the 89th were evacuating civilians from Thiaucourt, two
miles away, evacuating these innocents because the village had just been
liberated and there was no doubt that the Boche would bomb it ruthlessly. Taking the opportunity to talk to some of the refugees, Peixotto
noted that there were "nuns with placid faces; elderly men whose
shrunken bodies only half filled their Sunday clothes of before the war;
women in bonnets with strings tied under their chins, tired-looking and

*Beyond Seicheprey* by Smith. After the Saint-Mihiel victory, there was no time for raiding wine cellars;
the doughboys were immediately ordered to the Meuse Argonne region.

hungry after nights spent in cellars or in tending their peaked children—all of them leaving homes that they knew would now be destroyed, but happy, they said, happy in the thought that at last they were freed from the hated German yoke, freed by these sturdy, clean young boys from far-away America."

While Peixotto's language—"freed from the hated German yoke, freed by sturdy, clean young boys"—could be construed as histrionic or a bit ornate, the liberated Thiacourt residents were indeed exceptionally thankful when the doughboys marched into town. As one of the old men said to Peixotto: "We kissed them, we shook their hands, for it was impossible for us to express to them in words our joy and gratitude. Happily, we knew their uniforms, for we had seen a few prisoners pass—otherwise, we might have mistaken them for a new kind of German or 'other Bulgarian'!" But then he asked, "Our poor city—what will become of it?" Peixotto had no answer for the old man.[38]

On September 15, with the offensive effectively complete, Peixotto found a moment to write to Mary, opening his letter with the declaration, "I have just been passing three or four of the most impressive days of my life." He then recalled his harrowing experiences, which included the rude awakening: "It was a terrible morning," he wrote of September 12, "as you may imagine the noise of the great barrage." Coincidentally, Mary had also just endured a barrage—two air raids—while in Paris on September 14. "The barrage was fascinating and the strangest thing," she wrote Ernest the next day. As she sat in the dark she felt as though the sirens, the bombs, the people in the streets was all the perfect "theme for an . . . opera." In the noise and chaos, the final scene was clear to her: the fall of Germany. "And then a great silence."[39]

Having returned to Neufchâteau on September 15, Townsend was privy to communiqués arriving from the front, which all waxed euphoric. It was announced that U.S. troops had taken Woël and Wadonville to the north, thus flattening the former German bulge, with one of the corps taking eight thousand enemy prisoners. As for the prisoners, they seemed not just relieved, but rather pleased. "A Hun Major and his staff were led in today by his grinning orderly," Townsend jotted in his diary, "to the great amusement of the other prisoners." In total, the Saint-Mihiel Offensive netted fifteen thousand prisoners, while the U.S. 1st

Army suffered seven thousand casualties, which included only several hundred deaths. The relatively light AEF casualties prompted artist André Smith to label it the "bloodless offensive."[40]

In the sky over Neufchâteau, celebratory aviators treated those below to "several exhibitions of aerial acrobatics" that indicated they had enjoyed a good day against the Germans. It was a moment of artistic pleasure along with a measure of personal sadness for Townsend:

> One was struck by the very likeness of a bird's control of the air as they whipped and wheeled and looped, dropping and winging aloft again. To think that poor, dear old Henri once did this; that he was perfect, too, in his mastery of all the tricks, and that he had worked out several new manoeuvres that were quite his own, and then to lose his life thro some break in a petrol tube, perhaps. But he died in his duty, and got his wounds besides, over the Hun lines, from their shrapnel. So Glory to his name and to his memory. And that on the way home from his raid he should have this happen over his own airdrome and to fall from 100 feet just as he was trying to land with his own wounds for help—seems a cruel fate for even War to deal him. But, after all, we mustn't murmur or cry out in our grief. And he did get into the big fight for all he was worth, whereas many . . . give their lives before they have even tasted the wine of war in the air.[41]

Pershing and his staff also toasted the doughboys' success, while their French counterparts declared the victory "magnificent, superb, inspiring," and Premier Clemenceau telephoned GHQ to offer his congratulations.[42] In light of the fact that the Germans were retreating at the time of the attack, the measure of magnificence is up for debate; however, there was no doubt that the Saint-Mihiel victory was a morale booster for the Allied nations. And there was no doubt that those French citizens liberated were deeply grateful after four years of living hell under Boche reign. As for the foot soldiers—the doughboys—they found themselves with no time to raid beer and wine caches for spontaneous celebrations, because Pershing was determined to strike another blow against the staggered enemy. Columns of troops were already on the march, and the next offensive would not be so bloodless for the Americans.

# 13

# THE MEUSE ARGONNE
# AND THE
# GODDESS OF WAR

"WILL STAY HOME AND TRY TO COLLECT my scattered thoughts," Townsend wrote in his diary on September 17, "do some necessary reading and work out some ideas for pictures." With the Saint-Mihiel front relatively quiet on the heels of the German withdrawal, it was an ideal time to gather oneself— emotionally and physically. At the moment, the only action of note involved German soldiers surrendering in droves, their general mood one of disillusion and weary capitulation. "Prisoners speak of great discontent in Austria and of the great bitterness arising between Germany and Austria," Townsend jotted in his diary. In fact, a piece of intriguing news had just come out of Austria: it was appealing for a peace parley.

In contrast to Austria, the German air fleet remained aggressive; overnight, a horde of Gothas—a large, twin-engine bomber with excellent range—conducted a raid on Paris, resulting in dozens of casualties and inflicting material damage. Allied aircraft hit back hard. Townsend heard reports that all enemy airdromes were bombed heavily the next night, and, in a subsequent mission, Allied planes dropped ten tons of bombs on German troops at Mars-la-Tour, a strategic crossroads town about eight miles behind the newly drawn front line. Meanwhile, enemy pilots made a series of low-flying night missions along the front during which they dropped illuminating bombs; clearly they were worried about where the next strike would come. The Germans also bombed Saint-Mihiel, among other towns behind the lines, which, Townsend knew, meant it was only a matter of time before Neufchâteau was hit again.

On September 20, a full moon rose above the Bathos residence—a perfect night for raids on both sides—however, an exhausted Townsend forsook waiting up for the inevitable and went to bed. Sure enough, out of the silver night, the Boche bombers roared, but sleeping "the sleep of the '*bien fatigue*,'" the artist didn't hear the bombs hit buildings and streets. Slowly he drifted awake to what he perceived to be the *put-put-put* of machine guns; in a dream state, in a nightmare, he felt as though he was in a trench under Boche fire. Shaking his head clear, he looked at his watch: it was 11:30 P.M. He went to the window and saw two officers hugging trees, a rather silly scene. Scrambling from his room, Townsend immediately ran into Henri Bathos, who explained that after dropping two bombs, the enemy pilot had machine-gunned the streets.

As the artist milled with the lingering people outside, he discovered that they were infuriated by the random strafing of civilian areas that could kill children; there was talk of going into the fields for safety on such clear nights; and they couldn't understand why Neufchâteau had yet to receive the anti-aircraft 75s that had been promised. Having slept through the alert and then the bombing, as Townsend listened to the complaints, he found himself somewhat detached from the evening's events; instead of concern, he was filled with a perverse curiosity as to what had transpired and who had been killed. He realized there was a certain morbid delight in contemplating such horror, such deeds, a delight that you try to deprecate; yet, this suppression was difficult as the delight in destruction was an innate human quality.[1]

Encroaching on Townsend's "morbid delight" was the unsettling notion of a pilot randomly strafing the streets where innocent women and children could easily be victimized. These images in his mind extended to the strafing of soldiers, Allied or enemy, lying helpless in shallow trenches:

> I never get the picture quite out of my mind, the strafing of the Hun from the air as told by the pilots at Saints at the time of our work on the Marne battle. Of how, catching the Huns in their little holes dug in the ground each for himself, and just deep enough to protect him from rifle or machine gun fire, and to afford a degree of protection against flying shrapnel, they ran along the lines of these poor creatures, pouring onto them their streams of veritable liquid fire. And I can imagine how well they would do it too, these fellows who have become so skilled with their guns that they can catch the wary, darting, humming Hun. Somehow, dragonflies with bean shooters would seem an easy game for them. And I can imagine how those Huns there in their little shallow cups in the fields must have felt as they writhed around, knowing their utter helplessness, no place to hide, and how they must have longed even for a trench to dodge about in.

While lying in bed the next morning, a haunted and apprehensive Townsend listened to the anxious people passing by his window, their parade of footsteps evoking a scene he had witnessed many times as of late: the funeral procession with the stoic soldiers marching erect and the weeping women dressed in black. He picked up his diary and reflected: "Yesterday and today there has been a constant line of funerals, it seems, passing my windows here for the military cemetery. About evenly divided—French and American. . . . One is always hearing the volleys of the guns there over their graves."[2]

Despite the bleak cycle of funerals, the usual tantalizing question on most minds was, Where will the action heat up next? And for Townsend, that question was followed by the cynical thought, Who of the artists will attempt to sneak off in one of the motorcars, leaving the others in a rut? Townsend was still angry with Dunn, Harding, and Aylward for slipping away with a motorcar under a veil of secrecy on the eve of the Saint-Mihiel Offensive, leaving him and the others to miss the thrill of the opening charge, the dash across to enemy trenches. He didn't expect them to do so again, he noted in his diary on September 20: "But I certainly was the loser at the time of the great attack thro there being only the one car, and the secretiveness and the greed of the three of our men, who slipped quietly away in it, leaving three of us here cursing—for they could have taken two more with them. Oh well! Such is life! And War! And it's so that the human ego often works! But how can there be a real scoop in art, I'd like to know, and they surely know better."[3]

Townsend had once been a very forgiving man who embraced life, but a bitter cynicism was now creeping into his idealistic mind-set; the war was sapping Townsend's joy for living, and he was becoming melancholy. "Barren of interest, these days," he wrote uncharacteristically in his diary. "One works on at the regular task of getting his material together into pictures for the monthly delivery."[4] On the very day he made this entry—September 24—the artists received a tip that another offensive was impending, yet even this development failed to excite Townsend. He figured it would be another Saint-Mihiel, a relative walkover. He had this impression because he, as did many others, assumed the U.S. 1st Army would attack north and east toward Metz and then move on Germany through the Belfort Gap, near the Swiss border, a much easier task than striking toward the heart of Germany. It was a perception Pershing's staff propagated through deceptive communications and indiscreet shifting of some troops in that direction. In fact, tens of thousands of soldiers and weapons were being ferried well to the west of the Swiss border, toward the Argonne Forest, which lays to the northwest of Verdun. So, contrary to expectations, Pershing did indeed intend to strike at the heart of Germany.

As well as this rather vague tip, Townsend and the other artists received both a verbal reminder and a formal memo from Major James to confine their movements to the action in the Advance Zone. The blanket restriction still didn't sit well with the artists; as Smith put it, such an order was "a further example of the failure to consider us as individual artists working along our own clearly defined lines." Townsend and some of the other artists were now convinced that the General Staff's bellicose mood toward them was a result of Smith and Peixotto having "flooded" Washington with hastily made works of the SOS and other behind the lines scenes early in their tenure, before the AEF had entered the fight.[5]

At least GHQ now provided more definitive guidance concerning the next action. On September 25, Major James instructed the artists to meet him in Bar-le-Duc, where the entire Press Section had been relocated to be closer to the front. All of the artists except the doubting Townsend shipped out, and, when they arrived there midafternoon, James advised them to continue on to Clermont-en-Argonne, to the west of Verdun and about six miles behind the front. Furthermore, he ordered them to remove General Staff signs from their cars so as not to alert any Boche reconnaissance—eyes in the air and spies on the ground—that officers were on the move, which could indicate an attack was in the works. And again, he kindly reminded them to stay forward no matter how hot the fighting became.[6]

Still skeptical as to the significance of the tip and feeling depressed, Townsend planned to move forward once the offensive was rolling; for the moment he was deep into some aviation pieces he wanted to finish. But then, having second thoughts and not wanting to disobey orders, he decided to go to Colombey-les-Belles—by hitching a ride in the sidecar of a motorcycle belonging to the Red Cross—to visit with Brigadier General Benjamin D. Foulois, the AEF's assistant chief of the Air Services. Townsend wanted permission to join the aviators for the start of the action. With a dismissive wave that demonstrated little consideration, Foulois flatly rejected Townsend's petition. Aggravated, Townsend wrote in his diary, "If I continue to have as much difficulty put in my path as I've had of late, I'll feel like throwing up the game." The doors were supposed to be wide open to them, when, in fact, they were not. While it hardly took the edge off his disappointment, he found some consolation in the motorcycle ride: "It was a fine ride home cutting the air as we did in that bouncing, rollicking old motorcycle."[7]

Once he was back in gray Neufchâteau, Townsend's frustration with the AEF's bureaucracy and blackened state of mind was exacerbated by the arrival of a letter from one of his brother Henri's old friends. Not only did the letter remind him of Henri, of course, but it also reminded Townsend that he hadn't seen another friend, aviator Pat Maloney, for a long time. "I haven't been up to the fellows I know of so long," Townsend explained to Cory in a letter that day, "that I rather dread going for we've had these two big drives since I was with them and they have played a heavy part in them so I don't know who has been shot down and hate to ask almost—the poor fellows."[8] A distraction from such personal issues would come the next morning: the eruption of what would be called the Meuse-Argonne Offensive. Not the rollover Townsend envisioned, this lengthy offensive would involve several phases and would quickly become the bloodiest action experienced by U.S. forces.

As dusk was settling in on September 25, Peixotto, Harding, and the others arrived in Clermont-en-Argonne, located about six miles from the front and on the fringe of the Argonne Forest. At a regimental head-quarters belonging to the 37th Division, the artists learned they would see nothing of the battles from Clermont and were subsequently directed to track down a Captain Norcross over by Dombasle, a village to the northeast located directly behind the 37th and 79th Divisions, which were positioned in the middle of the line. Norcross knew the area intimately and could find them a good observation post. Finding the captain, however, became a harrowing challenge. "Twilight of late September was now deepening into dusk," an apprehensive Peixotto wrote, "and this dusk soon became a total darkness, utterly opaque, black as ink, unlit, in the early night, by any moon or star, for a foggy curtain hung low over the land." Afraid to use their headlights and wary of trucks roaring down the road, their motorcar crept along. When they finally reached Dombasle, they took a deserted road up a hill that was to lead them to Norcross, only he was nowhere to be found: "Not a being was in sight and a brooding mystery had settled down upon these black wildernesses of bleak landscape—an uncanny feeling enhanced by the fact that we knew perfectly well that within a very few hours hell would be let loose and everything would be on the move."

The artists attempted to retrace their steps but found themselves back on the road leading from Clermont to Dombasle; they had man-aged one big circle, not a comforting thought considering the Germans were in close proximity. Then, to their relief, near Récicourt they encountered 37th Division HQ situated in roadside dugouts. "Here a few officers sat poring over maps or talking quietly in corners where the dim candle-light threw huge grotesque shadows upon the wall," wrote Peixotto. Fortunately the officers were able to provide accurate directions to Norcross, who was hidden in a hollow near Brocourt. Norcross then pointed the artists to Montzéville—a village only some three miles behind the lines—where the American guns wouldn't deafen them and they'd be close enough to observe the ground action from a rise. Invariably, they again became lost in the "Stygian darkness" even though they were all too conscious of the fact that one wrong turn would find them in "Bocheland."[9] Finally, after 10:30 P.M., they rolled into the village of Montzéville, where the only shelter available was on a duckwalk leading into an *abri*, French for "safe place." It was already housing a group of doctors, who desperately needed the rest, for tomorrow they would find themselves severely tested.

Separated from the others, Harding found shelter in a shed, for a brief period, because the big guns jolted him awake before midnight. Later in the day, using a pencil, in tight, small script, he scratched in his diary:

> Got up at 11.30 when guns opened—
> Boche shelled hill while we were there
> stayed up—saw mist in valley could
> our gas shells falling drift with wind—[10]

Peixotto also witnessed the "preparation" for the ground battle; that is, the artillery softening the German lines. "Flashes like those of some prodigious electric storm swept the horizon," he wrote. "The booming of the distant guns, becoming less and less intermittent, rolled at last into one continuous roar." Then, a battery of 155s very close to them opened up with thunderous vengeance and rocked the ground under their feet like an earthquake: "Just before three o'clock the air was split by violent concussions. . . . In sudden lurid flashes the ruined houses of Montzéville leaped out of the night, lit as if by lightning strokes, then, as instantly, faded into darkness." Very few shells were coming back, but on occasion a dull thud could be heard followed by a shout of "Gas!"[11]

Around 5 A.M. on September 26, Peixotto stumbled into the muddy street to orient himself, and, as the streaks of dawn leaked into the sky, he watched the ambulances move out and the observation balloons—"huge bloated worms"—float skyward, although with fog blanketing much of the countryside they would serve little purpose until later. He also noticed that the roar of the guns had intensified (he would learn that this September 26 barrage was the greatest the world had ever known); in the American sector alone, there were some four thousand guns. There was no holding back in any respect; the doughboys' success was absolutely critical because this offensive was not merely an American maneuver in an isolated sector; it was one piece of a coordinated Allied push along the entire western front, from the North Sea to the Vosges Mountains.

Pershing's plan was to penetrate a depth of ten miles into the enemy's line to force the Germans from the Argonne Forest, then thrust forward another ten miles to outflank the Germans positioned along the heavily defended Aisne River, and, finally, clear the Germans from the heights located east of the Meuse River. The ultimate goal for Pershing's boys was to capture the city of Sedan to the north, which would break the network of railroads supporting the German army in France and Belgium. To do so, more than 250,000 soldiers had been assembled, many of them having been transferred from the Saint-Mihiel Salient, which involved covering sixty miles and reorganizing for the attack—all in less than ten days. In charge of the harrowing logistics was Colonel George

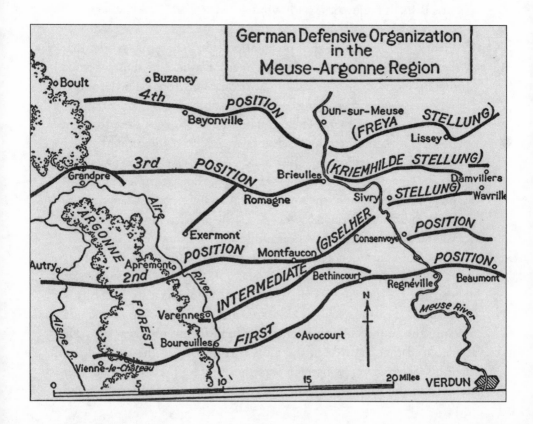

C. Marshall, who successfully aligned eight divisions across a thirty-mile front, from the Argonne Forest on the left to the Meuse River on the right. Conspicuously missing were the battle-hardened 1st, 2nd, 3rd, and 42nd Divisions.

The U.S. 1st Army was pitted against eighteen German divisions comprised of about 125,000 soldiers.[12] While the Germans were once again outnumbered, to their advantage they were entrenched in a treacherous landscape, which they had had four years to fortify. It was nothing like the Saint-Mihiel Salient, where the doughboys had found the land relatively flat and inviting. Now sitting in the center of the Germans' defenses was first the Vauquois Heights, followed by the thorny Montfaucon Woods and the town of Montfaucon, the latter a veritable citadel on a hill rising 1,250 feet above the surrounding land. Along the enemy's right flank, there was the impenetrable Argonne Forest, a tangle of ravines and hillocks and meandering streams reminiscent of Belleau Wood, except on a much grander scale. And along the ridges running parallel to the front, the Germans had built four successive lines of defense: the Hindenburg Line, followed by Giselher Stellung, Kriemhilde Stellung, and Freya Stellung. The first two Stellung lines were named after the mythic brother and sister of the ancient Burgundian royal family, celebrated in the epic German poem the Nibelungenlied; and the last formidable line of defense was named in honor of Freya, the goddess of love, sex, and war, who road astride a boar. Fortunately, the doughboys were oblivious to what these names forewarned.

As zero hour—5:25 A.M.—approached and the thunderous guns pounded the Germans up and down the line, Peixotto reflected on the many sacrifices being made, from the deprived women at home to the men stoking the furnaces in ships braving the U-boats, from the engineers who built roads to the front to the soldiers going over top. In hopes of witnessing the ground battle, Peixotto and Morgan moved up to Esnes, which was less than two miles from the front line. The village sat beneath the southern slope of Hill 304, which, along with the adjacent and aptly named hill Le Mort Homme, had been pivotal in the French defense of the Verdun sector. In the blood-drenched battles of 1916, the Germans had captured Hill 304 in the beginning of May and the Le Mort Homme toward the end of the month, only to lose both. "The Germans attacked in massed formation," a French officer recounted, "by big columns of five or six hundred men, preceded by two waves of sharpshooters. . . . It is absolutely impossible to convey what losses the Germans must suffer in these attacks. Nothing can give an idea of it. Whole ranks are mowed down, and those that follow them suffer the same fate. . . .There are slopes on Hill 304 where the level of the ground is raised several meters by mounds of German corpses."[13]

It was a hill of "tragic memories," Peixotto recalled as he stood there now. "Its denuded flanks, scenes of such bloody combats, rose bleak and barren, bereft of all vegetation, behind the ruined town that lay in the valley wrapped in a bluish haze."[14] The area was now just a tattered mess of collapsed trenches, craters, and twisted barbed wire, and destitute of life. Esnes itself was shattered and the roads jammed with beasts of burden pulling wagon trains; to maintain order the Military Police had posted a sign: "Play the Game Boys: Obey the M.P." In the village, Peixotto sketched troops marching through what resembled ruins of an ancient world, the disturbing scene accentuated by the difficulty of

*Troops Leaving Esnes* by Peixotto. Troops marching through what resembled ancient ruins captured the artists' imagination.

defining it in the drifting smoke and morning fog. While Peixotto contemplated the ruins, on the outskirts of Esnes Morgan linked up with a
machine-gun outfit, which he sketched in charcoal as it moved forward
under artillery fire. He worked feverishly as a reluctant mule pulled the
outfit's equipment and faceless soldiers struggled under heavy packs, the
heads of both man and beast hanging, exhausted but resolute profiles in
the gray light.

With tension and smoke in the air, to their frustration, the artists
again discovered there was little of the actual ground battle for them to
witness—no dashing cavalry, no staggering troops, and no rattling clash
of bayonets—as the soldiers ahead of them clamored through woods and
hollows. "But to the ear the war was a terrible reality," Peixotto noted, "a
terrific fact, for the noise was so deafening that it seemed as if one's ear-
drums would burst. Short, fat howitzers, long 120s, thin-nosed as grey-
hounds, 220s, all mouth, vomiting their big shells high into the air,
hidden in the ruined houses of the village or banked in tiers up the hill-
slopes, belched and barked and thundered."

Excited by the sounds of fighting, a frantic Peixotto climbed between
the guns stationed on Hill 304 in an attempt to gain a view of the battle.
The top, however, was shrouded in a heavy mist, and the officers there,
expecting a return barrage, ordered him off the hill. Forced back into
Esnes, Peixotto watched as both the wounded and the prisoners started

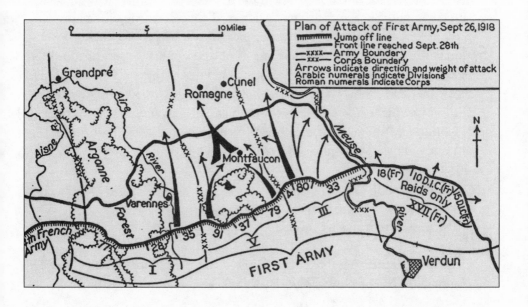

to filter in. The prisoners did not arrive in large numbers as they had during the Saint-Mihiel Offensive, which indicated that the Germans intended on putting up a stiff resistance. And he observed that most of the wounded were walking rearward; for several days there would not be enough ambulances.

Later in the morning, Peixotto decided he had to return to Hill 304 in spite of the danger, and, to his delight, the clouds had lifted: "It was a wonderful spectacle that lay spread before me, and, fascinated, I spent the remainder of the day wandering about, sketching and watching it."[15] The barren hill offered an unbroken view to Montfaucon, about four miles away and from where the kaiser, ensconced in his Eagle's Nest, had watched the 1916 battles around Verdun. Below, Peixotto could see the fight unfolding as the 79th Division pushed through the woods toward the broken village of Malancourt. Their ultimate goal for day one was Montfaucon, which stood in the center of the attack, its steep slopes rising above the doughboys. Failure to take the commanding Montfaucon would slow the entire American effort, and any delay would allow the Germans to summon reinforcements. This was an arduous task for a division that had only been in France since early August and had yet to see combat.

Embedded in the spectacle unfolding before Peixotto was his fellow artist George Harding, who had joined up with the tanks at their launching point in Avocourt and followed them into battle. He scrambled to keep up with the lumbering beasts as they pushed their way along dirt roads, through looping stands of trees, and across undulating fields toward the village of Malancourt. He inhaled the acrid fumes of burnt fuel and crouched in the tall grass, hoping to avoid the deadly shells, as he made his sketches with charcoal, pencil, and crayon, using crayon to add subtle touches of color to his pictures. Moving forward again, the images were quick and vivid:

> . . . the dead Boche
> near dugout the long stream of blood
> the shells arriving as we sat there—

German machine guns fired relentlessly. A tank exploded, its gasoline erupting in a ball of flame. Engineers worked feverishly to repair the road.

*Tanks at Meuse-Argonne* by Harding. Harding followed the tanks into battle, until he could no longer keep pace.

Eventually falling behind the advance, Harding sought refuge at a first-aid station near Varennes, where American wounded were being carried in by Boche prisoners. Using crayon and charcoal, the artist portrayed the boys slumped and bandaged, some grimacing and others passive, one soldier using two hands in an attempt to light a cigarette to comfort himself. Setting aside his sketchpad, Harding wrote in his diary:

> the first aid station the men coming
> in face shot off—arms broken legs,
> shot through . . .

A tank lieutenant stumbled in:

> eyes closed by gas . . .
> his hand full of bits of
> armor plate, face burnt, eyebrows,
> black skin, shot in shoulder . . .

Meanwhile, desperately needed ambulances were trapped some three miles rearward, courtesy of a massive crater in the road.[16]

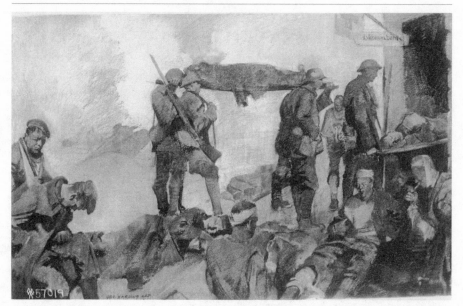

*First Aid Station with American Wounded* by Harding. Resting at an aid station, on September 26, Harding made a drawing of the wounded being carried in by German prisoners.

For Harding, the coming days would be sleepless, wet, and without warm food, but he took any privations in stride:

> You may follow this life for five days, during which you sleep none and eat but little. When the greatest offensive in the history of the world is going on, you don't think of sleep. At night you work, as in the daytime. There may be a burning village, with boche airplane flying above it, which makes a wonderful effect against the night sky. It generally rains, but occasionally there is a clear time when the moon breaks through the clouds over the battlefield. Or come across a German dugout, just captured, where you find a group of officers poring over their maps and making plans for the next day. You stop a minute to take notes of the scene, and find out, if possible, something of the possibilities for the next day, so that you too can make your plans. When you come across food, you stop and eat.[17]

Harvey Dunn was also with the tanks, remaining with the machines as they drove toward ominous Montfaucon, and from this experience he

*Prisoners and Wounded* by Dunn. As Dunn witnessed the carnage of the Meuse-Argonne Offensive, his work became ever more somber.

would create a bleak piece with sharp contrasts of light and dark titled *Tanks Before Montfaucon* (not pictured). Again, he portrayed the profiles of men stumbling and machine lumbering resolutely across a grim landscape, the shadowy figures evoking a ghostly netherworld. Another of his subdued but emotional pieces resulting from the offensive, *Prisoners and Wounded* (see above), depicted German prisoners aiding American wounded, with one young doughboy highlighted by white bandages looking utterly perplexed as to what has happened.

With the carnage Dunn witnessed during the Meuse-Argonne Offensive, the tone of his work became ever more somber as he became ever more absorbed by the feelings of helpless despair suffered during wartime. Except for expressing them in his artwork, Dunn kept his feelings mostly to himself—contrary to Townsend, who readily expressed his emotions in his diary and his letters.[18] On the surface, Dunn would still have his flashes of exuberance, but inwardly he was evolving into a subdued and restless man. Almost willing himself to not reflect on the horrors he had witnessed, Dunn would leave little in the way of personal writing and kept few pictures of himself—not exactly the behavior of a self-absorbed egoist as some claimed he was. Even with his war art he was hardly productive in the final analysis: yes, he was obsessed with experiencing as much of the war as possible and spent minimal time in the studio, but the very fact that he created less than thirty finished pieces strongly suggests that each of these works took an excessive emotional toll, and that this artist-soldier, accustomed to churning out pictures, could manage no more. Meanwhile, the other artists completed two, three, or four times that many. What Dunn did accomplish was to capture the feeling of war with exceptional quality; as he always told his students, they must use their art to convey a "feeling"—a simple notion, but not always easy to execute.

When he returned home from the war, friends and colleagues noticed a change in Dunn. "The war had been a tremendous experience for him," his friend Dean Cornwell observed, "and after it illustrating seemed tame and his work showed the change."[19] After the war, Dunn lost interest in what he now considered to be superficial commercial illustration work and would turn more and more to teaching—teaching art like it was a religion—in hopes of bettering his corner of the world. More focused on pure art, he would become famous as a painter of Dakota country pioneer and prairie scenes, a clear indication that he was a sentimental man who yearned for a simpler time, one from his own youth when he plowed his father's fields behind two oxen.

Still the morning of September 26, Peixotto watched men positioning a battery of 75s in a field near him—the men shouting curses as they bullied the lathered horses—and he joined the officers there. He looked through a powerful pair of binoculars they had set up on a tripod to view the damage they were about to inflict on the enemy machine-gun nests buried in the forest. From this vantage point, Peixotto finally grasped a real sense of troop movement, the heated action he had yearned to witness:

> Then, as the day wore on and the Bois de Malancourt was cleaned up, I could see, with beating heart, our troops emerge from these woods and start across the open to attack the Bois de Montfaucon beyond. Little khaki-colored toys they looked like, scattered out in open formation, just as I had seen them months before down in Alsace, training for a day like this, disappearing under the cover of any depression or shrubbery they could find, then reappearing at the sound of a whistle, half-rising or crawling on ahead.
>
> And then a thrill went up my spine as I saw the tanks come out,

strange lumbering creatures, crawling one after another, Indian file, rocking like ships in a heavy sea, but steadily creeping forward on their caterpillar feet toward machine-gun nests hidden in the woods, that are their special prey. Shells with lurid, saffron-colored smoke—the new antitank explosive—began to burst over them, and I could plainly see the hail of molten lead that shot directly downward from the ball of ruddy smoke.[20]

Behind Peixotto the battery of guns continued its relentless pounding of German positions. The din was like "giant sledge-hammers on an anvil" as the 75s "cleft the air. As its shrill whistling died away a moment later, a cloud of salmon-colored smoke mingled with debris and stones arose from the hill of Montfaucon opposite, drifting away finally on the afternoon breeze."[21]

The boys from the 79th—boys from Pennsylvania, Maryland, and the District of Columbia—were crossing open land now, following the ribbon of the Esnes-Montfaucon road along a valley that took them into the village of Malancourt, which they subsequently captured. As the 79th charged along the valley toward Montfaucon and across a belt of shell craters, the Germans could see the wave of khaki—just like Peixotto could—yet there was no rain of enemy artillery. Optimism was high that the boys would succeed with minimal casualties, but the situation changed rapidly: to their left on the valley floor was Cuisy Wood, which was littered with machine-gun nests that now opened up with a vengeance. They were caught in the open, in a field of interlocking fire. Although the 79th would make it to the base of Montfaucon by nightfall, they would be pinned down, forced to dig into the sides of ravines to protect themselves from the unrelenting machine-gun and artillery fire.

Regardless of the mounting casualties, Peixotto was entranced: "After months of peering through periscopes or peeping furtively over trench parapets, it seemed strange indeed to stand thus in the open and watch even a fraction—though it was an important one—of the greatest offensive in history. . . . all the pressure of men and transport attacking from all sides upon Montfaucon, their main objective in this sector, the whole forming a panoramic picture we had never been able to see before this war."[22] For the remainder of the afternoon, Peixotto watched as the infantry, supported by tanks, worked its way forward. All the while,

American field artillery was being positioned around him, on the crest of the hill, to support the advance. Camouflage units worked feverishly to do what they could to disguise these batteries. By chance, Peixotto ran into his friend Captain Homer St. Gaudens, the son of the renowned sculptor Augustus St. Gaudens and also an artist, who was assigned to a camouflage unit. On the exposed ridge, there was little time to catch up on personal news; in fact, a distraught Peixotto later learned, just fifteen minutes after leaving his side, St. Gaudens was wounded in the head by exploding shrapnel. He would survive.

The 79th failed to take Montfaucon on day one—partly due to green troops and weak leadership in the field—a costly delay that gave the Germans the time needed to reorganize and bring in reinforcements. Overall, the doughboys pushed forward only three miles, a good five miles short of Pershing's rose-colored goal for day one; so, the 79th was not the only division to hit an impasse. Because the countryside was so varied, so disjointed, so difficult to negotiate, soldiers became lost, messages and supplies went to the wrong points, and supporting artillery batteries were bogged down. To the left of Varennes, a village that Peixotto and Morgan were planning to visit the next day, the 35th Division suffered a catastrophe on the morning of September 26, and Peixotto would personally be drawn into the aftermath. Positioned just to the right of the Argonne Forest, the 35th, made up of Kansas and Missouri National Guardsmen and draftees, had been charged with taking the legendary Vauquois Heights, the historic town of Varennes, and Cheppy, a pivotal town along the Hindenburg Line, all of which would take them across terrain called "pestiferous" by one veteran.[23] Their first target was the front-and-center Vauquois Heights, a maze of tunnels and mine craters the French had unsuccessfully attacked repeatedly in 1915. Such obstacles were made all the more daunting by the dense morning fog that left the soldiers disoriented and regiments intermingled.

While elements of the 35th tangled with the Vauquois Heights, its 138th Infantry Regiment charged toward Cheppy, the 138th under the leadership of Colonel Harry S. Howland, a forty-one-year-old veteran of the Philippines campaign. He had retired in 1915 but was then recalled, and once in France, he subsequently requested assignment to a combat unit. While he was granted his wish, he was given the command a mere two days before they would go over the top. His being thrown into the fire, albeit voluntarily, reflected the entire division's situation: having only been pulled together in France in time for reserve duty at Saint-Mihiel, they lacked field experience. But now, on September 26, Howland's boys would suffer so much bloodshed that he would feel moved to write his friend Ernest Peixotto with a special request, along with a complete report of what transpired.

While under heavy artillery and gas fire, during the night of September 25, Howland's men had marched to their jumping-off points. As they made final adjustments the next morning, the fog was so thick that visibility was down to forty feet and platoons quickly became disoriented. Once over top, it was all the more difficult for the successive lines to stay in touch with each other, and Howland had no choice but to follow his compass, knowing that Cheppy and the 2nd German Guard Division of Berlin were somewhere in front of him. Suddenly, at 6:55 A.M., they came under direct and severe fire from a nearby battery . . . it was high-explosive shells. The men scattered and "dropped onto the ground for protection," Howland reported. "However, the shelling was so heavy that more than a score of them were instantly killed, several blown into shapeless masses of blood, flesh and clothes." Others were killed and wounded by machine-gun fire that materialized from seemingly nowhere. The slightest movement now invited lethal bursts.

*An American Graveyard* by Morgan. American troops paid a dear price in attacking Cheppy and Varennes; Morgan captured the troops exhausted from their burial detail work.

The men became desperate when the well-hidden machine-gun nests couldn't be located. Thankfully, two French tanks appeared; however, through some misunderstanding they proceeded to the rear. A French officer went in search of tank support at 9:15, almost two and a half hours after the initial attack. Meanwhile, Howland crawled forward to gather any men still alive, but in the shell holes he found only dead soldiers. Then, Howland was hit with a shell fragment; it shattered his hand, but he fought through the pain to organize his men. His surviving boys slowly made their way to an existing ditch and dug deeper for better protection. Under blistering fire so heavy it knocked down any parapet they attempted to build, they held on for the next three hours, when, at last, eight tanks wallowed forward. Howland's men dashed behind them, forming squads, and started raking the hillsides. After they knocked out all the nests on the left side, groups of soldiers swept across the ground directly in front of the Germans and eliminated the remaining positions. Howland continued to lead his men, but by 1:30 P.M. he was feeling faint from the loss of blood, and a French doctor ordered him to an aid station.[24]

While lying in Base Hospital No. 23, Howland wrote his report, in which he could not say enough about the heroics of his men and he recommended a number of them for the Medal of Honor and Distinguished Service Cross; he himself would be awarded the Distinguished Service Cross. "Under his leadership the regiment bore the brunt of a heavy attack on Cheppy," a New York Times article extolled, "considered one of the pivotal points of the Hindenburg line, and, cut to pieces in the early stages of the battle, went forward to its objectives after three hours of grueling punishment."[25] The punishment would continue: over four days and six miles, Howland's infantry regiment, along with the entire 35th Division, would lose a total of six thousand men of the fourteen thousand in the engagement.[26]

Still confined to the hospital, Howland urged his adjutant, Lieutenant Clarence Sonnell, to interview those who survived so that a complete history of the action could be recorded and both the living and the dead could be honored.[27] With a third of his men casualties, Howland also wanted the battle commemorated in painting, so he next wrote to Peixotto, whom he knew from California:

It may not come within the scope of your official duties but, for me, for my regiment, and possibly for our dear Bohemia, will you consider going to the battle field at Cheppy, and exercising your art in a vision of what happened there? When you read the report you will understand what I mean.

Shortly after I saw you at Menil-le-Tour last month, I was suddenly promoted to full colonel and assigned to command the 138th Infantry, of which I took command two days before going over the top. The regiment is made up entirely of St. Louis men, over one-third of whom now, however, are dead or wounded.

I have no other desire but to get back into shape as soon as possible and return to the regiment. My hand is badly shattered but will soon be patched up.[28]

To give Peixotto some perspective, Howland enclosed a sketch map and the official report he had submitted.

Peixotto would indeed sketch scenes from Cheppy and the surrounding area; however, he informed Howland that Harding, whom Peixotto acknowledged to be the best qualified, would also make a study that could be used for commemorative purposes. Not until late November did Howland receive the artist's response, prompting him to vent to Peixotto that it was "utterly absurd" that it took a month for letters to be exchanged in France. Nevertheless, he was very excited that Harding was to make a drawing of Cheppy. One for dramatics, in his letter he proceeded to describe his hand to Peixotto as looking like a Thanksgiving turkey drumstick. The hand would require surgery.[29]

As the artist André Smith, who was also in the area sketching, contemplated the initial failures of the offensive, he concluded that one of the major contributing factors was the fact that the AEF was engaged in a new kind of warfare in the Argonne countryside—open-field warfare—where boundaries and responsibilities were less clear than those when aligned in trenches:

So long as there were trench lines and ribbons of wire to designate them, the rules of the game were evident; but the moment one side had pushed the other beyond these ditches and into the open, the whole aspect of the game changed. No longer could he see the "sides," nor could his imagination picture the invisible line of division that separated, by hill and dale, one group of antagonists from the other. The maintenance of "contact" between separate units along the front is a necessity which would seem obvious to him, and yet one that impressed him as being almost impossible of execution, especially where the natural instinct of an advancing force is that of stealth and concealment. You can keep in contact with something that you can see, but if you cannot see it—well, the result is only too obvious: Lost companies, lost battalions, lost regiments, and lost battles![30]

In his semisardonic conclusion, Smith was alluding to the 1st Battalion of the 77th Division, which, on October 3, would become cut off and surrounded by the enemy in the Argonne Forest; the Lost Battalion's exploits to become the subject of books and movies.[31] Not until October 7, when the 1st, 28th, and 82nd Divisions attacked the eastern side of the forest, would contact be reestablished. By then, the Lost Battalion's survivors numbered 252—just 195 without wounds—of the original 679 men who had found themselves trapped in the isolated pocket.[32]

Despite the confusion and soaring casualties, Townsend observed that back in Neufchâteau members of the U.S. command were congratulating themselves. On the afternoon of September 26, reports came in stating that aviators had observed sixteen German columns, along with heavy artillery, retreating to the rear. That night communiqués indicated that U.S. troops had advanced seven miles—which was faster than the initial Saint-Mihiel advance—and had taken five thousand prisoners. On hearing this report and that casualties were light, Townsend wrote in his diary, "So much for the battle—what tomorrow?"[33]

There were also glowing reports concerning the tank brigades; the reports claiming they were instrumental in capturing Varennes and Cheppy. "Great numbers of tanks are in operation and," Townsend noted in his diary, "as in the recent fight, they starred brilliantly. There is little doubt but that a great part of the credit for the apparent break in the morale of the enemy, and rapidity of our advance, is due to the effect both of the fire and the dread of these Juggernauts of Behemoth!"[34] But the truth was the tanks had performed poorly; too often they lagged behind or roared ahead, with the soldiers refusing to support them because they were juicy targets for German guns. And at Cheppy they had failed to support Howland, which resulted in such high casualties the U.S. Congress would eventually investigate the incident. Once again Townsend and GHQ staff officers had fallen prey to extreme overstatements of success.

The only sour news coming into Neufchâteau was a report that George Patton was fatally wounded, but there was no confirmation. "Poor Colonel Patton," wrote Townsend. "He was a most interesting man, and most enthusiastic and active and progressive as a Tank Commander. I shall never forget the ardour and joy with which he pulled off the tank manoeuvres there at Bourg on the 16th of Aug. This was, in fact, to give the more or less doubtful members of the General Staff an idea of just what the possibility of the tank was. . . . The manoeuvres seemed to impress them too, and I remember how happy Colonel Patton was after it. How enthusiastic and pleased he was . . . to have an artist picture them and their deeds when they got into action."[35] As it turned out, the rumor of his death was yet another piece of misinformation. Patton's tank had been disabled, but, hardly calling it a day, he climbed out, gathered up about a hundred soldiers, and attacked German machine-gun nests. Although severely wounded in the leg during the assault, Patton survived and would be awarded the Distinguished Service Cross.

After a relatively quiet night of reorganizing themselves, on September 27 the 79th Division renewed its attack on Montfaucon, and, finally, at 11 A.M., soldiers from both the 79th and the 37th captured the fortress town. The tardy victory was bittersweet, for over the next two days the Germans would barrage the town and surrounding roads so very mercilessly and with such accuracy that Smith noted the enemy was "open to rounds of applause" for their brilliance even as they retreated to their next line of defense.[36] It was becoming increasingly apparent that the Germans were not going to roll over as they had at Saint-Mihiel, and Pershing was not going to easily win the glorious victory he so desired.

Just behind the lines, Peixotto and Morgan motored westward to Varennes, a storied and strategic town on the eastern side of the Argonne, to see how the fight was developing in that sector. Early on the road was traffic free, but then a mile or so beyond the picturesque village of Neuvilly there was the worst traffic jam Peixotto had ever witnessed. For miles, the road was blocked. Three lanes of traffic—every description of vehicle imaginable—were paralyzed. The ammunition could not be moved forward and the wounded could not be moved rearward. "I saw colonels and even a brigadier-general on foot in the road," Peixotto wrote, "acting as 'traffic-cops,' directing, swearing, 'bawling out' every officer in sight, but the blockade never budged."

While there was a certain humor in the noisy chaos, it was no laughing matter as the shattered roads hindered the advance with as much tenacity as the machine-gun nests. And at any moment, the Germans could unleash an artillery barrage against these crowded streets that would do unspeakable damage. Feeling vulnerable, Peixotto and Morgan figured they had best keep moving, so they pulled the car off to the side and started walking forward with alacrity. It wasn't long before they found the cause for the traffic jam: a massive mine crater more than 150 feet long and 40 feet wide, a crater that could swallow ammunition trains whole, a crater so spectacular they took time to sketch it. From this disaster point, Peixotto soaked up the surrounding landscape:

> Fields of wire, shell-holes filled with water, quagmires, rank grass, and a few blasted trees—these were the objects that composed the tragic landscape across which, by muddy side-roads, like ants toward an ant-hill, crept long lines of horse-drawn vehicles, diminutive, almost lost in the vastness of the desert waste. Off to the east rose the sinister slopes of the Vauquois, denuded, stripped of their forests, ravaged and ploughed up by shells and high explosives, with the old French and German first-line trenches running almost side by side up and over their summit. To the westward the heights of the Argonne, rocky and precipitous, succeeded each other, hill after hill, from the southern horizon to the northern, green and densely wooded, save for the portion that had lain so long between the enemy lines—the portion where the trees had been reaped as with a giant sickle, only the stumps standing like stubble in a wheat-field.[37]

Peixotto's gaze then fell on a nearby hillside where several German prisoners were digging a grave for a fallen comrade while a sergeant read a simple prayer.

Continuing their march northward on a road running parallel to the Aire River and the Argonne Forest—the source of continuous bursts of machine-gun fire—the artists patiently picked their way through the unrelenting traffic. About a mile from Varennes, Peixotto walked into the village of Boureuilles, where engineers had just finished repairing the main bridge into town, to allow the ambulances to evacuate the wounded who had been waiting for hours. The town itself was "razed to the ground and honeycombed with wrecked trenches," Peixotto wrote, "destroyed by our barrage and just abandoned by the enemy. Some of our tanks were still crawling about it, moving farther up over the narrow-gauge tracks that afforded them better support than the roadway."[38]

Anxious now to capture the action, Peixotto and Morgan quickly pushed on to Varennes, which the 35th had recently purged of Boche. Like so many French villages in the war zone, it had been picturesque, Peixotto reflected, and, in addition, it had been memorialized by a historic event. During the French Revolution, in 1791, King Louis XVI and his wife, Marie Antoinette, had attempted to flee the bloodthirsty revolutionaries but were arrested while attempting to enter Varennes. Both the king and the queen would lose their heads. More than a hundred years later, the 35th Division also paid a considerable price entering Varennes as they were forced to clear it in vicious house-to-house fighting.

When Peixotto arrived, engineers were throwing up shaky bridges while under continuous artillery fire. He looked around at the historic village ruefully and concluded succinctly, "Now the ancient place was smashed to bits." At a carrefour, miraculously, a Virgin still stood in her blue niche, but the chapel was more than destroyed; it had completely disappeared. In the village's main square, forty or fifty tanks—in "gaudy camouflage"—wallowed in the sticky mud like African beasts, while the main force had settled just beyond the town. "The unburied dead lay in the streets," Peixotto noted. "The dressing-stations were crowded and groups of prisoners kept filtering through on their way to the rear. The roar of the artillery was very close and sharp, and the rattle of musketry and of machine-guns over in the forest where the Seventy-Seventh was trying to dislodge the Boche was incessant and insistent."[39] It would be so for days to come as the saga of the 77th's Lost Battalion continued to unfold.

. . .

"And just what does it all portend?" Townsend reflected on the first days of the Meuse-Argonne Offensive. "Will there be an immediate collapse? I think not. But how can they be foolish enough to keep on?" Foolish enough apparently. Townsend, along with many others, sensed that the German leaders had no choice "but to fight on to their own destruction, throwing their poor deluded pawns into the game to be swallowed up— into the maw of that gigantic military monster that we have been forced to breed and rear and throw into the field here to stop the depredations of their blind, mad God?" He understood that the German leaders were in too deep. If they didn't die at the hands of the Allies, they surely would at the hands of their own people. There was a strong feeling that the German people would welcome peace immediately; however, Townsend speculated that only "a social revolution" would put a swift end to the madness. "But somehow this seems impossible in Germany; the people seem to have been under too long. But oh when will the end be?"[40]

As Townsend suspected, the German leaders were indeed far too committed to readily capitulate, in spite of being grossly outnumbered: they quickly reinforced their line facing the doughboys with three more divisions, each filled with seasoned veteran troops who fought savagely.[41] And, as the doughboys moved across open land or through heavily defended forests, the sheer size of the U.S. 1st Army presented such an easy target that the Germans couldn't help but inflict serious damage. Recognizing that casualties were mounting rapidly and confusion was spiraling out of control, a shaken Pershing called a temporary halt to the offensive operations on September 29, so his staff and he could digest their failure to break the Germans, and mull over their next move before the situation became a stalemated bloodbath.

# 14

# THE FESTIVAL OF
# THE DEAD

AFTER THE FIRST FORTY-EIGHT HOURS OF THE
Meuse-Argonne Offensive, several artists returned
to "the office" to prepare their monthly submission
of art, but not the youthful risk takers Dunn and
Harding, who really didn't give a damn about art
shows for staff officers. Neither did the oldest of
the group, Ernest Peixotto, who, along with Bill
Aylward, fell back to centrally located Rarécourt, where they were
offered a room behind the Graves Registration Bureau, a "cheerful
neighborhood" Peixotto noted sarcastically. This depressing situation
was made all the more surreal by his barren chamber with its leaking
ceiling, useless fireplace, and a broken armoire door that opened at
random times. As Peixotto explained, the room happened to contain
"a placard with a broken door from which various articles of feminine
apparel—sordid dresses and hats trimmed with bedraggled feathers—
insisted on emerging at most unexpected intervals." Dresses and hats

trimmed with feathers in one chamber, the dead being processed in another.

"And from Rarécourt I proceeded to make my various sketching trips," Peixotto wrote. "Rain and slush; mud and dirt; my paper wet and soggy, my hands numb with cold—these were the conditions, none too propitious for sketching." While the offensive was stalled, he revisited the recent battlefields that yielded the same desolate remains: "From the slits of the P. C.'s I looked out over the grim wastes of Hill 304 and Le Mort-Homme and saw the same tragic landscapes that the Kaiser and his son must have seen as they watched the heroic defense of Verdun. I ploughed through the mud that was ankle-deep in the old German trenches. Heavy clouds, thickly charged with moisture, drove low over the lofty hilltop and swept the ruined arches of the martyred church with their misty filaments. The clipped trees of the Place de l'Eglise, once neatly trimmed and umbrageous, now stood like charred skeletons, reaching out their bony arms, leafless and branchless, in gestures of mute despair and ardent supplication."[1]

Peixotto spent a couple of rain-soaked days sketching the German defenses around Montfaucon; the woods and hollows around Very and Cheppy, veritable fortresses once held by the Second Guard Division of Berlin that had punished Howland's boys; and a ruined church in Neuvilly.[2] "Neuvilly itself tempted us to linger," he wrote, "for it was very picturesque. Its ancient houses are, for the most part, of half-timbered construction, the spaces between the beams being filled in with plaster and mud spread on heavy laths. The concussions of the various bombardments had blown all this mud filling out, so that only the timber-work was left to support the red-tiled roofs that remained fairly intact though the walls that held them up were open to the four winds of heaven."[3]

The artists also continued to venture northward into the Aire Valley, where localized fighting remained vicious. They toured Exermont, which the 28th Division had captured on September 28 and was now occupied by the 42nd—only after a grueling two-day march.[4] From Exermont, Peixotto and Aylward motored north to Cierges (the artists visited two villages named Cierges), which the 37th Division had entered on September 28th but could not hold. The next day the doughboys again attacked, but concentrated enemy artillery fire beat them back. Not until October 1 was it seized and held by the 32nd

*Neuvilly—Interior of Ruined Church* by Peixotto. Even though the
church at Neuvilly was gutted, the edifice with its majestic columns
still impressed the artists.

Division, which had moved into the line.[5] Over the next weeks, as
Peixotto remained in the field, his exposure to the elements—what he
called "the four winds of heaven"—would take its toll on his health. It
was a precarious time to become sick, because influenza was reaping its
own share of soldiers and civilians.[6]

In Neufchâteau, as Townsend prepared pieces for their monthly submission, it was difficult for him to focus, because, regardless of Pershing's
temporary halt to the 1st Army's offensive, encouraging news was coming in from battlefields across Europe. On the Macedonian front, the
Allies had broken the Bulgarian line—Bulgaria having joined the Germans in 1915—and that country was now pleading for an armistice.

The Belgians, Townsend noted, were "advancing with little resistance from the Boche" and "beginning to once again occupy their own little country." The Brits were attacking in the Cambrai sector with such ferocity that by October 5 they would push through the last defenses of the Hindenburg Line. This triumph included an assault on the 6,500-yard Bellicourt Tunnell of the Cambrai–Saint Quentin Canal, a virtual underground city that housed German troops. Aiding the British were the AEF's 27th and 30th Divisions, which would suffer a total of more than fifteen thousand casualties in taking the tunnel.[7]

When André Smith later toured Bellicourt, he discovered a "crumpled" village that left him shaken to the marrow. "It was a place of depressing solitude and desolation," he wrote. "Here one felt the cold silence of death; not a sound reached one's ears, and one's eyes could find nothing that even suggested the presence of human life. The thought that not so long ago this street had known the laughter of children at play was now inconceivable. And, after all, this was but one street in only one of the hundreds of villages which have suffered the full horror of war."[8]

There was one artist who had been following the 27th Division in the weeks before the Hindenburg Line was cracked in the British zone: John Singer Sargent. Still in search of his epic, the artist had pushed to the extreme northwest of the front, to Ypres, Belgium, where, he had heard, American soldiers were going into the line. In the Ypres Salient, he linked up with the 27th Division, which was indeed about to encounter some heated action. Comprised of New York National Guard units, the division had sailed for France in early May 1918, was assigned to the British and placed in reserve, until late July when it slowly rotated to the front line in relief of the British 6th Division. Now, in the last days of August, Sargent hoped there would be an opportunity to see the doughboys fighting in partnership with the British.

On August 30, elements of the 27th—with the U.S. 30th on its left and the British 34th on its right—attacked a German stronghold on the Vierstraat Ridge. Closely following the 27th, Sargent promptly set up his easel and equipment, including, as reckless as it was, his big white umbrella to shade him from the sun. Disbelieving American officers immediately ordered him to camouflage his umbrella, which was like a bull's-eye for German gunners. Unfortunately for Sargent, other than incoming artillery fire and aerial assaults, there was no vivid combat to be witnessed and no British-American hand-in-hand assault on the Germans, no intermingling of forces. In fact, the 27th's 107th Regiment would suffer less than two hundred casualties, indicating a relatively light engagement.[9] The most interesting aspect of the battle was that the Americans were fighting under a handicap: command had decreed that they were not allowed to damage any unharvested wheat farmed by the Flemish, who, as the war raged about them, kept at their yokes.

Still yearning to witness actual combat before this particular skirmish ended—and against the wishes of the 27th's commander Major General John F. O'Ryan—Sargent persuaded one of the general's staff members to take him closer to the front lines. They immediately found themselves in the midst of a gas attack and had to withdraw to the ruined city of Ypres, where they subsequently found themselves under artillery bombardment. Back at 27th HQ, Sargent ducked down into General O'Ryan's dugout—a steel Nissen hut—and, hoping to salvage the day, requested permission to sketch the general. Amid the staccato shrieks and explosive roars, Sargent remained unperturbed and executed a lovely portrait of the general, while his men were capturing and holding the Vierstraat Ridge. One can only imagine what O'Ryan, a hardened veteran of the Mexican wars, thought of the bon vivant artist.

After two days of fighting, the 27th was relieved, and Sargent was again left with his quandary of finding British and U.S. troops fighting hand-in-hand. While the Germans pulled back to their impregnable Hindenburg Line, the artist knocked around the zone for several weeks. Having survived artillery barrages and aerial bombardments, he was finally laid low by the cold, wet weather. In late September he came down with the flu and was taken to a casualty clearing station near Roisel. There he spent a week in a tent surrounded by the "groans of wounded and coughing of gassed men, which was a nightmare," he wrote. "It always seemed strange on opening one's eyes to see the level cots and the dimly lit long tent looking so calm, when one was dozing in pandemonium." He was soon relocated to the officers' ward, where he enjoyed the comfort of an oil stove.[10] However, he couldn't forget the gas casualties in the tent, who, in turn, reminded him of the blinded boys he had seen at the dressing station on the road to Arras. The grotesque line of blinded boys. The distorted bodies. The frieze. That was the one image that kept playing vividly in his mind. That was to be his epic.

Even so, Sargent remained in the zone in early October, making his studies. In Peronne, while observing hundreds of German prisoners locked in a cage in ankle-deep mud, he was caught in another artillery attack. Undeterred, as shells burst around him, the artist merrily pushed his canvases, equipment, and supplies about in a wheelbarrow. From there, on October 5, Sargent wrote a Major Lee, who was connected to the War Memorials Commission, that he was very happy at the moment, "and that bombs are coming from all directions," which was just what he liked.[11] At this time, however, Sargent also wrote a letter to Alfred Yockney, the secretary of the British War Memorials Committee, in which he complained, "For a long time I did not see any means of treating the subject given to me of 'British and American Troops Working Together.' They do this in the abstract but not in any particular space within the limits of a picture."[12] Sargent was now convinced that he was wasting his time—even as American forces were assaulting the virtual fortress of the Bellicourt Tunnell just to the east and would suffer severe casualties.

Still feeling the effects of the flu, at the end of October, Sargent returned to his Tite Street home in London and set to work on his war masterpiece, which he completed and delivered in March 1919. However, nowhere in the majestic painting were there British and American troops

*Gassed* by Sargent. An epic piece depicting American and British troops together in heroic battle was not to be for Sargent, but this subdued work put the war into perspective.

fighting heroically in concert. To the contrary, his work was a quiet commentary on the horror of war titled *Gassed* (see the previous page). In his epic painting—the canvas measuring nine feet by twenty—there are about sixty-five soldiers, all gas victims. In the foreground are nine soldiers marching blindly toward the dressing station, with help from two orderlies. The third soldier in line is lifting his foot to an exaggerated height—an awkward, pathetic gesture—to avoid tripping. Other wounded are lying about in the field, distorted and collapsed figures. White bandages wrap around their eyes. The sun is low in the yellow sky, reminiscent of the heinous gas.

The work shows restraint, impersonality; it is not tainted by sentimentality. The soldiers' gestures, while invoking pain and despair, are subtle. Yet, the very understatement strengthens the piece and its condemnation of war. In reviewing the work, Sir Claude Phillips wrote in the *Daily Telegraph*: "Of singular beauty and singular impressiveness is this halting, broken rhythm marked in timid advance of the shattered band which but an hour before marched out in all the elastic gayety of youth and self-confidence. . . . Reticent as the artist has been in the expression of supreme tragedy—perhaps, indeed, on account of this very reticence—he attains to a height of pathos such as has not been reached as yet in any war picture."[13] Work by both Harding and Dunn presented similar dramatic scenes of the wounded. Not so surprisingly, the venerable Sargent's grim but magnificent piece won high praise, while the AEF artists suffered unfair criticism for their pictures depicting the devastating results of war.

In the Meuse-Argonne sector of the Western Front, the first few days of October were relatively quiet for the doughboys, as Pershing reorganized his divisions for a series of attacks to be launched on October 4. However, there were still incidents of horror to digest. One such incident that particularly struck Townsend involved an American pilot who was on a mission over Hun lines when anti-aircraft fire hit his load of bombs: "At any rate, horrible to think of, there was a terrific flash and explosion, and nothing but tiny fragments remained or were found later. This same thing happened, I remember hearing, along early in the summer in one of our other sectors. What a fate!"

While mired in the violence around him, Townsend also worried incessantly about his family, which added to his burden. He worried about his daughter, Barbara, eating too much candy because she had recently had a cavity; he worried about whether she was enjoying her new school in Chicago; and he worried about the effect of his absence as she grew older. The list continued, as he feared he was shirking his duties as a husband and a father. Realizing his wife was under duress, too, in a letter he urged her to attend a concert or the theater, even though their personal finances were extremely tight. He reassured her that he would be able to forward money soon; however, before he could, he might have to buy a new uniform because the General Staff was considering a new design. Redesigned uniforms while men died regardless of their attire; it seemed absurd, part of a perverse satire.

As Townsend sought to give his family advice and comfort, he wondered if his letters were even reaching his wife. From Cory, he had just received her sixty-seventh letter to him—literally numbered so he could see what came through and what didn't. In fact, some did go missing. Regardless of his letters' fate, Townsend continued to write lengthy letters to purge his troubled mind. One letter that most definitely reached Cory was that in which Townsend finally informed her about Henri's confessional letter because she wrote in response, her response less than wholly empathetic. Feeling that their relationship was already strained, Cory now questioned why her husband had hidden the existence of Henri's letter from her; she wondered what else he might be hiding. Townsend again explained that he simply had not possessed the emotional strength to divulge the letter until months later. "What an unfortunate thing his going was and particularly before we got a chance to see each other," he wrote. "It came back to me the other day again his going, his presence now. And a considerable sense of loss." Townsend was now embracing the painful emotions intertwined with his brother's death because he never wanted "to get so callous that I forget."[14]

Amid this emotional carnage expressed in early October, there came a glimmer of hope: the Germans had made peace overtures to President Wilson. It all sounded as though the boys might be going home sooner than thought, Townsend wrote to Cory excitedly on October 6, as everyone awaited Wilson's response.[15] The president's reply was blunt: before there could be any negotiations, Germany had to withdraw its troops from all occupied territories. Of course, the Germans balked. The killing continued. And Townsend would be in France for more than another six months, recording history for posterity's sake.

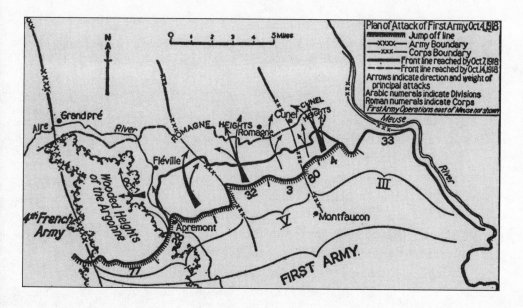

. . .

In hopes of reinvigorating the offensive, Pershing reinserted the seasoned 32nd, 3rd, and 1st Divisions into the line and, on October 4 at 5 A.M., relaunched the attack in what was phase two of the Meuse-Argonne. Despite the shake-up, on the edge of the Argonne Forest, almost directly west of Exermont and Cierges, the doughboys remained thwarted by the enemy. Decimated by German artillery sitting atop the Argonne bluffs, not until October 6 did the 28th and 82nd capture Châtel-Chéhéry, a village they had expected to liberate days earlier.[16] When Peixotto motored to Châtel-Chéhéry from Apremont, the latter captured on September 28, he realized just how bogged down the offensive remained, because Apremont was less than two miles to the south. It had taken the doughboys a week to advance less than two miles. "After its initial push forward," Peixotto observed, "our Argonne offensive moved slowly, for it encountered the bitterest opposition. One hard fight succeeded another. Through one cold night after another our infantry camped in the open, wet and freezing, sheltered only by their pup-tents and exposed to a continuous harassing fire from the enemy's artillery. Slow and steady progress was being made, to be sure, but only by 'paying the price.'"[17]

Also now touring the advance zone, Townsend was witness to the continuous carnage, and, reflecting on the Meuse-Argonne Offensive, he determined it to be a "terrible struggle and blight of death for our men, an offensive in which the losses were actually the heaviest of the whole war for the number of men involved. What terrible things I saw here, and how sick of the war I had become. And yet how fascinated too."[18] Like so many soldiers and civilians, he continued to wrestle with the dichotomy of these emotions.

Another week of high casualties yielded little ground, so, on October 11, Pershing again halted offensive operations to reorganize his divisions. The next day he announced the formation of the 2nd Army of the AEF and placed Lieutenant General Robert L. Bullard in charge, while Lieutenant General Hunter Liggett took command of the 1st Army and Pershing took the title of Army Group Commander. The hope was that by decentralizing planning and transportation, among other logistics, the execution of the battles themselves would be more efficient and effective as the 1st Army continued to drive for Sedan and the 2nd Army directed its forces eastward, toward the city of Metz. Phase three of the Meus-Argonne Offensive would be launched on October 13, with Pershing growing more anxious to break Germany's backbone.

While the doughboys suffered at the front and Pershing fretted, the mood in Paris had improved considerably since the bleak summer days. "Paris we found so different . . . from my last visit of the 14th of July," wrote Townsend, who, along with Smith and Duncan, had traveled there on October 10, "for now she has quite her old spirit back again and her people. They, who had hid themselves away when the air raids and Big Bertha made their days and their nights troubled and anxious ones, have hurried back now that the menace is over. . . . The Café de la Paix in its palmiest days never catered to such crowds, nor more carefree and good-natured ones."[19] Officers crowded the cafés, as did the flirtatious French girls, who were a cheerful bunch. They were proud to practice their English, doing quite well at it, and thus made great company for the doughboys at the cost of a mere drink or meal. For Townsend, it was amusing entertainment to watch the officers stumbling over the girls and trying to communicate with them.

With the big German guns no longer threatening Paris, the city was indeed returning to its old lively self; however, along with the increasing

crowds came exorbitant price increases even though the French government was attempting to prevent gouging. Townsend felt a little guilty
about splurging on fine meals and still preferred to find the cheaper
places, which earned him a reputation for being "close" with his money.
Meanwhile, he explained to Cory, his fellow artists were "like all the
other officers here—nothing is too good for them as long as their money
lasts." Duncan completely let himself go when he purchased a set of
reproductions of Rembrandt etchings for 300 francs, while Townsend
sent what money he could to Cory.

Townsend wasn't too frugal; their first night in Paris he went to the
Théâtre Michel, an intimate playhouse that advertised only by word of
mouth. Andrée Spinelli, a well-known French actress who starred in
light musicals and comedies, was currently starring in a revue called *Plus
ça Change*. Both a farce and a lovely musical, it was a recounting of
human history beginning with prehistoric animals and ending with a
futuristic scene set in 2018. Townsend purchased a fourth-row ticket
that cost him 15 valuable francs, but he needed desperately to lose
himself in an entertaining farce to escape the horrors he had witnessed.
Not disappointed, Townsend found Spinelli to be "the finest thing of her
kind" and pointedly noted that there was no need to know French
because "there are perfectly stunning girls in costumes brief enough to
please the most fastidious"—and they could act.[20]

Perhaps not having fully comprehended how detrimental the war was
to his emotional health, Townsend now realized its effect when he surprised himself by feeling compelled to visit the Church of Christ Scien-
tist in Paris. To rekindle his faith, he conferred with a church leader, a
Mr. Norlidge. "We had quite a good talk and he seems very practical
and I think that his talk will help me to keep straight in my thought,"
Townsend wrote to Cory. "It was all along the line of 'Mind's business'
and he realizes what a fellow is up against in the matter of contact with
material evidence all the time." The next morning Townsend attended
church, further proof that while in gay Paris, away from the war, he desperately needed spiritual renewing.[21] Regardless of any doubts in God
he was harboring, he needed to retreat into his religion to survive the
bloodbath around him. In an October letter to his daughter, he asked
her to "tell mother that I have been reading my Science and Health and
that I know Love is taking care of me, and that I will be all right at once
and am now." That he would "be all right at once" suggested that he had

indeed been struggling with his faith and that his emotional health had been suffering.[22]

In addition to some well-earned rest and relaxation, the artists were in Paris to secure studios for the winter, under the assumption that the war would be over. Even though, as Townsend put it, he nearly "chased his legs off" hustling around, it was impossible to find any space. Because the Parisian artists who had gone off to the war had been permitted to keep their studios without paying rent, they had not relinquished them, making for a tight market regardless of how many of them were still alive. So that the trip was not a complete loss, the Americans purchased art supplies to bring back to Neufchâteau.

Before departing Paris, Townsend ventured into the Montparnasse Quarter, a working-class neighborhood where he did not find the same marked, upbeat change he had elsewhere in the city: "It still has the sad calm that has been so noticeable before. For its inhabitants are the ones who were permanent and they have gone—to the war—or those that the war left there perhaps sought their families in the country, till their loved ones came home. And the city still shows this loss here. Many of them will never come back, no doubt."[23] In contrast, on their return journey to Neufchâteau, Townsend and gang enjoyed "a wonderfully beautiful ride down thro the autumn foliage and faint, hazy sunshine that seemed to turn everything into a blaze of color that was unreal." They stopped in Provins for dinner and passed through Troyes, an ancient city with a thirteenth-century cathedral, which Townsend found to be "one of the most picturesque old places we had yet seen."[24] His ebullience would not last.

On his arrival in Neufchâteau—the 192-mile journey from Paris having taken a long seven hours—Townsend found the gray stone buildings to be depressing in the low October sun. His disheartened mood anticipated the news awaiting him: Townsend's friend Don Martin, a correspondent with the *Herald*, had died suddenly of cholera. With his wife having already passed away, he left behind a fifteen-year-old daughter. In addition, at GHQ there was intensified concern over a rapidly growing outbreak of influenza—the outbreak having started over the summer—which Townsend noted with detail in his diary:

Am informed on our return that the casualties in Neufchâteau from the Spanish grippe have been enormous—that it has

approached a real epidemic, and everyone is more or less frightened over it, for everyone has a bad cold and feels that they are
going down with it, so that it's all one can do to fight this universal belief. There is a steady stream of funerals passing my studio all
the time, and alas many, many of them are American soldiers, too.
The loss in the civil population, tho, has been very heavy, I am
told, as many as three or four a day, they said, in the week passed.
I have counted as many as three some days, since my return, and
the military ones have run as high as six U. S. and three or four
French in one day, and there's never a day goes by that there isn't
the more or less regular count of them, so that it can well seem
alarming to a people whose belief in sickness is already keen. The
rumors, too, that reach us of the number of cases in our army at
the front are amazing. But it's an epidemic that hits the enemy
even harder than it's hitting us, we are told, so there is consolation
in that. . . . Our medical corps, I understand, are going into the
thing hard, trying to discover the germ and a remedy, which the
French authorities to date have been unable to do. In the meantime, our hospitals are overflowing with our boys, and many of
them start West as a result of the ineffectual treatment. It's a hard
death for one who has come so far, thinking at the worst, to die
fighting the Hun.[25]

The chief of staff of the SOS, Brigadier General Johnson Hagood,
reported on October 7 that he had received information that indicated
soldiers were dying "at a rate of about one every ten minutes." It
appeared to Hagood that the trouble had originated in the United
States, with the sick being loaded right onto the transport ships instead
of being sequestered. Soon some 11,000 soldiers would contract
influenza and pneumonia weekly, and, ultimately, according to esti-
mates, 43,000 doughboys mobilized for the war would die of influenza.
Between 450,000 and 675,000 Americans would die in 1918 and 1919.
And somewhere between 20 million and 40 million worldwide would
die.[26] Naturally, each side of the conflict kept the effects of the influenza
on its respective armies as secret as possible—no potential weakness
could be intimated or displayed.

Exacerbating the gloom, according to Townsend, there was little
Allied enthusiasm for a negotiated peace with Germany, which had

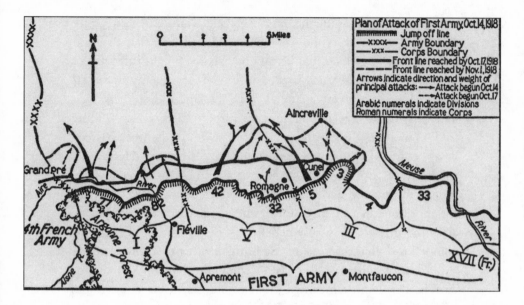

been a hot topic as of late. More bloodshed was certain as there remained the feeling, as much as one wanted to deny it, that the war would have to be fought to the bitter end. Allied forces would have to ruthlessly drive the Boche soldiers into the Rhine River and the kaiser from his palace. Indeed, even as there was talk of peace, President Wilson accused the Germans of inhumanity in their submarine warfare and on the battlefield, which they vehemently denied. Reading this back-and-forth rhetoric, Townsend saw the German rebuttals as "shoddy propaganda," and, he noted, the misinformation so incensed the Allies that they were determined to bring the German leaders to "their knees" and render them "impotent."[27] However, it was not going to be easy bringing Germany to its knees.

"Our 1st Army has struck a snag in its offensive north of Verdun," Townsend recorded, concerning the broad attack Pershing had launched on October 13, "in that owing to the nature of the country there, and the fact that it's . . . such a vital sector to the Boche, he is throwing in all his available strength there to stop the American advance. These facts, and the fever, are a hindrance, but in spite of it all, our troops make slight but steady progress. The Germans are launching ceaseless counter-attacks, preceded by artillery fire, but we have been able, in all cases, to stop them, and generally to turn them to our advantage."[28] It appeared that no reorganizing and retooling on Pershing's part could break an enemy well entrenched in a daunting countryside.

The artists continued to follow the troops, including their old friends with the 42nd, who were pushing straight north through the Romagne Heights to the Kriemhilde Stellung, the third of the four German defensive lines. Exemplifying the fierce enemy resistance, over four days, the 42nd's 84th Brigade under Douglas MacArthur suffered three thousand casualties as they attacked the Côte de Châtillon, a fortified section of the Kriemhilde Stellung. One private with the 42nd experiencing the harrowing assault with searing vividness was Albert Ettinger, who was trapped in a foxhole while the enemy pounded them with artillery. All he wanted was to smoke a lousy cigarette to steady his nerves, but he needed a light, so, as shells exploded around him, he jumped over to the adjacent foxhole. He borrowed some matches from his color sergeant, Bill Sheahan, and returned to his own hole. "No sooner had I rolled and lit a cigarette than there was a terrible explosion!" he recalled. "Both

*Working Back to Aid Station* by Harding. Due to traffic jams, ambulances often could not reach the front, so the wounded were left to struggle rearward.

Sherwood and I were stunned and buried in mud. We managed to dig ourselves out of our hole, heard shouts, and discovered that the shell had landed in the adjacent hole where those two fellows had been. There was no sign of Bill Sheahan, and the other fellow had both legs blown off; he was being carried down the slope to the aid station." Once the morning sky lightened, they searched for Sheahan—all that remained was what "appeared to be a piece of roast beef strapped by a web belt."[29]

To the west of the 42nd, the artist André Smith followed the 77th Division into St. Juvin, a village just north of the Argonne Forest that they captured on October 14. "After the men of the Seventy-seventh Division," Smith wrote, "citified New Yorkers whose previous knowledge of forests had not extended much beyond the orderly boundaries of Bronx Park, had made a clean sweep of the Argonne wilderness . . . it added as a full measure of its accomplishment the capture of the village of St. Juvin. It was no easy job. St. Juvin was on the second line of the Kriemhilde defenses, and had the advantage of position on high ground with the precipitous walls of the citadel of Grandpré as a vantage point for any attempted advance from the forest in that direction."[30] Fighting was intense; it took three attacks before St. Juvin fell.

It was hoped that the 77th would smash through the Germans and quickly capture Grandpré, a significant town on the Aire River, but it was not to be. At 10 A.M. on October 14, the 3rd Battalion of the 308th Infantry attempted to cross the river and establish a line, the commanding officer recorded in his report; however, "harassing artillery and machine gun fire on our positions prevented our troops from reaching the Corps Objective until 12:30 A.M. . . . The enemy appears to be determined to continue a strong rear guard defense."[31] Still pinned down the next day and suffering heavy casualties, the 308th was relieved in the early morning hours of October 16 by the 311th Infantry Regiment of the 78th Division, another green division, made up of boys from mountainous, rural New York and New Jersey.

On October 22, Harding and Morgan motored into the northern area of the Argonne Forest and visited with an artillery unit with the 77th, before pushing forward to where the 78th was dug in outside Grandpré. The situation was perilous, as Harding noted:

the air plane activity enormous . . .
Boche forced down into woods
about 200 yards from us.
Coming back—they dropped bombs
on road about 200 yards ahead &
where we left our car—

Amazingly, amid this carnage, God's creatures survived, for Harding observed birds migrating and rabbits hopping through trenches. The surrounding hills reminded the artist of Newfoundland, after a forest fire, or better yet, he decided, the landscape resembled desolate Nevada. There was little time to ruminate over such matters as the war encroached on his daydreams, and, again, he pulled out his small notebook paper:

The wire the trenches. The rusted
gear out there—the utter desolation
the trucks in shell holes the broken
tractors, the machine gun fights . . .
horses unable to get
up skinny & worn out.

Harding and Morgan attempted to spend the night in their car, positioned reasonably close to the front, however, between big naval guns on nearby railroad tracks firing continuously and incoming enemy shells, they were forced to relocate. The next morning, they hitched a ride in an ambulance, going forward two miles before being forced to walk into a seething, bubbling cauldron straight from hell. Just ahead of them, an enemy plane dropped its bombs, killing three doughboys. As Harding passed by the dead, he noted that one soldier's legs and side were blown open so he looked "like skinned rabbit." Further forward, they encountered a doughboy who had accidentally dropped a live grenade in his own trench; he lost his testicles and both hands.[32]

Harding had become somewhat calloused to such scenes, as they were repeated day in and day out, and at times he pushed ahead blindly until completely exhausted:

*Going through Gas* by Harding. Even though both sides were no longer surprised by gas attacks, American and German artillery continued to use gas.

After five days, or even less, in the offensive, everything becomes commonplace. You go with your army, often with the Germans behind you, while whole companies have wedged through the enemy, often leaving the boche behind, so that as you pass through villages, you find many Germans still there, sniping at you from the windows. You go on and on, until at last you realize that you have absolutely lost all power of observation and that everything appears commonplace. It gradually sinks into your tired mind that you need sleep, a hot meal and a chance to get the stuff you've seen out of your head. Then you drop behind, get a good sleep, something to eat, and a larger piece of paper to work on, which is a relief after the six-by-eight sketchbook. Then you get out again for the big show. If there is a lull of four or five days, you use it to work at top speed in transcribing your notes into sketches, so as to be ready to start out again at the opening of the next offensive.[33]

. . .

Now charged with taking Grandpré, the 78th discovered what the 77th had and what André Smith summarized with an appreciative eye: "This strip of France which was turned over to us for capture was the most treacherous and difficult battleground on the entire Western Front. . . . It was nasty going all the way." Not until October 27 did these boys, whose nom de guerre was "The White Lightnings" after their fancy for moonshine, take the citadel town of Grandpré. The battle climaxed with hand-to-hand combat across the town's terraced roofs and the 78th suffered five thousand casualties in this visceral engagement.[34] Harding captured the frantic and fractured nature of this fight:

> The citadel the barn with gas
> shell in it. The machine gun
> fight about citadel the americans
> in lower part of town the Boche
> sniper in back part of citadel

*A Counter-Attack* by Harding. The fighting became ever more vicious, with villages changing hands multiple times, as Germany became a desperate animal backed into a corner.

in a room . . .
The Americans attack from the
hill opposite cemetery with
trees cut in half . . .
The men looking
for quarters to sleep some on
doors among ruins.[35]

"It was a hot place," confirmed André Smith, who made sketches of Grandpré and the surrounding area, "the Germans were slow to relinquish it, and the town changed hands several times before we were finally able to make it our own. And in this back-and-forth struggle Grand Pré was mauled and battered and stirred up as if by one of our western tornadoes, and for that matter it was, only worse . . . it was struck by the fury of the 'Jersey Lightnings' in the shape of the 78th Division."[36]

In the field for almost the entire Meuse-Argonne Offensive, in his October report Harding informed their chief that he had visited the Verdun sector and Argonne Forest "where the heaviest fighting had been. I devoted considerable time to making notes of the way our troops lived in the open, a new phase of American campaigning in France."[37] He captured the smoky, disorienting scene of early morning artillery fire with the loud reports rendering men senseless, and the more chaotic scene of troops following the subsequent creeping barrage, with soldiers stumbling over chewed up earth and hand grenades spinning through the air. And then there was always the aftermath, the repeated aftermath: the grim-faced wounded making their way back to advanced aid stations, carrying each other and stepping over the dead entangled in wire.

Through these cold and wet days of October, the forty-nine-year-old Peixotto had dedicated most of his time to following the troops, to making good; however, the elements took their toll and he finally succumbed late in the month. In his diary, on October 27, Townsend noted that Peixotto "was suddenly stricken with a sort of a heart attack the other day." Artist Walter Duncan was also taken ill, Townsend added, so "that the artists are hit a bit, too."[38] Peixotto was ill enough that Smith felt it necessary to report his case to their chief, Major James; it was hoped that the artist would recover enough to travel to his home in

Samois-sur-Seine, where his wife could care for him. The cause for concern was well justified considering the influenza epidemic.

The Meuse-Argonne Offensive was simply one vicious battle after another as the doughboys cracked one line of defense after another. Over six weeks, the AEF witnessed 26,277 killed and 95,786 wounded, the kind of bloodshed witnessed in the most horrific of World War I battles before America's entry. Toward the end of October, the ground was literally thick with the dead, as discovered by Private Arthur Yensen of the 5th Division, who was following the advance in a mule wagon. He recalled a grisly scene he came across while he was arguing with a comrade over whether it was morally right to take souvenirs off dead soldiers: "He said it was wrong to take anything off a dead soldier for a souvenir; I said it was all right and just about had the argument won when I heard a popping noise. I looked down and saw I'd run over a dead Yank and broke his legs! Later we saw lots of dead men. Half a man here and another half across the road, bled white and spattered with mud. I felt sorry for the poor boys; they looked so pitiful." Yensen would take no souvenirs.[39]

"More funerals today," Townsend jotted down on October 27. "Both civil and military." Complementing the funerals in a morbid fashion was the autumn weather. "Last night was very cold and it froze," the artist wrote. "There was a heavy, white frost on everything this morning that lasted way into the slow, pale sunlight."[40] As casualties mounted at an alarming rate, about the only good news Townsend heard was that the Advance Section of the SOS was moving into Neufchâteau, which meant the artists would be able to get ample supplies of wood for their fires rather than being forced to pay extortionate prices to the French. Electricity and thus lighting, which the artists desperately needed as the days grew shorter, would also be more widely available thanks to the SOS crews. But then their hopes were unceremoniously dashed as the wood they had so anxiously anticipated would not burn. "Too damp, and how they expect a fellow to get any heat out of it is beyond me,"[41] Townsend noted caustically in his diary. He couldn't win.

In terms of raw numbers, American casualties were negligible, because there were still plenty more soldiers to send to the front: as of October 23, the AEF's strength was over 1.2 million men and officers.[42] Perhaps because the Central Powers recognized the inevitable—the overwhelming force of the Americans—toward the end of October there were reports that they appeared to be more serious about their peace overtures; however, this news elicited "no feeling of joy" in Paris as a negotiated truce remained anathema. Still, with the end of hostilities on the horizon, Townsend sat down in front of his fireplace and, on the morning of October 27, penned a letter to his family in which he mulled over postwar life. He explained to Cory and Barbara that he was considering where he'd prefer to live: New York City or France. While he enjoyed the "spirit of things" in New York, he concluded that he would not be content to live there. In France there were too many lovely villages nestled among the hills to be explored and everywhere he looked there seemed to be "a new delight for the eye." In New York, on the other hand, you had to hunt around for "a thrilling spot."

As Townsend also pondered what he would do in terms of work, he knew something would develop, but not necessarily related to war art, because "I suppose from everyone's attitude now they will be so sick of the war after that they won't want to see a war picture, or think a war thought." However, he didn't look forward to "grinding away at the measly dollars of old." Magazine and book illustration would be too mundane, too commercial, too trifling in this embattled world. Like Dunn, who would also shun commercial work, Townsend wanted to do something meaningful with his art. Yes, the war had changed him and the other artists; everything now had to have a deeper spiritual significance, and each of them was intent on making profound statements. They were driven to leave a legacy. In sharp contrast to his reflective mood, American planes soared playfully across the sky over Neufchâteau and performed stunts to celebrate battlefield victories, albeit costly victories.

When Townsend picked up the October 27 evening paper, it announced Ludendorff's resignation; he had fallen from favor with the kaiser for supporting capitulation. No longer welcome in his country, Ludendorff donned a false beard and dark glasses and escaped to Sweden. It was also reported that Germany had accepted some of Wilson's conditions for opening negotiations, such as a representative government. Adding to the pressure on the kaiser, Germany's newspaper editors believed they as a people must now follow through even if it meant abdication by the kaiser. Yet, while the politicians were taking steps toward peace, the fighting continued unabated because the Allies were intent on pressing home their victories.

"The battle up on our front seems to have assumed a sudden fury that the papers say has not been exceeded in the war," Townsend wrote in his diary that night. "There is much troop movement thro here by train again, and there are rumors that another big offensive is being prepared, tho there is talk that it is out of the question at this particular moment, on account of the fact that it is necessary for us to keep all our experienced troops up above Verdun, and that we have none but green men for a new attack. But I doubt it if that is a true condition."[43]

Late in the day on October 28, news came that Austria had requested a separate peace, regardless of how the negotiations with Germany proceeded. Meanwhile, Germany's leaders claimed that their government was already representative of the people and the government was waiting for proposals for a "preliminary armistice." As Townsend put it, "There can be but one answer to such a nation. Unconditional surrender!" In a letter to Cory he wondered how the American public was taking the Austrian overtures, and informed her, "There's no great enthusiasm here save that it makes it a bit easier to force Germany to her knees tho there are many who would rather fight her down than have her forced to give in by her allies dropping away."[44]

Regardless of Germany's continued peace overtures, it appeared the country would indeed go down fighting, prompting Townsend to note in his diary "how bitterly Germany is still fighting." There was a sense that the enemy wanted to inflict as much pain as possible on the Americans before finally settling on peace. In fact, in those last days of October, battles were so vicious that Townsend felt it necessary to assure Cory that he was not in the thick of it. He was working diligently on his pieces due at the end of the month.[45] Determined to create masterful renderings of the war, Townsend even recruited models from the men convalescing in the local military hospital so he could accurately portray the doughboys.

In October, Townsend created several dramatic pieces, including *Soldiers of the Telephone, Infantryman* (not pictured), and *Helping a Wounded Ally* (not pictured),—all three rendered in charcoal to create a subdued mood and dramatic lighting. In all three pieces, depicting six soldiers in total, Townsend allows only one face to be seen: that of a grimacing soldier hunkered down in a trench working the telephone. As with the other artists, especially Dunn, who created his universal soldier, Townsend understood that expressions told too much of the horror, they were too dramatic; it was best to keep faces in the shadows or turned away. In *Soldiers of the Telephone* (see page 104), he inserted sharp, vibrant lines slashing through the picture to provide the necessary sense of tension as the men hunker down in their trench, jaws clenched, vigilant, wary of enemy fire, while attempting to relay information to HQ. Overhead the sky is dark except for an unnatural burst of light to the right, the fierce contrast unsettling and ominous.

While Pershing struggled to break the enemy, the artists finally scored their own victory: the mood in Washington toward their work changed suddenly and dramatically to the positive. Even though he had been scolded for writing to Smith directly, Banning, who was quite encouraged by the most recent group of artwork to arrive, did so again: "From an artistic standpoint they are regarded highly," he gushed. In a conciliatory tone, he informed Smith that steps were being taken to arrange for an exhibition in Washington that would then become a traveling show. "I can assure you that every effort will be made to give the pictures the widest possible publicity," he wrote. Even so, the nitpicking Banning still desired "to establish a more definite point of view toward the functions of the official artists . . ." and noted that the whole matter was "now being gone into thoroughly." Of course, by the time Smith received the letter it was late October—many of the artists were six months into their work—and there was serious talk of the war ending. Smith immediately forwarded Banning's letter to Major James, with a note stating that the "tone of it is quite different from any previous communication."[46]

Washington was particularly impressed with Harding's work, prompting Banning to write to him directly, as well. It had received "favorable comment" from everyone, Banning relayed, including Herbert Adams, the president of the American Federation of Artists, and Charles Moore, the chairman of the Fine Arts Commission. The ever-opinionated Banning thought Harding had chosen excellent subjects and the artist understood precisely what they needed in Washington—action pieces so the public could revel in the glory of battle. However, his one complaint was that only twelve pieces of Harding's had arrived—Banning assumed there were more and naturally wanted them posthaste.[47]

Morgan also received a personal letter from Banning, in which he reiterated that not only was Harding's work "enthusiastically received" but pieces by Morgan and Townsend "were liked." This latest review, however restrained, was a relief to Townsend, who immediately reported the good news to Cory. He also noted that Harding's pieces were so well received, in part, because many were in color or "were black and white and had color in them." While still feeling the pressure to churn out at least two polished pieces every week, Townsend was now determined to get into "the color game hard," and, feeling "a bit better" about their work, he was finally settling into a groove. Townsend realized it "sounds strange to be only sort of getting into good working condition" so far into the war, he explained to Cory, however, it took all of them time to adjust and settle in. "I've no doubt that they will want and expect us to do a lot of the most important work after things have let up or are finished," he concluded. "It seems to me too it's the only way to collect the necessary material for painting for you simply can't do it now."[48]

A traveling show would indeed be organized in November, as Banning promised, and one of the first stops was in New York at the Allied War Salon, founded to benefit American war relief. Sweeping aside any early misgivings in Washington, a review of the show by Royal Cortissoz, an art critic with the *New York Tribune*, was glowing:

> If the war has produced anything for us it has produced these snap shots in water color and pencil. They vary in appeal according to the temperament of the draftsman. Capt. George Harding is notable for his dramatic spirit, for the picturesque élan with which he sketches our troops. Capt. J. André Smith is interested in making literal transcripts from nature. He and Capt. Peixotto and Capt. W. J. Aylward are students of topography rather than of military action. They supply the setting of the war, so to say, the traits of scarred landscapes and ruined buildings. In Capt. Wallace Morgan's drawings, as in those of Captain Harding, we get more of the soldier type, more of military movement. . . . Looking at all these drawings in the mass—and they are so numerous that it is frankly impossible to deal with them otherwise—one kindles to their truth, to their unmistakable value as records.

Because the artists had their own, self-designated specialties, their work did have to be studied collectively to begin to grasp the magnitude of the war and the importance of their work as a historical record.

In evaluating the quality of the pieces, the art critic for the *New York Times* noted that the artists were capturing the truth of war:

> Much of this talent is of a high order, and the quiet, unobtrusive manner in which it is used is of the very essence of its quality. . . . There is a characteristic absence of sentimentalism in all the records and freedom from insistence on any one feature of the scene at the expenses of others. The tired men at Château-Thierry are just tired men, not exhausted heroes, under Capt. Harding's pencil. The French light tanks are making their way across the

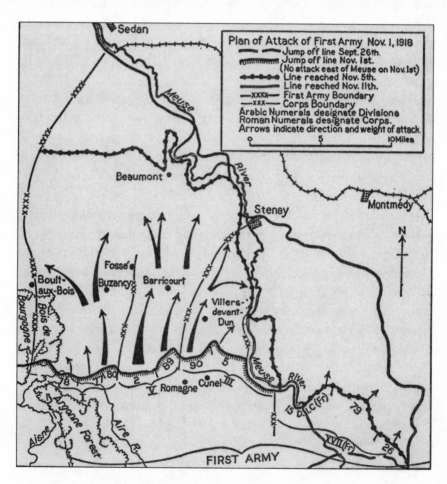

fields with businesslike precision. It is reserved for the artists at home to draw the agony of Belgium and the sorrows of women and children.[49]

The artists certainly received a measure of well-deserved redemption; however, conspicuously missing from both reviews was any mention of Harvey Dunn, whose pieces would eventually become the most popular. Demonstrating that he was already becoming far less interested in the commercial acceptance required in his work as an illustrator, Dunn simply didn't care what Washington thought or what the critics wrote. Instead, he remained obsessively focused on spending as much time with the troops as possible in what would be the final weeks of the war.

The rhythm of the Meuse-Argonne Offensive had an ebb and flow quality to it, and as Halloween approached it was obvious that the doughboys were gearing up for another violent push forward. Indeed, on November 1, at 5:30 A.M., the 1st Army under General Hunter Liggett attacked, their goal to break the Freya Stellung, Germany's last defensive line, and take Sedan. North of Verdun the artillery fire was terrific, according to reports, but as Townsend noted ruefully, he was not there to observe the action: "As before, we were in no way given any tip as to the move, so were not there. And why GHQ continually does this is more than we can understand."[50] Meanwhile, they still had standing orders to confine their activities to the forward zone.

Casualties promised to be high in assaulting the Freya Stellung, which, Townsend observed, was apropos in a perverse sense because November 1 is the Fête de Tous Saints—All Saints' Day. So, while the doughboys flung themselves into the enemy's fire, throughout the day the locals closed their stores and businesses, and took flowers and potted plants to the cemeteries. The next day would be the apt Fêtes de Mortes, Festival of the Dead, with more ceremonies in the cemeteries, all of which prompted Townsend to observe wryly in his diary that most fetes now revolved around the dead.

The rain continued on November 2, yet, in spite of the horrid conditions, as Townsend learned back in Neufchâteau, the American drive had turned into a rout. Positioned in the center, the 2nd Division advanced six miles the first day and another five miles over the next two. The Germans were fleeing so quickly it was difficult to stay in contact with them and large numbers of prisoners were being taken. The German backbone had finally broken.

The only delay in the advance was along the right side of the 1st Army, along the Meuse River, where the 5th Division faced formidable defenses in trying to cross the river and seize the village of Dun-sur-Meuse. But, as Smith pointed out, with the Vaterland just over the horizon, the doughboys were highly motivated and succeeded in throwing the Boche beyond Dun within a few days. When Smith arrived there to sketch the battlefield, he discovered a large munitions and gasoline dump, indicative of the importance of this village to the Germans. Reflecting on the ugly scene before him, he wrote:

> Occasionally a sweep of landscape enlivened by troops, or some monumental ruin rising against a bank of clouds will carry your interest above dull elements that compose it. But, as a whole, the background of war is a confusing mass of drab-colored dreariness. There are too many miles of tree-smashed roads, too many acres of mud and ruptured fields, too many villages of monotonous ruins, too many long wooden barracks, ammunition dumps, storage piles, horse sheds—in fact, too much of everything that is sordid, colorless and ugly. And yet, it is all part of the picture, a vital setting of this tremendous performance of war. And so it must be drawn.[51]

And so he made a drawing of the munitions dump with a horse in the foreground, a horse broken under the weight of caissons and set free to die.

After days of steady rain, the sun broke through on Sunday, November 3, and Townsend went for a stroll, along with the columns of U.S. troops moving through Neufchâteau. With Pershing intent on intensifying the pressure, doughboys were being transported toward Toul; a large pursuit field was being built near Manonville, relatively close to the front; and stories of plans for a concentrated attack toward Metz were circulating. Meanwhile, still driving for Sedan, doughboys with the 42nd Division were a mere hour behind the retreating Germans. Eager to see the latest phase of the Meuse-Argonne, Townsend wrote to his daughter, Barbara, that "we may go up to the new offensive that had just well begun, and which as you have read there in the papers has turned into a terrible rout with the Huns on the run so fast that we can scarcely keep up to them with autos."[52] In a sharp transition in his letter to Barbara—a surreal juxtaposition of home life with war—Townsend asked her how she was liking Chicago and told her he had had some rabbit and mushrooms for a meal the other day. He often had mushrooms, he explained, because there were lots of them and they were cheaper than meat.

Before Townsend could motor to the now-more-distant front, there was the monthly art to submit, so, on November 4, Townsend and Harding took their work to Chaumont and hung it for display in the exhibit hall. Townsend's seven new pieces—including *Helping a Wounded Ally*, *Infantryman*, and *Soldiers of the Telephone*—brought his total submissions to forty-one. While at Chaumont, Townsend discovered that their last month's work had yet to be shipped to Washington, another typical AEF bureaucratic bungle. As for the delay, he was told the crates weren't marked with large enough lettering, prompting Townsend to simply note, "It's always someone else's fault."[53] That was the army—only large print accepted. Meanwhile, Washington still complained of not receiving enough pieces; in fact, as of December 4, the Historical Branch of the General Staff would have received not one piece by Dunn, only twelve pieces by Harding, and but eighteen of the forty-one Townsend had submitted to date.

On their return to Neufchâteau, news reached the artists that Austria had signed an armistice. "Austria gives up," Townsend wrote on November 5. "Terms are signed and fighting ceased at 3 P.M. yesterday. The Kaiser, in a speech, bemoans that the old order has passed but says ruefully that he is willing to do his part in a new order. But he doesn't abdicate just the same, tho it can only be a matter of days till he must, surely."[54] On this same day, U.S. units were on the hills overlooking Sedan; however, they were subsequently ordered to shift eastward so that the French 4th Army could have the honor of capturing the town. First defeated at Sedan in 1870 and still feeling humiliated almost fifty years later, the French desired a measure of redemption, the kind of redemption that starts future wars.

On November 6, word filtered into Neufchâteau that German armistice delegates had left Berlin under a white flag to request terms

*German Plane Falling in No Man's Land* by Harding. The sight of an airplane being driven into the ground made even the toughest man recoil.

from Foch; of course, the only term he was interested in was unconditional surrender. Excited to witness the German delegation crossing the lines, Duncan, Harding, and Morgan commandeered the one and only available motorcar and motored for the front. "At the present and this morning and after the usual display of thoughtfulness and consideration each for the other Wallace, Jack and George Harding managed to break away without too much of a struggle," Smith wrote with sarcasm to Peixotto, who was still recuperating at his home in Samois-sur-Seine. While Smith referred acerbically to Neufchâteau and the artists as "the same dear sweet place and the same lovable companions," he informed Peixotto that he would wait for his return to make a trip forward. To cheer up his fallen comrade, he noted, "Exhibition of official masterpieces was hung on Monday. . . . Your drawings look bully and have brought forth praise even from the great Dunn. Let that make you happy!"[55]

Even though the war's end appeared imminent, Harding, Morgan, and Duncan discovered the roads north to be more congested than ever—with troops and weapons being rushed into the line—but persevered until they reached Granpré, where rumor had it the war was over. A band was playing and the town, according to Harding, was "all lighted up like Coney Island." And then the Boche bombed it that night, the strike killing some men in a church right next to where Harding was sleeping. The artist awoke to an MP yelling to put out the lights and the angered soldier actually fired his revolver at a lit room.

It took all of November 8 for the artists to slog north about twelve miles to Sommauthe, located a couple of miles behind the line and under sporadic enemy artillery fire. After a night in a loft with enlisted men, Harding ventured to the local brigade HQ, where he attempted to squeeze information from a major "who looked wise [but] knew nothing." Wandering through town, he passed by a hospital with tents for the wounded, the gassed, and the sick. Hunkered in a church were refugees, including war baby mothers—one fourteen, the other nineteen—a one-eyed man, the schoolmaster and his two grandchildren, the mayor, a dog that barked at any uniform, and a goat. They were surviving on hard bread and coffee and dressed in old patched clothes. Looking through a church window, Harding could see that other mothers had chosen to escape the battered town; they were pushing their baby carriages across the open field.

Continuing northward to Beaumont, the traffic was so heavy it took the artists a half day to go half a mile. From the road, Harding watched as thousands of troops pushed across open country, through fields and ravines; he watched the burial details hard at work; and he watched the dead horses sinking into the liquid mud. The collage of images left a vivid impression:

> . . . the rockets the
> heavies coming in the machine
> gun the Boche plane—the
> stillness at night the cold

ice, frost frozen boots
man out of fog voices in
the distance . . .
the beauty of mist[56]


The bitterness felt by the artists trapped in Neufchâteau toward Duncan, Harding, and Morgan diminished somewhat when the trio returned to report that the roads were in such bad shape and congestion so horrific, it took forty-eight hours to get to the front. Even though the artists never encountered the German delegation, the newspaper correspondents in town pumped them for information because they had not been allowed to the front for over a week, relying instead on communiqués coming over the wires. While their trip had not been particularly exciting, Harding, Morgan, and Duncan did tell stories of crazed soldiers firing their artillery guns absolutely relentlessly, for in not knowing when the war would be declared finished, each battery wanted desperately to have the last shot.[57]

Although the roads along the front were hell, Townsend, who had been in Paris to see an exhibit of Boche aeroplanes, attempted to procure a motorcar on November 10 so he could venture to the front to witness the soldiers' reactions when the impending armistice was signed. He was too late. This time he discovered that Aylward and Dunn had taken it, even though Dunn knew Townsend had returned and wanted to go. "But it's his selfish way," Townsend wrote in his diary bitterly, "and I was thoroughly mad about it, for with the only car left, they have no right to take it without seeing that the rest of us were provided for. . . . But no, they think only of themselves, till one is sick of it all. This pose of Dunn's of having seen more actual fighting than any one of the rest, and of being the only one who has really gone over the top, is unbearable sometimes. When he goes back, of course, he will take the whole war with him!" Now Townsend regretted having left Paris because everyone knew that when the armistice was signed, a celebratory Paris would be a sight to behold.

# 15

# THE RESTORATION
# OF LIGHT

ERNEST PEIXOTTO HAD SPENT TWO WEEKS at his home in Samois-sur-Seine convalescing from what he called the flu, but was now anxious to return to the front; he deeply regretted that he had missed what appeared to be the final days of combat.[1] On the other hand, a historic moment was upon them. Rumors had coalesced into certainties: the armistice was to be signed in the early morning hours of November 11, and take effect at 11 A.M. on the eleventh day of the eleventh month—a very tidy conclusion to the Great War. To return to Neufchâteau, Peixotto had to travel through Paris, where he arrived on November 10, to discover the boulevards already filled with people anticipating the great event. However, while vendors selling little flags did a brisk business, the general mood remained somber; many civilians, while not outwardly mourning, were dressed in black or muted colors, and the numerous limbless soldiers wandering the streets had little impetus for song and dance.

That afternoon Peixotto went to the Café de la Paix and took a seat on the terrace, where he was surrounded by officers in colorful uniforms from every Allied nation: French, Americans, English, Canadians, Australians, Portuguese, Serbs, Belgians, Poles, and Italians. Peixotto then walked down to the place de la Concorde, where a crowd had packed the square; their eyes gazed with content and receding detestation on the various war trophies assembled there:

> Coysevox' horses and figures that stand at the entrance to the Tuileries Gardens and the Champs Elysées, precious works of art that had been protected by sand-bags during the bombardments, were now further embellished with strings of Boche helmets that hung over them arranged in symmetrical designs. The terraces that overlook the Place were lined with captured planes of every type and description—Fokkers, Rumplers and other Taubes, and the big black Gothas and bombing-planes that had terrorized Paris at night for so long a period. Around the obelisk and the fountains that decorate the center of the square, big guns of all calibers, trophies of the last offensives, pointed their grim noses toward heaven, encircled by armies of smaller pieces—37s, 77s, trench-mortars and *minnenwefers*—over which the children were climbing and sporting.[2]

Yes, the way for children to conquer that which had terrorized them was to turn the weapons into harmless toys, into jungle gyms. Yet, their growing familiarity with such weapons would make guns all the more comfortable to handle in a future war.

The next morning, November 11, Peixotto stepped out onto the balcony of his hotel room and took in the sights—majestic arches, domes, and towers—of the city before him: the Arc de Triomphe, the Panthéon, the Invalides, Notre-Dame, and Sacré-Cœur. Below him, in a hospital yard, recuperating soldiers were playing tenpins. The world almost seemed righted. But the morning newspaper brought no definite news of the expected armistice, which was troubling. The people needed closure. Peixotto decided to go to G.2's office on the rue Sainte-Anne for information; he, too, was anxious for confirmation that the war was finished. Yes, the intelligence officers told him, the armistice had been signed at 5 A.M. and would take effect at eleven. "I looked at my watch," he wrote. "It stood at eleven-ten. The war was over!"

When he again took to the streets, the news was spreading and flags were flying, the place de la Concorde was filling with a joyous crowd and singing students. For lunch, Peixotto went to a restaurant on the rue Royale, taking a table by the window to watch the ever-growing throng of people: "A troop of *chasseurs d'Afrique* came up the street mounted on Arabian horses . . . looking exceedingly picturesque in their pale-blue tunics and red fezes. . . . Grizzled veterans, in battered helmets and uniforms faded by years of campaigning, were singled out of the crowds, hoisted on youthful shoulders and, *drapeau en tête*, borne careering down the boulevard." Soldiers of different nationalities marched arm-in-arm. Factory girls were hoisted onto trucks—decorated with swathes of bunting—and passed loosely overhead by the celebrating soldiers. A group of Australian troops marched down the rue Royale, led by their band. "Ah, the music, that was what we needed—what we wanted!" Peixotto wrote. "But there was little of it and little cheering—and no brazen noises like those we make at home. Underlying the joy that the long nightmare was over, I distinctly felt an undercurrent of sadness, pain at the thought of all the dear ones who were gone forever and could not be there to share the hour of rejoicing; vivid recollections of years of anguish that could not be dimmed even in this, their hour of triumph." When a group of wounded soldiers—some sightless, some armless, and some legless—came through, the crowd parted reverentially.

Fighting the growing mass of people, Peixotto made his way over to the place de l'Opéra, where the images and colors continued to strike him: "The brown-gold trees, the gray houses, and the Opéra itself, with Carpeaux's Dance hidden behind sandbags covered with war posters, served as a background to a solid a mass of humanity, black for the most part, but thickly sprinkled with spots of blue and khaki, jostling, joking, good-humoredly pushing, seething up from the Metro like ants from an ant-hill." Then, as a great Handley-Page aeroplane roared overhead, every face turned upward.[3]

Overwhelmed by the emotional scenes, Peixotto recounted them in a letter to his mother: "Flags appeared as if by magic from every window; groups of men and women started to parade the streets; captured cannons were hauled from the Place de la Concorde and dragged along the boulevards with soldiers riding astride of them; sad mutilated soldiers appeared from the hospitals and the crowds stopped and made way for them to pass, reverently, with faces between laughter and tears. That was the spirit of the day for the rejoicing in ultimate victory was saddened by the thought of four years of anguish and the memory of all those who were gone. Toward evening the streets were crowded from curb to curb and I have never seen such excitement and probably never will again."[4]

In Neufchâteau, Townsend's bitter mood brightened when the anointed hour finally arrived. "At noon, the bell began a joyful ringing that lasted for a full hour," he wrote in his diary, "everyone decorated their houses with the Allied flags and coursed thro the streets singing and dancing, for now singing and dancing is again permitted." He could only begin to imagine the relief the French people felt after four-plus years of war, of bondage, of suffering, and of hardship. Two regiments of doughboys who had been ordered to the front but now had nothing to fear came roaring through town on camions, shouting and singing at the tops of their lungs. People in the streets shouted back. There was talk of champagne for dinner.

After indeed having champagne at dinner, Townsend went with the Bathos family to the place Jeanne d'Arc, where there was to be a ceremony and singing of the "Marseillaise." "What excitement there was everywhere," he reflected. "And how strange it seemed, even to me, to see the streets all lighted, the first time since the war began, and no one had to close their shutters tight tonight in fear of the raiding Hun as he has had to do the full four years. So you can imagine it looked gay and it was all like some very pleasant dream come true." In the square, there was an Italian band playing and rousing cheers bursting from the crowd.[5]

The next day the newspapers printed the terms of the armistice, terms Townsend, among others, recognized immediately as too stringent. "There is one ray of hope in them, tho, and that is that it seems the Allies have obligated themselves to see to the victualing of the German population." A considerable promise. The other big news was the kaiser's flight to Holland. While leaving his wife behind when he slipped out the country didn't appear to trouble his conscience, rumor was the crown prince had wept uncontrollably as he signed away his right to the throne. And then there was a wondrous story circulating that the kaiser's own troops had shot him, but no confirmation.

While the German government appeared to be moving in the right direction, toward a more open and democratic institution, the Allies still had little trust in its leaders. Townsend noted that "there seems to be a strong feeling that there is something suspicious about the new government, and those at its head, since they are friendly to the old regime. But I imagine the Allies are clever enough in their plans now to block any later attempt of any party there that may rise up to get the kaiser back at the helm again."[6] No, that would be reserved for one Adolf Hitler, a corporal in the German army who had been decorated for his bravery.

Another prickly, disconcerting issue at GHQ, according to Townsend, was the fact that the doughboys had not been permitted to march into Sedan in the last days of the conflict. The French had insisted on assuming the privilege, although they had yet to make their historic occupation. The same situation had arisen at Saint-Mihiel, where the French were given the honor of retaking the city even though the Americans had shed the blood. Now, more so than ever, there were strong feelings that the battered doughboys should be given their due. In fact, on the morning of November 11, the 5th Marines were still positioned outside of Sedan and were still taking potshots at anything they saw moving when the order to cease-fire came down the line. The subsequent celebrations in the field were more joyous than those in Paris. "We built a roaring fire," marine Private Malcolm Aitken wrote, in describing the festivities, "salvaged some wine and other rations that we had staked out. . . . There was plenty of yelling and dancing around as we made bets as to who fired the last shot."[7] To Aitken's right, elements of the 89th Division were still fighting that morning, ordered to cross the Meuse and keep the pressure on the enemy, the order resulting in some eleven hundred casualties. Meanwhile, their commander—the commander of V Corps—Major General Charles P. Summerall, was ensconced in a château, safe from a last-minute bullet with his name on it.

Townsend heard that the Germans had scored the final hit; in the last hour they had thrown over gas, and then, in the waning moments, a German shell had hit an American battery, killing five men.[8] However, the honor of being the official last AEF death belonged to Henry Gunther, who was shot through the head at 10:59 A.M. He was with the 313th, which had, fifteen minutes earlier, been notified of the cease-fire. Not so astoundingly, perhaps, in a final fit of bloodlust, during the last six hours of the war—from the signing of the armistice at 5 A.M. until the cease-fire went into effect at 11 A.M.—all sides on the Western Front witnessed a total of almost eleven thousand casualties, including over twenty-seven hundred deaths. The U.S. Congress would investigate, an activity they relished.

To fully record this history, Townsend, Peixotto, Smith, Harding, Dunn, and the other artists motored immediately to the recent battlefields. Outside of Dun-sur-Meuse, Smith encountered a U.S. field encampment where the soldiers were rejoicing in the simple fact they could now burn open fires and stand erect without fearing a sniper's bullet:

> Only those who have felt the tangible darkness at the front, nights when the blackness was a solid that pressed against your eyes and confused your senses, when you stumbled along roads and only through the grace of the sixth sense that you never before possessed, avoided collision with man and beast and motor-truck, only then could you fully appreciate one of the blessings of the cessation of hostilities: The restoration of light. Relieved from the dull threat of suffering or death, one was quick to take the fuller joy in the regained freedom of simple acts—fires at night, lighted roadways, and the immunity from all the petty restrictions that governed your life for its own preservation. But best of all was one's resurrection from the narrow confinement of trenches and dugouts into God's open country, to stand erect without menace and danger, to feel against your face the freshness of unpoisoned breezes, and to look once more without dread upon the fullness of the moon.[9]

# 16

# THE OCCUPATION
# AND THE STORIES
# OF HARDSHIP

"THE WORLD STILL SEEMS TO BE RUBBING ITS eyes to see if it is awake or still dreaming of a time long way off. But they smile as they have never done before, and they laugh as they haven't in four years," Townsend wrote in his diary two days after the armistice. "And there are many kisses thrown the Americans these days, and no doubt as in Paris the other day, so throughout France, there are many real kisses bestowed on our boys by women and girls out of real gratitude and love." The resounding consensus among French citizens, according to Townsend, was that if the United States hadn't arrived on the battlefield when it did, the war would have been lost. They would have faced a fate worse than death: German subjugation.[1]

There remained the Herculean task of rebuilding the annihilated countryside, villages, and cities. Meanwhile, the AEF's Army of Occupation was on the march to occupy a zone in Germany, including the cities of Mainz, Coblenz, and Cologne; and the artists were expected to remain in the field, on the heels of the army. As the artists journeyed into the heart of Germany—into the Fatherland—they would hear many stories of heartbreak from both sides of the war, they would witness more inhumanity to man, and they would be threatened by the bitter vanquished.

Excited to return to the front after a prolonged absence, on November 15, Peixotto joined up with Morgan and Smith to travel to Sedan, where they hoped to record the city's reaction to being liberated after almost fifty years of enemy occupation, the city lost to Germany in the War of 1870.[2] Would a return to France be a blessing or not for the residents? Would there be Boche sympathizers prepared for violent protest? The artists motored there via the valley of the Aire, a trip that took them through a succession of ravaged towns, including Grandpré.

On the approach to Grandpré, where they would spend the night, the fierce effects of Allied artillery were evident: along each side of the road the fields were pockmarked with overlapping craters—gaping mouths

*Pathway to Peace* by Smith. Faith in man and God was sorely tested; with irony, Smith chose this title for his symbolic rendering of a church.

with gnashing teeth—while the road itself had been spared for the advance. On the outskirts of town it was apparent where the Germans had placed their main defenses—machine-gun nests and artillery batteries—because these locations were absolutely smashed. In town that night, the artists had their choice of the houses for a billet; it was matter of finding a home with four sound walls to stave off the sharply chilled wind. For dinner they went to the officers' mess, located in a modern villa, but, with the building crowded, they were forced to eat outside under a tarpaulin and gulp down the food before it turned cold. Sitting opposite Peixotto was a bitter Frenchman who had just returned home to dig up some money and valuables he had buried in his garden before abandoning the town four years earlier. Realizing Peixotto spoke French fluently, the man suddenly exploded, all his frustrations and despair spilling forth. Later, in a more reflective mood, he said to Peixotto, "This afternoon I found the graves of two of your men down by the little stream below my house. I shall always care for them as if they were the graves of my own sons; they shall never lack for flowers."[3]

In the morning, the streets were coated with ice, and wheel tracks from the vehicles "glistened like bands of polished steel."[4] At breakfast, the north wind chilled the hotcakes before they could be eaten, and soldiers slapped their hands and stamped their feet to keep warm. Peixotto, Morgan, and Smith pushed north to Sedan, where they expected to encounter doughboys and French soldiers celebrating victory in the streets.

The artists proceeded along a lonely road through the Forest of Dieulet, which had been lacerated by shell fire in the early November 4 hours as the 89th Division pressed the Germans back to the Meuse River. On the approach to Raucourt, Peixotto found the road extremely treacherous; it had been deeply furrowed by the retreating Germans and was now thus frozen by the winter temperatures. Still nailed on church towers and factory chimneys were white flags; the locals had been desperate to save their means of existence from the calloused armies. Here the road became strangely deserted; they passed but one family pushing a baby carriage filled with their meager personal property. Once on the main road running north along the Meuse, progress was slow as they struggled to avoid mine craters and became entangled in snaking telephone wires.

At the last railroad crossing before entering Sedan, a French sentinel halted their car and asked to see their papers. Regardless of their passes, he insisted that no one could enter the city; amazingly and incomprehensibly, no soldier—French or American—had yet to enter Sedan. "The sentry's information that no troops had yet entered it," Peixotto recalled, "though it had been 'captured' about a week before, was indeed surprising." Apparently, the war had given away to pomp and circumstance as the poor people of Sedan awaited for a properly organized parade to liberate them. In hopes of winning permission to enter the city, the artists were forced to see a French colonel, who fortunately saw no harm in permitting them to sketch the environs.

Back at the railroad crossing, the still reluctant sentry pulled aside the barrier and they drove down a tree-shaded road to the city. "The faubourg was hung with flags—not flags such as one might ordinarily see," Peixotto observed, "but pathetic flags that had lain hidden in cellar or garret for years, mingled with others of a home-made variety, French flags, stitched together clandestinely in back rooms with reds and blues of varying intensity, British flags of strange design and, most touching to me, American flags, presumably copied from photographs, for their starry fields were out of ill proportion and their red stripes were very often black."

In the center square, the place de Turenne, they encountered one elderly man who had dressed himself in well-brushed but well-worn clothing. Sadly, with watering eyes, he looked up at Peixotto and said, "When are the French coming in? We need them. We have neither heat nor food."[5] The French were to enter in grand fashion the following day—necessities could wait. What also astounded Peixotto was that Sedan had apparently been captured without troops swooping in, but, in speaking with the locals, he soon discovered how this came to pass. As soon as the Americans had approached Sedan, the Germans opened negotiations and agreed to abandon the city, leaving it intact, as long as they were unmolested in their retreat. That was a week ago. It was now Saturday, November 16.

For the night, the commissaire de police assigned the artists to a large, imposing house—the hotel Marie de Sedan—on the square.[6] With hotel cupboards bare, Peixotto and Smith shared what canned goods they had with the lady of the house, who, in turn, made chamomile tea to warm them. While they sat in the kitchen—the only heated room—the woman proceeded to tell them her strange story. Before the war she and her husband had been living in Paris, but once drafted into the army he was stationed near Sedan. As fate would have it, when she came to visit him, she was caught in the Germans' unexpected lightning advance. On interrogating her, the enemy discovered she had managed a hotel in Paris, so they forced her to organize a rooming house in Sedan for the officers. Despite her many tribulations, they treated her well enough. For the German garrison, she recounted, all had been dandy until a few weeks ago when communiqués with superiors had suddenly halted. Arguments immediately erupted and soldiers brazenly told their superiors, "We won't go any further; the war's over for us." When the zone's commanding general retired to the rooming house from his forward headquarters, everyone knew the situation was dire. "He sat most of the time with his head in his hands," the woman told Peixotto, "silent and dejected."[7] And then came the distant sound of guns. Not long after, the Germans packed up and departed.

On the morning of November 17, Peixotto was awakened by the sound of hooves clattering along the paving stones. In the dim morning light, all he could see through the window were the sparks flying off the horses' shoes and the glowing Matinal cigarettes dangling from the soldiers' mouths. Realizing it was the cavalry patrol that preceded the advance guard, Peixotto and Smith joined the townspeople gathering in the square: "And as we stood there together I heard the same sort of stories that I had heard before at St.-Mihiel: the same tales of mute suffering, of the haughty, overbearing officers; of girls being ordered to report at certain places at midnight; of underfed men obliged to work overtime at hard labor." In a letter to his mother, Peixotto wrote, "It was a morning ever to be remembered in that historic city."[8]

After watching the French troops enter Sedan, Morgan, Peixotto, and Smith drove southward along the Meuse River, passing the columns of doughboys who were marching on Germany. "We saw too thousands of prisoners returning after their long captivity—Russians, Tommies, Yanks, French, Italians—poor half starved creatures," Peixotto wrote to his mother, "some of them scarcely able to totter along, yet buoyed up with the great hope of seeing their homes and dear ones again. That night we slept in the citadel at Verdun, through the kindness of the commander! Can you imagine our thoughts and dreams?"[9]

Another city worthy of visiting was recaptured Metz, which had also been lost to the Germans during the War of 1870 and was now potentially volatile due to a strong pro-German contingent among its residents. On the morning of November 17, Townsend, along with Dunn, Harding, and Aylward, pushed off for Metz, located northeast of Saint-Mihiel. Lunch was had in Pont-à-Mousson, the town square very Spanish in character, the entryways to the surrounding buildings arched or arcaded, yet all barricaded with sandbags and filled boxes to protect the stores from what had been fairly regular air raids. Any surviving stores now fell victim to subsequent raiding by wayward doughboys passing through.[10] Remaining there for dinner, the famished artists appreciated the food. "What a wonderful mess they had," Townsend wrote. "Real American food. As Captain Dunn puts it, 'Honest to God food.'" Apparently he did not find French cuisine agreeable.

Continuing on to Metz, they passed intersecting side roads still marked "Mined" that left them pensive about the relative safety of the main roads. As they approached the city, over countryside that had been ripped up by Allied artillery, a sentry waved them to a stop by brandishing his gun. As the car rolled up to him, he backed away, clearly ruined psychologically by the war and frightened of being run over, yet still waving his gun. Metz is off limits, he declared. Thinking quickly, Townsend handed over their French pass, which no doubt was of little use—it had even expired—but he figured it had a better chance of carrying them through than their American one. He was right; the flustered guard, seeing the French language and esteemed signatures, waved them on.

Eagerly the artists roared into this historic, fortified city on the Moselle River, which boasted France's oldest church, dating from the fourth century. Due to the lack of material damage to the city, it was apparent to Townsend that during the ground advance, American artillery had used great restraint to avoid unnecessary destruction— although they had "longed to pay their respects to the Boche on its outskirts." When they rolled into the Grand Place Empereur Guillaume, a crowd quickly gathered and they were forced to stop. "Little children . . . tried to climb on our car as we passed," Townsend wrote in his diary. "Everywhere there were waving arms and kisses thrown us, and cries of 'Vive la France!' In a couple of instances, there were cries of 'Vive L'Amérique!' . . . There were plenty of hostile residents in the crowd, too, and there were menacing looks. There were girls in the crowds who besieged the car, shouting and ready to kiss us. . . . We were showered with attention from the time that they learned we were Americans, and they lost no time in telling us how much they owed to the Americans." As it turned out they were the first Allied soldiers to make an appearance, the French soldiers still awaiting orders.

Townsend asked if there was yet a French HQ established. No, came the answer. And there were no gendarmes. The only French soldiers in town were released prisoners. In fact, the Germans were still in one end of the town making their departure. "We decided it would be best to keep moving," Townsend wrote, "so we drove slowly around, picking and forcing our way through the crowds, which, as we got farther down to the cathedral, grew more dense and took on a different tone. Their looks gave them away. They were Boche, and they had evidently been seeing their troops away. And their attitude was decidedly unfriendly and, in a number of instances, menacing."[11] They were hissed and spit at, Townsend recounted in a letter to his wife. "We were a bit scared for a minute tho we had our revolvers."[12] Even though Townsend's anxiety level did escalate, later that day he concluded that "nothing could really hurt us, coming as we did on a peaceful mission to a freed people." Of course, the Germans didn't know of their mission; not the Germans, who had annexed the city in 1871 and populated it with some of their own blood.

They edged around the town, but soon found themselves right back at the Grand Place. "So we pulled up in a corner," Townsend wrote, "and the crowd had its way with us for a time. By this time, the word had gotten round that the Americans were there, and there was all the town around us by the time we were stopped. I talked to as many as I could at one time, answering all the questions I could. 'When were the French coming? When the Americans? Were we going to stay and please do?' And with pointing fingers, they would show us 'sales Boches' in the crowd around us."

There was a discussion among the artists about pulling out of the city for the night, for darkness could very well bring violence. But then Townsend found a boy who appeared to be very much French Lorraine, someone who could be trusted, and he guided Townsend and Dunn to a hotel—Ancien Hôtel de l'Europe—that would be suitable and safe. Because it had been used by the high German officers, the German billeting notices were still posted in the hotel rooms, notices the bellboy— the garçon—tore down hastily when he escorted Townsend to his room. Going back downstairs, the artists met a contingent of French officers, who were pleased to see them but disappointed they had been beaten to town. The officers advised them that the remaining Boche were indeed in a foul mood and not to venture out that night unless in a group.

At dinner, the hotel owner, Herr Hafen, told the artists that the kaiser and the empress had stayed here, as had the crown prince, who was really "a very fine fellow." While showing them the register in which all these luminaries had signed their name, Hafen grew so excited that Townsend concluded the Herr was still a loyal subject to the crown.[13] Meanwhile, outside, the raucous celebrations continued: the Lorrainers were running through the city, shouting and singing the "Marseillaise." Unable to resist the excitement, the artists joined the crowd sweeping through the streets. Whenever they entered a section of town that was Boche, the crowd would chant, "Boche, Boche, Boche" and then continue on its way. Coming upon statues of Kaiser William and Kaiser Frederick on horseback, they danced around them in a circle and there was talk of tearing them down, but no action was taken. Later that night, poor forsaken Kaiser William would fall.

The artists enjoyed a nightcap at a café, and throughout the evening, the French and the American liberators were toasted and the girls smothered them with kisses. As the artists were leaving, the madame of the café warned them not to sing at that hour in the streets because they might attract the ire of a German who happened to own a gun. Just the night before shots had been fired into a raucous crowd.[14]

The next day, November 18, as Townsend, Harding, Aylward, and Dunn wandered through the shops, they couldn't help but notice the prisoners now filtering through the city. "We see many prisoners," Townsend wrote, "who are coming in great numbers now from the German prisons on foot, in all sorts of conditions, many barely able to walk, and some barefoot. All hungry. They are being looked after, and the hospital has been taken over by the Red Cross, we hear. Today a big truck of supplies arrived. The hospital was found in terrible condition, I hear."

Townsend talked with a number of prisoners and recounted the conversations in his diary:

Accounts of their experiences vary. Some insist they were well looked after, save that the food was scarce, even for the Germans with whom they came in contact. Others insisted that they had rotten treatment and were worked near the front. Others were in mines that were being raided all the time by Allied aviators. Some, who were wounded and bandaged up, said that they had no treatment for their wounds because there was a shortage of bandages and drugs. Many of them were dressed in captured Russian uniforms, black with a wide stripe down the legs. But they were motley and wore whatever they could get. They were all eager for news, too. They knew nothing of the world outside, or what was happening. They had suddenly been freed and told the direction to the rear.[15]

That day the first French newspaper in four years was printed in town, and an article mentioned the arrival of American officers the prior afternoon, they being the artists. "So we go down in history," Townsend wrote playfully. "And what a history Metz has."[16]

Not until November 19, eight days after the armistice, were the French troops scheduled to enter Metz en masse. That morning the streets were filled with girls and women dressed in traditional, colorful Lorraine costumes that included a towering white bonnet draped with ruffles and lace, and there were old men in long frock coats and silk hats. The troops were to arrive at 11 A.M. but would not until 2 P.M., the delay making for a restless crowd. A scuffle broke out with a Boche citizen that quickly escalated into a fistfight, until a cavalryman rode his horse into the crowd and escorted the Boche away. That was not the worst of it. A short while later, areoplanes soared overhead—wheeling and cutting capers—but then one pilot swooped too low and caught his wing on a telephone wire. Immediately spiraling out of control, the plane crashed into the crowd in the Grand Place. Two children were killed instantly and other victims died later, at least seven killed in total. The pilot, unfortunately for him, survived. Still, in a letter to Cory, Townsend wrote that it was a magnificent day he would never forget; in particular, the soldiers marching by and saluting Pétain was a stirring sight.[17]

During the artists' last day in Metz, a little boy came running up to Harding and Townsend as they were walking in the street and tried to take their hands; however, a woman shouted immediately at the Americans to shun the boy because he was Boche. The Germans and their sympathizers had been marked, even the children; none of them could be trusted—apparently, their martial intent was in their bones.[18]

. . .

Townsend and gang returned to Neufchâteau on November 21, but only for the night; Major James had again given them orders to "be in the field as much as possible."[19] To follow the Army of Occupation, the next day the artists departed for Luxembourg and then Coblenz, Germany, where the doughboys would cross the Rhine en masse into the heart of Germany. When passing through Metz, Townsend, along with Dunn, Harding and Aylward, learned that some four hundred Boche civilians living in the city had been rounded up quietly and interned in Nancy, and could possibly stand trial for sundry war crimes. Townsend also learned that wayward American soldiers were being rounded up in the city: Metz was officially off limits to the doughboys, yet they kept coming in droves for unofficial R&R, only to be arrested by highly efficient MPs. "They have put the screws on tight, it seems," observed Townsend.[20] Clearly, thousands of doughboys frolicking across the countryside, getting drunk and contracting venereal disease, was the last thing Pershing wanted.

On his arrival in Luxembourg, Townsend determined it to be "quite a lovely city" with "aristocratic houses, wide streets, wonderful-looking shops and hotels, and apparently no very poor quarter." In his conversations with soldiers and citizens, Townsend learned that Luxembourg had given the doughboys a royal welcome, a grand fete that lasted several days, and they had been feeding and housing the Americans for nothing: "Some Americans pretend to think that a lot of this is really put-on, but from what I have seen of the people here, they won't go to this length of financial sacrifice to show it." According to Townsend, the Luxembourgers, as did the Lorrainers, credited the Americans for delivering them from the German menace. However, as he spent time in Luxembourg, his view on their attitude would soon change.[21]

After a dinner at the press mess, the artists went to the Grand Hotel, where there was yet another reception, a striking scene as a general from the Luxembourg army—sporting a long, waxed mustache and a monocle—received guests in the foyer. Already awakening to an element of pro-German sentiment, Townsend was not completely fooled by the warm reception: "The people seem very friendly on all sides, but there seems to be a decided undercurrent of Boche looks, in spite of the protestations of the staunch ones."[22]

Peixotto also had his suspicions, even though the entire city's popu-
lace appeared to be in the streets celebrating and there were national
flags fluttering everywhere. As he analyzed the situation, the city
appeared to have not suffered under German rule; if anything, it had
benefited since the time it was invaded in August 1914. In this city surrounded by a sylvan countryside, the civilians were too well dressed and
the waiters too polite serving food that was too good. When they went
out for drinks and music, Peixotto made careful observations: "The café
was packed; up-stairs there was music and dancing. I watched the crowd
with the greatest interest, for the German physiognomy was everywhere
apparent and the whole atmosphere of the place was distinctly 'Boche,'
resembling in every particular some German Verein in East Fifty-ninth
Street. Yet by word and action the people were receiving us with open
arms, happy, they said, to be freed from German rule and assuring us
repeatedly that no Prussian officer had ever been admitted within the
precincts of this club."[23]

In evaluating the attitude in Luxembourg, André Smith summed it
up best: "From the point of view of the people of Luxembourg our
apologetic use of their country as a thoroughfare into Germany, preceded by a polite proclamation explaining the military necessity of our
temporary and friendly invasion, was open to two degrees of acceptance:
Those who welcomed us with open arms and those who merely welcomed us."[24]

After several days in Luxembourg, in the last week of November, the
artists continued to follow the doughboys marching toward Germany's
"frontier." Motoring along the Moselle and then Sauer rivers, both of
which flowed along Luxembourg's borders, Townsend found the countryside to be ever spectacular with its rolling hillsides patterned with
vineyards—except for the ubiquitous machine-gun emplacements and
military patrols with rifles on shoulders. By the end of November, the
doughboys were in position to enter Germany. As they awaited the long-
dreamed-of orders for a simultaneous crossing of the border by all Allied
forces, tension built, for no one was certain how Germany would react
to its turn to play host to foreign troops.

During this pause on the eve of the occupation, Townsend's group
returned to Luxembourg for a Thanksgiving dinner. It was raining
heavily—always raining it seemed—and they passed by troops spending

the holiday huddled in trucks. That night the artists, along with a number of correspondents, celebrated Thanksgiving with a dinner of roast pork, peach pie, champagne, and wine. Afterward, Dunn and a Major Bulger played the violin, while Major James led them in song, and, Townsend wryly noted, they got "out of their systems about all the army songs ever sung."[25] The artists then discussed their plans with James: they would go to Paris to continue their hunt for studio space, but then quickly rejoin the Army of Occupation, which would soon be moving into Coblenz, Germany, located on the Rhine River. As for Major James, their chief, in the coming days, while in Luxembourg, he would suffer a nervous breakdown and be hospitalized. The real toll of the war could not yet be tallied.

# 17

# PENETRATING THE FATHERLAND

AS SOON AS THEIR ORDERS CAME THROUGH in the second week of December, all of the artists pushed off for Coblenz, traveling via Treves, a German city on the Moselle River and now GHQ's forward HQ. The artists had been warned about visiting Treves, or Trier, because, like Metz, there was a real potential for spontaneous violence. At dusk, as the motorcar carrying Townsend, Dunn, Harding, and Aylward crossed the Moselle at Wasserbillig and entered enemy country, Dunn celebrated by playing his harmonica, playing "Yankee Doodle Dandy" and the usual patriotic numbers. His song list now included the "Die Wacht am Rhein" ("The Watch on the Rhine"), a popular German tune with war overtones, which he played in a decidedly mocking manner. When they arrived in Treves—where all signs of German nationalism had disappeared, including the German flags that had greeted the retreating army—it was only 4:30 P.M., yet ominously dark. They found rooms at the Reichshof and had a dinner of meat, vegetables, and bread they had acquired from the Red Cross, confiture for dessert, and coffee. That night, as rain fell, Townsend wrote in his diary:

> We are in Germany at last, and eating in a real German restaurant, with our hated enemy around us at the other tables, looking at us, most of the time, in strange ways, it seemed to us, tho not too unfriendly. But it is a queer feeling that I have—the realization that I am here with the Army of Occupation in an enemy country, an enemy that has been judged the most brutal and treacherous that has ever fought. . . . And now we were entering her country, not to plunder, pillage and burn as she had been doing, but to see merely that she lived up to her new contract, and to hold, as it were, as a guarantee, to control, and if necessary, to take, should she fail. A bitter pill, surely, for them to swallow. What wonder if they might a bit resent it all."[1]

Also in Treves, Peixotto took a room at the Porta Nigra Hotel, his window overlooking the partially finished great arch Caesar had ordered erected more than a thousand years earlier. After dinner and in spite of possible retaliation, he walked the streets, analyzing the city and its inhabitants with an artist's eye:

> Its shops were brightly lighted and filled with attractive wares. The people looked neatly dressed though their shoes were not of leather. Though but a few miles from the border, all seemed so tranquil, so undisturbed that my gorge rose within me as I walked down street after street, where handsome houses stood intact, their windows freshly curtained, their door-steps neatly swept, and I thought of all the devastation that I had seen, of the sufferings that I had witnessed, of the homes systematically robbed and pillaged, and in my mind I contrasted the forlorn refugees wandering they knew not whither with these smug middle-class people who even now were strumming their pianos and singing in their comfortable homes.[2]

Hardly endeared to the people of Treves, Peixotto's group continued on to Coblenz. As they passed village after village, he noted, "The inhabitants stood in their doorways, silent, furtively watching us as we passed. The children, on the contrary, dashed out from doors and alleyways, and, at the risk of their lives, boisterously greeted the honk-honk of our horn."[3] Near Coblenz, they passed the 1st Division, which was due to enter the city the next day. Then, at the city's perimeter, sentries stopped them—there were four checkpoints in all—because only those assigned to G.2.D., that is, intelligence, were allowed to enter. Fortunately, that was precisely what the painters were, those strange birds, so on they proceeded. At the moment, the only soldiers in the city itself were the 2nd Battalion, 39th Infantry Regiment, 4th Division, sent in to guard the stores from vengeful combatants and remorseless looters.

Peixotto was given a room in the Coblenzer Hof, a very elegant seven-story hotel just finished before the war. It had a magnificent terrace running the length of the third story, arches running the length of the ground floor, and a promenade between the edifice and the water. His third-floor room commanded a view of the Rhine River and the very pontoon bridge the American troops would use to cross over. Looking down, he was moved emotionally when he saw "sentries in khaki from far-away America guarding the bridge-head over the Rhine in the name of liberty, justice, and humanity!" In the hotel's dining room, he was surprised to encounter a contingent of Germans officers; they were there to make arrangements with their American counterparts regarding the city's occupation.

In Coblenz, Townsend's group also took a suite rooms at the Coblenzer Hof, a stay that started off with bumbling unpleasantry. Harding went to the wrong floor and accidentally barged into a room filled with German officers, a sudden confrontation fraught with tension. Afterward, of course, the incident was worth a few laughs. The whole concept of sharing hotels and streets with the enemy was not only uncomfortable, but for obvious reasons it lent itself to possible conflict. Adding to the artists' nervousness was the fact that they had been ordered to bring sidearms with them in case of an emergency. Later, as they walked the streets, they received some sullen glances, but there were no remarks made against them.

At the hotel mess, the artists received an excellent meal for 2 marks, which would be applied against their allotted 57 cents a day for rations. That night Townsend and several of the artists attended a performance of *Carmen*, the opera put on by a local company. The theater was filled with American officers, many of them generals and colonels, who, along with the entire audience, appeared "to enjoy it all thoroughly," wrote Townsend, who also thought it an excellent production. In warily observing the Germans at the opera, as well as in the streets, he was impressed by their upbeat mood:

> They seemed to take our presence as a matter of course. They could even smile naturally at us, or speak to us at times, as tho we might have been casual visitors in their town. Nor, I might add, was the attitude of the Americans there that of conquerors grinding a vanquished people under their heel. Perhaps the Germans sense this too. For it's no secret that they like the Americans, even as victors, and despise the French and the English.[4]

After the opera, the artists were at a café enjoying Moselle wine when a drunk German came over and explained, in German, that even though he had been wounded four times, he, as well as his fellow countrymen, intended to be a good host. This surprising German tone, one of polite acceptance, was corroborated at HQ, where Townsend spoke with a Lieutenant McGrath, the adjutant, who gave him the lowdown on how the Germans had prepared for the arrival of the Americans. To his surprise, McGrath said, the sleeping quarters for the officers—the caserns—had been thoroughly scrubbed and fresh sheets put on all the beds; the officers' club had fresh beer on tap and was stocked with food; the canteen was also shipshape and fully supplied; and there were enough neatly stockpiled potatoes to feed a small army. The Germans were absolutely gracious. In complete contrast, whenever the Americans had moved into a French zone, the departing officers had left a mess.

On December 13, a Friday—with fog heavy in the valley and a steady rain falling—the artists had an early breakfast of wheat cakes, bacon, toast, and coffee. Early because the troops were scheduled to cross over the Rhine at 7 A.M. sharp, an event they awaited eagerly in the winter darkness. "Just before dawn I heard a sound I had been listening for: the sound of shuffling feet on the wooden Bridge of Boats below my window," Peixotto wrote, "and, looking out, could see, in the first dim light of day, a long yellowish serpent crawling slowly across the bridge. Longer and longer this serpent grew, until its head had disappeared under the railroad viaduct on the opposite bank of the river. Yet its sinuous body, bristling with guns and plaited like chain mail with steel helmets, kept ever wriggling and writhing across the river."[5]

Waxing euphoric over the noble modesty with which the Americans carried themselves, Smith also wrote down his observations of the Rhine crossing:

> At Coblenz, where it was my good fortune to view it, it was an event that was typically American in that it occurred without pomp or ostentation. . . . There was no flare of bugles, no beating of drums or martial music to mark the occasion of their advance. Only the brief order to "march" set in motion the stream of American soldiers that for days continued to flow across the river and spread out into the arc that formed our area of occupation. One needed but to witness the sight of the "Stars and Stripes" moving forward above dull ranks of khaki and shining like a bright flower against gray, vine-clad hills of the Rhine to know that this was the fulfillment of our dreams, the final curtain which ended our military participation in the greatest and grimmest of wars.[6]

After sketching the bridge crossing from above in their hotel rooms, Peixotto and the other artists made their way to the streets and spent hours gazing in wonder at the troops marching over the bridge. At the same time, columns of U.S. soldiers also entered Coblenz proper, which the Germans thought would involve a raucous entrance with bands playing and colors flying. "But instead of a procession of triumph," Smith observed, "our men made their entrance into town quietly, but with a suddenness and completeness that filled the streets in every direction that one looked."[7]

While most inhabitants continued to remain indoors with their shudders latched tight, later in the day Peixotto did notice that some townspeople eventually came out to watch, muttering, "How young they look; how handsome!"[8] The smell of food brought others into the streets, he also observed, and soon changed some citizens' attitudes:

> The field-kitchens began to smoke and the smell of "slum" and hot coffee filled the air. What the marching troops—the entrance of an Army of Occupation into their city—had failed to do, these culinary

odors accomplished. First the children, then the housewives, drawn by these odors as if by irresistible magnets, began to issue from the houses, gathering furtively at first, then more and more boldly, around the steaming wagons. . . .Though tinged with a distinct touch of humor, the picture was in the main a pathetic one, telling its tale of months of privation.[9]

Harding was also impressed by the German attitude but believed that there was little evidence of deprivations in Coblenz: "The only evidence that there was a war was the fact that there were no shoes to be bought, except of wooden and canvas, and no rubber. Bicycles were equipped with rope tires. And there was no soap. I took six cakes with me to use as tips. I used one and the other five were stolen from my bag at the hotel."[10] A German woman on the street audaciously told Harding that the Americans and the Germans were friends, and other residents went so far as to say that the two countries should have been allies in the war. Contrary to such intimations of friendliness, Harding heard from an MP that local leaders had decreed that any German girls seen with doughboys would have their hair hacked off—so, Americans were not to be accommodated in every respect. Still, there were the usual groups of women on the street at night, smoking cigarettes and looking for well-moneyed escorts.

As Townsend mingled with the people on the streets, he mulled over the possibility of the average German actually being pleased with the change in political climate: "I shouldn't be surprised if there were very many who truly welcome it all, who welcome their defeat even, and see better times and a government more to their liking ahead of them, tho they must one and all dread . . . the realization of the ultimate and inevitable peace terms, for they all know that in spite of President Wilson, Marshal Foch has the whip hand."[11]

The attitude of the French was indeed another matter; it was clear to Townsend that France was "an embittered and unrelenting victor." In Treves, the German locals had already filed a complaint against the French for pillaging valuables and for raping two girls.[12] In mulling over the friction between the various nations, Townsend now sensed there was more animosity between Americans and Frenchmen than between Americans and Germans. Townsend, like others, was disturbed by the fact that a group of French officers had been permitted to lead the Americans over the Rhine, at Coblenz, an honor not necessarily deserved, considering the heavy price the doughboys had paid during the Meuse-Argonne Offensive. It was yet another repeat of what had happened at Saint-Mihiel and Sedan, when the French had insisted their troops march into the cities after the Americans had expelled the Germans.

In fact, the relationship between the French and the American soldiers was becoming increasingly acrimonious, Townsend observed, as it appeared the French command was taking more credit than due them. "I must confess that there has been growing in my heart a hatred for the French officer and his supercilious aloofness from the world about him," Townsend wrote in his diary. "If the German ever had a superman idea, it has a real counterpart in the mind of the average French officer. The very spick-spanness of their uniform has gotten to express their spirit to me. A fleck of dust on it becomes an humiliation." This attitude was much different from the early days of the American involvement, when the artists admired the French officer walking dignified as artillery shells fell around him. "And they are jealous as can be of the Americans," Townsend continued. "They lay much of it to the fact that we have, as officers, so much more money to dispense, and this, and our freedom in spending, and the interest in their women so many of whom are becoming engaged to and marrying American men, is one of the main causes for their jealousy."[13]

On December 16, the U.S. Army was still crossing the Rhine River, and on that day, hauling over a long line of gleaming 155 guns pulled by healthy, large horses, which prompted Townsend to note, "We certainly have been careful in picking the best we have for this occupation, and its effect is worth all it will cost us, too, in increased respect for our power or potentiality."[14] As he was watching the spectacle, a little woman—a Mrs. Condear—standing next to him suddenly turned and asked in excellent English if he knew where the guns were going. If her English wasn't a surprise, her next comment was: she said it was good to see Americans after four years. Elaborating, she explained that she was born in the United States and was "American to the core"; however, her husband was born in Coblenz, where they had been visiting when war broke out. Although New York City citizens, they were unable to leave, and her husband was pressed into service as a construction worker.

Confirming previous insights into the German perspective the artists had garnered, she said that the Germans were astounded by the American military might and couldn't believe all these soldiers had made it to Europe. How was it possible, the woman asked, with the submarines? Townsend explained that they had lost very few ships to the submarines, which was a revelation to her; she and all Germans were under the impression that the subs were a great success. As a whole, Mrs. Condear elaborated, the German people had been against submarine warfare; they blamed it for bringing the Americans into the war. "She said that the feeling of the German people for the Americans was not one of hatred," Townsend recounted, "as it was against the British and the French, and would never, and could never, be, on account of the blood ties, tho they did regret our coming into the war, for without our entry, they would have won."[15]

Because U.S. officers with a rank of major or higher had now completely commandeered the more elegant Coblenzer Hof, Townsend found a room at the Bahnhof Platz. In speaking with the madame of the hotel, he learned that she had lost her son in the final days of the war. Although the mother was in deep mourning, Townsend observed with a measure of astonishment that she was "kindness itself."[16] Also forced to relocate, taking a room at the Hotel Monopol in Coblenz, Ernest Peixotto witnessed a scene in contrast to the forgiving kindness Townsend had encountered. For Peixotto, it was a fitting, conclusive scene to the war. He had come down to breakfast, the dining room facing the street, the windows covered with muslin curtains, and taken a table next to a group of arrogant German officers:

> We were about to begin our meal when an infantry column came down the street and just as it reached the window at which we sat the band at its head struck up a stirring and triumphant Sousa march. One of the younger German officers impulsively jumped up and, with boyish curiosity, held back the muslin curtain the better to see the American troops. Their colonel rode by at the head of his regiment, and then came the Stars-and-Stripes again, uncased, flaunting its bright folds in the fresh morning breeze.
>
> I watched the Prussian major's face and it well repaid my scrutiny. From a deadly pallor it turned pink, and then, as the

blood mounted to it, crimson, until I thought he would be seized with a stroke of apoplexy. Every muscle was tense and rigid, but he never moved, remaining still and silent, with folded arms, watching. My cup of happiness was full. I had seen a typical Prussian officer humiliated in the heart of his own country.[17]

Townsend did not gloat over the American victory; no, he had lost a beloved brother, and his life had been irrevocably altered. Yet, he struggled with feelings of revenge. These feelings came to the surface in full force after he received notification that he could attend the upcoming Paris Peace Conference—the only AEF artist permitted to—and was on the road back to Neufchâteau. Not long after returning to French soil, on December 18, he suddenly came upon a destroyed farmhouse and then a ruined village, which wakened him from his daydreams of the week in Germany, where the only ruins had been ancient Roman: "Now we are in the midst of ruin, the work of the Kaiser's guns, and we begin to think and to wonder about this question of retribution. We ponder the problem of turning the other cheek! Not a mark had we seen in

*Coffin Guards* by Smith. The American army was forced to post coffin guards, as they did here at Menil-le-Tours, to prevent thievery and desecration.

Germany that was the work of the Allied guns. Air bombs may have made their scars, but we saw them not, so that now the contrast was complete and startling."

Doubts surfaced in his mind as to how sincere the German people were about peace: "And the words 'guile,' 'craft' and 'cunning' creep into our thoughts, and we wonder if, after all, the French have a truer perspective than we have as to this old, old neighbor of theirs. But I insist that the people and the militarists in Germany are two distinct things, much as they overlap, thro the Army being made up from the people. For, after all, they surely prefer peace to war, this mass of common clay. For they must have interests and hearts that are human, same as we."

On Townsend's arrival in Neufchâteau, a stack of always-savored mail awaited him. "I find, oh joy! a bunch of letters from Cory and Barbara, and I see a Christmas package has showed up for someone at the Press," he wrote in his diary. "Christmas just one week away. Everything spoke of Christmas in Germany, too. Shops full of toys and everyone shopping. Men carrying sleds and skates home, for, I take it, deserving boys."[18] These images of Christmas, images of innocence and joy, would do much to erase the searing memories of a brutal war just ended, would do much to purge the stark images of sinister landscapes and desolate no-man's-land. For Townsend, the image of a loving father with a toy under his arm for a "deserving boy" infused him with hope and renewed his faith.

While Townsend spent Christmas with the Bathos family and rejoiced in the bittersweet peace, the artist George Harding was on the road, touring the battlefields.[19] He spent Christmas Eve in Épernay, located straight east of Château-Thierry, sleeping on a bedroll in an abandoned café. He awoke to rain and celebrated the gray Christmas morning with a meal of chicory bread and plum pudding. Then it was onward to Soissons, on the Aisnes River, a route that carried him through the Marne Salient with its lasting scenes of the grim summer harvest, some of the harvest left rotting in the fields:

The dugouts in valley in the hollow
road winding up it shellholes
full water tree chopped off—
concealed entrances concrete—

log—sand bag—gear around
French guns etc some French
dead still around . . .

Now standing in a chilling sleet, with stark white birches and blemished blue hills in the distance behind him, on this Christmas day, Harding watched as dozens of war pilgrims searched battlefield cemeteries for the graves of their loved ones. If lucky enough to find the grave, and, if infused with a necessary fortitude, they methodically exhumed the body, gently placed their soldier in a wooden coffin made by the locals, and wearily began their long journey home.

# AFTERWORD: THE ARTIST-SOLDIERS

The war is certainly over here. And I am struck at once with the smug satisfaction they all seem to have here. . . . Its really disgusting the seeming degree of prosperity that everyone enjoys here and they tell it is real too. Spite of the war or rather because of it every one has gotten rich it seems. Somehow it makes one mad to think of it as all the old world has suffered.

—Harry Townsend to Ernest Peixotto,
New York City, July 5, 1919

## Their War Art

On January 28, 1920, the U.S. National Museum, part of the Smithsonian Institution, took charge of the art created by the eight AEF artists. At 507 pieces, the collection was too large to show at once, which deeply disappointed the artists. However, over the years, selections of their work have appeared and continue to be shown in numerous exhibitions around the United States. Some of these pieces are on display at the Smithsonian National Museum of History and, from time to time, are loaned to other institutions. An online gallery of their war art can be viewed at www.petekrass.com.

## William James Aylward (1875–1956)

Born in Milwaukee, Wisconsin, Aylward studied art at the Art Institute of Chicago, the Art Students League in New York City, and under Howard Pyle, the venerable father of American illustration who had a school in Wilmington, Delaware. An award-winning illustrator and author, he worked for *Scribner's* and *Harper's* and illustrated books by top authors such as Jack London and Jules Verne. When he joined the AEF, he was married and had a five-year-old child. After Aylward shipped home, in June 1919, he resumed his career as an illustrator and a writer, specializing in marine and naval subjects. He taught at the Pennsylvania Institute of Art, the School of Fine and Industrial Arts in Newark, and the Pratt Institute in Brooklyn. Aylward died while living in Bath, New York.

## Walter Jack Duncan (1881–1941)

Born in Indianapolis, Indiana, Duncan studied art at the Art Students League in New York, where he remained from 1899 to 1902. His specialty was pen and ink. Beginning in 1903, he worked for such illustrious magazines as *Century Magazine, Scribner's,* and *McClure's,* which took him across the country and to Europe. In late December 1918, Duncan took a studio in Paris, as did many of the artists, and worked on drawings and lithographs. After returning to the United States, in June 1919, Duncan continued working for magazines and illustrating books, and he taught at the Art Students League in New York for several years. In 1939, he published *First Aid to Pictorial Composition.* Two years later he died of a stroke while working in his New York studio.

## Harvey Thomas Dunn (1884–1952)

Born in Dakota Territory, Dunn studied art at the Art Institute of Chicago before joining Pyle in 1904 for two years. He then embarked on a career of illustration. After the end of hostilities, Dunn hoped to have months to create his visions of the World War I; however, he was shipped home in February 1919 and discharged in April. Dunn opened a studio and modest art school in Tenafly, New Jersey, where he taught hundreds of students and was a major influence on the next generation of illustrators. Years later, beginning in 1928, he painted a series of World War I scenes for covers of the *American Legion Monthly*. Dunn was invited to rejoin the service as a combat artist during World War II but declined. In 1945, he was awarded the coveted rank of national academician by the National Academy of Design. From 1948 to 1951, he served as the president of the Society of Illustrators and was voted into its Hall of Fame. Dunn gave a substantial portion of his work to South Dakota State University before his death in Tenafly, New Jersey.

## George Matthews Harding (1882–1959)

Born in Philadelphia, Pennsylvania, Harding studied architecture briefly at Boston Tech before studying art at the Pennsylvania Academy of Art and then under Pyle. Beginning in 1903, he worked for top magazines, which took him around the world. After the armistice, he spent much time in the field before being shipped home, in February 1919. Although discharged that May, he dedicated the remainder of the year to creating a magnificent portfolio titled *The American Expeditionary Forces in Action*, which he published in 1920. In 1922, Harding became the head of the department of illustration at the Pennsylvania Academy of the Fine Arts. He created the mural department and became head of it, remaining at the school until his retirement in 1958. He also taught at the University of Pennsylvania. During World War II, at age sixty, Harding was commissioned a captain and shipped out to the South Pacific, the only AEF artist to again create combat art. Over the years he earned many medals and awards. In 1945, Harding was elected as a national academician by the National Academy of Design. He died in Wynnewood, Pennsylvania.

## Wallace Morgan (1873–1948)

Born in New York City, Morgan studied art at the National Academy of Design. In 1897, he went to work for the *New York Sun* as a sketch artist before moving on to work for popular magazines and illustrating books.

After being ordered home, in March 1919, Morgan continued to illustrate for magazines and authors, including H. G. Wells. Morgan's work appeared in *Collier's*, *Cosmopolitan*, the *New Yorker*, and the *Saturday Evening Post*. He also dabbled in advertising and occasionally taught at the Art Students League in New York. From 1929 to 1935, he was the president of the Society of Illustrators and then made honorary president for life. Morgan was elected a national academician by the National Academy of Design and voted into the Society of Illustrators' Hall of Fame. Considered one of the best artists in black and white of his time, he was referred to as the dean of American illustrators. During World War II, he traveled to veteran hospitals, making sketches of the wounded and cheering up the men. Morgan died in New York City.

## Ernest Clifford Peixotto (1869–1940)

Born in San Francisco, Peixotto studied art in that city at the Fine Arts at the Mark Hopkins Institute and then at various schools in Paris from 1888 to 1890. He became a prolific author and illustrator, penning several travel books. After the war, Peixotto remained in Paris as the head of AEF's Art Training Center, which was dedicated to providing education for doughboys remaining in Europe during the occupation of Germany. After the school closed, in June 1919, and he was discharged, he took up residence at his home in Samois-sur-Seine. In 1923, Peixotto returned to the United States and became the director of the mural department at the Beaux Arts Institute of Design in New York. After several years, he retired from teaching and dedicated himself to his murals. In 1935, New York mayor Fiorello La Guardia appointed Peixotto to the New York City Municipal Art Commission, a post he held until 1940. In his later years he served as a consultant for many high-profile mural projects. Peixotto died in New York City.

## J. André Smith (1880–1959)

Born in Hong Kong, Smith majored in architecture at Cornell University, earning a master's degree in 1904, before dedicating himself to art. By 1915, he had established himself as an award-winning etcher, whose work was in demand by the country's top collectors. After the armistice, he toured the Belgian and British fronts. Not long after Smith was discharged from the AEF in April 1919, he published *In France with the American Expeditionary Forces*, which included a hundred of his war pieces. The book helped launch his career as a freelance illustrator and painter. He settled in Connecticut and pursued his evolution as an artist, which was briefly derailed due to poor health. When in officer training in 1917, he had injured his right leg on barbed wire and it never properly healed. In 1924, a massive embolism developed, and he had to have the leg amputated above the knee. Smith would forever suffer from phantom pain. For health reasons, he began to summer in southern France but was soon attracted to Florida. In 1938, he opened a studio and art school in Maitland, Florida, now called the Maitland Art Center, largely funded by Mary Louise Curtis Bok, the widow of the philanthropist Edward Bok. Considered an architectural jewel, the studio was placed on the National Register of Historic Places. A pioneer in surrealism, Smith published *Art and the Subconscious* in 1937. He died in Maitland, Florida.

## Harry Everett Townsend (1879–1941)

Born in Wyoming, Illinois, Townsend studied art at the Art Institute of Chicago, joined Pyle in 1900 for a brief period, and then studied in Paris. He worked for the country's top magazines and illustrated books, while studying sculpture and other artistic disciplines. In 1912, Townsend, his wife, and his daughter relocated from New York to London, where he worked for British magazines. In 1919, he attended a number of the Paris Peace Conference sessions, which he found to be more pomp than substance. He also flew in an airplane that spring, a poignant experience that helped bring closure to his brother Henri's death. After being discharged in June 1919, Townsend settled in New York City for a short time, then moved to Norwalk, Connecticut, where he built a studio in an old barn. He was a charter member of the Silvermine Guild of Artists, founded in 1922, in New Canaan, Connecticut, serving as its president from 1926 to 1927 and on the board for the remainder of his life. He died in Norwalk, Connecticut.

# Acknowledgments

In working with historical subjects such as the AEF's "Eight," it is very important to find connections to the past to better bring the subject to life. Toward that end, I was fortunate enough to become acquainted with the children of the artist George Harding. Specifically, I owe a deep debt of gratitude to George Harding Jr. for sharing his family's personal papers and offering his thoughts. In expressing my appreciation to Mr. Harding, I also must thank Anita Harding Kistler, for opening her home to me, and Charlotte LaDow Reinhard, for her assistance.

There are a number of institutions and individuals who were particularly helpful as I researched the book, and for their efforts I am grateful. They include: Terry Brown, Society of Illustrators; James Copp, New Britain Museum of Art; Mitchell Yockelson, National Archives and Records Administration; David Kessler, Bancroft Library, University of California, Berkeley; Sarena Deglin, Helen Farr Sloan Library and Archives, Delaware Museum of Art; the Brandywine River Museum; Renée Klish, U.S. Army Center of Military History; Maitland Art Center, Maitland, Florida; U.S. Army Military History, Carlisle Barracks, Pennsylvania; Smithsonian National Museum of American History Library; Pennsylvania Academy of Fine Arts; Alfred Cornebise; and Steve Budlong.

Thanks also to Kristen Getchell and Joe Mas for their assistance in research; Dad for giving me a book on World War I art for Christmas (which is what sparked the idea for this book); Hana Lane, my editor at

Wiley, for her support; everyone at Wiley involved in the production and marketing of the book; and Ed Knappman, my agent for the book. Last but not least, I must always thank Diana, my personal editor and honest critic, to whom the book should also be dedicated—as always.

# NOTES

## Manuscript Collections and Abbreviations

Archives of American Art, Smithsonian Museum, Washington, D.C.

Brandywine River Museum, Chadds Ford, Pennsylvania

Delaware Art Museum, Wilmington, Delaware

EPBL—Ernest Peixotto Papers, BANC MSS 88/75c, Bancroft Library, University of California, Berkeley

Harding Family Papers, in possession of the Harding Family

MPBL—Mary Hutchinson Peixotto Letters, BANC MSS 90/39, Bancroft Library, University of California, Berkeley

NARA—National Archives and Records Administration, College Park, Maryland

NBMA—Harry Townsend Files, New Britain Museum of Art, New Britain, Connecticut

Pennsylvania Academy of Fine Arts, Philadelphia, Pennsylvania

Society of Illustrators, New York City

U.S. Military History Institute, Carlisle Barracks, Pennsylvania

## Prologue

1. Ernest Peixotto, "Effects of War Upon a Small French Town," typed manuscript, Ernest Peixotto Papers (EPBL), BANC MSS 88/75c, Bancroft Library, University of California, Berkeley. For other background material, see Ernest Peixotto, *The American Front* (New York: Charles Scribner's Sons, 1919), Introductory Note; and Peixotto Interview with DeWitt McClellan Lockman (hereafter Peixotto Interview), typed manuscript of interviews of artists and architects associated with the National Academy of Design, 1926, Archives of American Art, Smithsonian, Washington, D.C., microfilm reels 502–504.

## 1. The Journey into the Maelstrom

1. Mary Peixotto (MP) to Ernest Peixotto (EP), March 14, 1918; MP to EP, March 17, 1918, and March 20, 1918, University of California, Berkeley, Bancroft

Library, Mary Hutchinson Peixotto Letters, BANC MSS 90/39 (hereafter MPBL), 14 March 1918–31 March 1918 Folder.

2. Peixotto Interview with DeWitt McClellan Lockman (hereafter Peixotto Interview), typed manuscript of interviews of artists and architects associated with the National Academy of Design, 1926, Archives of American Art, Smithsonian, Washington, D.C., microfilm reels 502–504; and André Smith to Major A. L. James, October 21, 1918, National Archives and Records Administration (NARA), College Park, Maryland, Record Group 120, Box 1, Folder 4. (Hereafter only the folder will be listed for artist-related material at the NARA as all other locator information is the same.)

3. George Creel, *How We Advertised America* (New York: Harper & Brothers, 1920), p. 5.

4. "The British would eventually train over five hundred artists." Col. H. Avery Chenoweth, *The Art of War* (New York: Friedman/Fairfax, 2002), p. 92. Copy of Statement to the Press in Regard to Appointment of Official Artists, February 21, 1918, Folder 10; *New York Times*, February 22, 1918.

5. Major General William M. Black, chief of engineers, U.S. Army, at the War Department to Harry Townsend, February 15, 1918, Folder 2.

6. See document dated March 6, 1918, EPBL.

7. Gary Mead, *The Doughboys: America and the First World War* (New York: The Overlook Press, 2000), p. 349. Russia suffered 1.7 million lost; Germany, 1.6 million; France, 1.4 million; Britain, 900,000; Austria-Hungary, 800,000; Italy, 364,000; Turkey, 250,000; and the United States, 50,300.

8. www.history.navy.mil/danfs/p8/pocahontas-iii.htm, May 6, 2004.

9. Lejaren A. Hiller, "A Word or Two Concerning Wally Morgan," undated two-page typed manuscript, Society of Illustrators, New York, Wallace Morgan Folder.

10. Ernest Peixotto, *American Front*, p. 4.

11. Wallace Morgan to his sister Bess, reprinted in the "The Wallace Morgan Story," typed manuscript, pp. 8–11, Society of Illustrators, New York, Wallace Morgan Folder; Peixotto, p. 6; and Peixotto Interview.

12. "The Wallace Morgan Story," pp. 8–11.

13. Major General W. M. Black, Chief of Engineers to Commanding General, Port of Embarkation, March 1, 1918, Folder 3.

14. For more on the black experience, see Mead, p. 76.

15. Peixotto, *American Front*, p. 9.

16. Mead, p. 104; and Peixotto, *American Front*, p. 10.

17. Peixotto, *American Front*, p. 10.

18. The SS *Philadelphia* was later renamed the USS *Harrisburg*. For more information, see www.history.navy.mil/photos/sh-civil/civsh-c/c-paris.htm.

19. George Harding, "Drawing the War," *American Magazine of Art* 32, no. 10, October 1939, pp. 570–572; and Harding Diary, April 16–18, 1918, George Harding Jr., Collection. Harding made all his original diary entries on 3.5-by-5.5-inch sheets of paper that he later tied together with string. Some of the entries that he included in his article, "Drawing the War," are more developed than what is in the original diary. Most of the original entries are fragmented and with little punctuation, reflecting the unsettling conditions under which Harding was working. I note when quoting from the original diary versus the article.

20. Harding Diary, April 16–18, 1918.

21. Ibid.

22. The USS *Cassin* was torpedoed twenty miles off Ireland, with one killed and nine wounded; and the USS *Jacob Jones* was torpedoed twenty miles off English coast, with sixty-four killed. See www.usmm.org/ww1navy.html, May 6, 2004. This Web site cites its sources as: *American Ship Casualties of the World War, Including Naval Vessels, Merchant Ships, Sailing Vessels, and Fishing Craft*, Corrected to April 1, 1923, compiled by Historical Section Navy Department, Washington: Government Printing Office, 1923; *American Ship Casualties of the World War, Including Naval Vessels, Merchant Ships, Sailing Vessels, and Fishing Craft*, Corrected to April 1, 1923, compiled by Historical Section Navy Department, Washington: Government Printing Office, 1923; and *The U.S. Merchant Marine at War, 1775–1945*, edited by Bruce L. Felknor, Annapolis, Md.: Naval Institute Press, 1998.

23. "The Wallace Morgan Story," pp. 8–11; Peixotto, *American Front*, p. 6; and Peixotto Interview.

24. MP to EP, March 20, 1918; March 22, 1918; March 26, 1918, MPBL.

25. Peixotto, *American Front*, p. 11.

26. Harding, "Drawing the War."

27. Ibid.

28. Harding Diary, circa April 28, 1918.

29. For more description, see Smith, *In France with the American Expeditionary Forces* (New York: Arthur Halo, 1919), p. 1.

30. S. L. A. Marshall, *World War I* (Boston: Houghton Mifflin Company, 1964), p. 343.

31. Mead, p. 213.

32. "The Wallace Morgan Story," p. 6.

## 2. Into the Trenches

1. www.firstworldwar.com/diaries/firstgasattack.htm; and www.firstworldwar.com/weaponry/gas.htm, September 14, 2004; Harding Diary, August 11, 1918.

2. Peixotto, *American Front*, pp. 18–19.

3. Ibid.

4. Ibid., p. 21.

5. Ibid., p. 22.

6. Smith to Major A. L. James, October 21, 1918, Folder 4.

7. Peixotto Interview.

8. Peixotto to Chief G.2.D., May 8, 1918, Folder 3. All of the artists had to submit monthly activity reports, which can be found in their respective folders in the NARA.

9. Marshall, pp. 371–372; and Mead, pp. 225–226.

10. Peixotto, *American Front*, p. 29.

11. www.42id.army.mil/history/patch.html, accessed March 22, 2006.

12. Field Exercises, May 23, 1918, 42nd Division, NARA, RG 120, Box 29, Field Exercises Folder.

13. Smith, p. 10.

14. Smith, p. 40.

15. Peixotto, *American Front*, pp. 31–33.

16. Smith, pp. 11, 19.
17. Quoted in Helen Wright, "J. André Smith—Etcher," *The American Magazine of Art* IX, no. 12, October 1918.
18. Smith, p. 8.
19. Ernest Peixotto, *Through the French Provinces* (London: T. Werner Laurie, 1914), p. 32.
20. Peixotto, *American Front*, p. 38.
21. Smith, p. 9.
22. Peixotto, *American Front*, p. 38.
23. Ibid., p. 40.
24. Ibid., p. 42.

## 3. A Brother Goes to War

1. From undated photocopy of news article from *Toilet Requisites*, Townsend Files, New Britain Museum of Art (hereafter NBMA). Henri "Hank" Townsend was a manager for a toilet supply company.
2. War Department, Office of the Chief of Engineers, Washington, to Mr. Harry Townsend, February 15, 1918, NBMA.
3. Alfred E. Cornebise, ed., *War Diary of a Combat Artist* (Niwot: University Press of Colorado, 1991), p. 9. Alfred Cornebise transcribed Townsend's war diary, which is at the New Britain Museum of Art. Having compared sections of the original material against Cornebise's work, I decided to use Cornebise's book for all diary references due to ease of format and readability.
4. Harry Townsend (HT) to Cory Townsend (CT), August 19, 1918; HT to CT, August 20, 1918, NBMA. In these letters Townsend reviews in detail the letter from Henri.
5. Lieutenant Rex Willey, RAF, to HT, April 28, 1918, NBMA.
6. Dan Chase to Pat Maloney, May 11, 1918, NBMA.
7. HT to CT, August 20, 1918, NBMA.
8. Ibid., August 19, 1918, NBMA.
9. Ibid. and August 20, 1918, NBMA.

## 4. Last Peaceful Forays

1. Robert F. Karolevitz, *Where Your Heart Is* (Aberdeen, S.D.: North Plains Press, 1970), pp. 51–52. Karolevitz also published a brief biography of Dunn titled *The Prairie Is My Garden* (Aberdeen, S.D.: North Plains Press, 1969).
2. For descriptions of Dunn, see Edgar M. Howell, "Harvey Dunn: The Searching Artist Who Came Home to His First Horizon" (*Montana Heritage Series*, Winter 1966).
3. Henry C. Pitz, "Four Disciples of Howard Pyle," *American Artist*, vol. 33, January 1969, pp. 38–43.
4. Anonymous, "I am My Work; My Work Is Me," Society of Illustrators, Harvey Dunn File, a Harvey Dunn pamphlet.
5. Karolevitz, *Where Your Heart Is*, p. 53.
6. Ibid., p. 37.
7. Ibid., p. 53.
8. Harding Diary, May 2, 5, and 7, 1918.

9. William Henry Holaday III, *Harvey Dunn: Pioneer Painter of the Middle Border* (Columbus: Ohio State University Ph.D. Dissertation), p. 26.
10. Stanley Olson, *John Singer Sargent, His Portrait* (New York: St. Martin's Press, 1986), pp. 255–257; and Charles Merrill Mount, *John Singer Sargent: A Biography* (New York: W. W. Norton, 1955), p. 353.
11. Smith, forward, no page number.
12. Ibid., p. 13.
13. HT to CT, May 7, 1918, NBMA.
14. Chief, G.2.D. to Morgan, Peixotto, Smith, Townsend, Dunn, April 30, 1918, Folder 10; and Smith to Major A. L. Banning, October 21, 1918, Folder 4
15. General Policy Reference to the Work of Official Artists, June 7, 1918, Folder 10; and Peixotto Interview.
16. Marshall, pp. 244–249.
17. For their movements in May, see Morgan to Chief, May 31, 1918, Folder 5; and Peixotto to Chief, G.2.D., June 1, 1918, Folder 3.
18. Peixotto, *American Front*, p. 44.
19. www.army.mil/cmh-pg/mohwwi.htm, September 20, 2004.
20. Peixotto, *American Front*, pp. 48–55.
21. Harding Diary, May 14–15, 1918.
22. See Morgan to Chief, May 31, 1918, Folder 5; Dunn to Chief, June 1, 1918, Folder 7; and Smith to Chief, June 1, 1918, Folder 4.
23. Smith, p. 14.
24. Townsend Diary, May 22, 1918, pp. 19–20.
25. Ibid., p. 21.
26. See Mead, p. 226; Marshall, p. 372; and Laurence Stallings, *The Doughboys: The Story of the AEF, 1917–1918* (New York: Harper & Row, 1963), p. 55.
27. Townsend Diary, May 22, 1918, pp. 22–23; May 23, 1918, p. 23; and May 25, 1918, p. 26.
28. Ibid., May 23, 1918, p. 25.
29. Ibid., May 24, 1918, pp. 25–26.
30. www.baseball-almanac.com/treasure/autont2002b.shtml, September 22, 2004.
31. Harding Diary, May 30, 1918.
32. Ibid., June 2, 1918.
33. www.32nd-division.org/history/ww1/ww1.html, September 21, 2004.
34. E. R. W. McCabe, Assistant Chief, G.2.D. to Chief, G.2.D., June 1, 1918, Folder 3; Covell to W. G. Haan, Commanding General, 32nd Division, June 7, 1918, Folder 3; Haan to Chief of Staff, A.E.F., June 8, 1918, Folder 3; and "The Wally Morgan Story," p. 13.
35. MP to EP, April 25, 1918; MP to EP, April 26, 1918, MPBL; Letters from MP to EP 8 April to 26 April 1918 Folder; MP to EP May 20, 1918; MP to EP, May 24, 1918; letters from MP to EP 1 May to 24 May 1918 Folder.
36. Peixotto, *American Front*, p. 64.

## 5. A Grim Harvest along the Marne

1. Peixotto, *American Front*, pp. 67–69.
2. MP to EP, June 16, 1918, MPBL; Letters from MP to EP, 16 June 1918 to 21 June 1918 Folder.

3. Lieutenant Colonel Davidson to Commanding General, 3rd Division, June 12, 1918, NARA, RG 120, Box 48, Folder 131. This report details the actions of Bissell and the 7th Machine Gun Battalion.
4. Ibid.
5. Harding Diary, June 5, 1918.
6. Harding, "Drawing the War."
7. Karolevitz, *Where Your Heart Is,* p. 49.
8. Illustration Class Notes, p. 2, Society of Illustrators, Dunn Box.
9. Dunn Letter to Parents, reprinted in local paper August 14, 1918, which was, in turn, reprinted in Judith Miner Hine Luedemann, *Ancestry of Harvey Dunn* (Chester, Conn.: Pequot Press), pp. 304–305.
10. Harding Diary, June 5, 1918.
11. Harding, "Drawing the War."
12. Dunn Letter to Parents, *Ancestry of Harvey Dunn,* pp. 304–305.
13. Townsend Diary, June 5–8, 1918, p. 27.
14. Ibid.; HT to CT, June 7, 1918, NBMA.
15. Peixotto, *American Front,* p. 70.
16. Townsend Diary, June 5–8, 1918, pp. 28-29; HT to CT, June 7, 1918, NBMA.
17. Mead, p. 196.
18. Marshall, p. 6.
19. Townsend Diary, June 5–8, 1918, p. 32.
20. Ibid., p. 32–33.
21. Ibid., p. 33; see also HT to CT, June 7, 1918, NBMA, in which he details these experiences.
22. To illustrate how alien combat is to human beings, the war historian John Keegan quoted an official U.S. report on combat exhaustion: "There is no such thing as 'getting used to combat.' . . . Each moment of combat imposes a strain so great that men will break down in direct relation to the intensity and duration of their exposure . . . psychiatric casualties are as inevitable as gunshot and shrapnel wounds in warfare." And no matter how much inward hardening occurred, Keegan pointed out, all men's resolution would be challenged to a breaking point. Modern warfare only exacerbated it: "Impersonality, coercion, deliberate cruelty, all deployed on a rising scale, make the fitness of modern man to sustain the stress of battle increasingly doubtful." See John Keegan, *The Face of Battle* (New York: Viking Press, 1976), pp. 325, 329.
23. Peixotto, *American Front,* p. 73.
24. Quote recorded by Harding, Harding Diary, July 4, 1918.
25. HT to CT, June 7, 1918, NBMA.

## 6. Questioned Sacrifice in Belleau Wood

1. www.firstworldwar.com/battles/cantigny.htm, December 23, 2004; and Smith, p. 45.
2. Mead, p. 243.
3. Ibid., pp. 243–244.
4. Townsend Diary, June 5–8, 1918, pp. 36–37. The war historian Glenn Gray explains that there are "secret attractions of war" that include "the delight in seeing, the delight in comradeship, the delight in destruction." See Glenn Gray,

*The Warriors: Reflections on Men in Battle* (New York: Harcourt Brace, 1959), p. 52.

5. Townsend Diary, June 5-8, 1918, pp. 37–38.

6. www.firstworldwar.com/source/belleau_daniels.htm, September 29, 2004. Also see Townsend Diary, April 17, 1918, p. 221. He visited the battlefield in April 1919 with Marine Majors Larsen and Kingman and all three men were deeply moved by the slaughter that had occurred in the open fields leading to Belleau Wood.

7. History of the 6th Marines Regiment, NARA, RG 120, Box 68, History of the 6th Marines Regiment Folder.

8. Robert B. Asprey, *At Belleau Wood* (New York: Putnam, 1965), p. 202.

9. Townsend Diary, June 5–8, 1918, p. 40; HT to CT, June 7, 1918, NBMA.

10. Smith, p. 48.

11. Peixotto, *American Front*, pp. 74–75.

12. Smith, p. 51.

13. Mead, p. 245.

14. Wayne to Folks, July 1, 1918, NARA, RG 120, Box 68, 6th Regiment Marines History Folder.

15. Ibid.

16. Peixotto, *American Front*, p. 79.

17. Mead, p. 249; and www.firstworldwar.com/battles/belleau.htm, September 29, 2004.

18. HT to CT, June 7 and 10, 1918, NBMA.

19. Townsend Diary, p. 40.

20. Asprey, pp. 208–209.

21. Harding Diary, circa June 8–20, 1918.

22. Karolevitz, *Where Your Heart Is*, pp. 54–55.

23. Henry C. Pitz, pp. 38–39.

24. Harding Diary, June 7–8, 1918; Philadelphia *Public Ledger*, March 3, 1919, quoted in Walter Kelly Hood, *Words, Wars and Walls: The Art Life of George Matthews Harding* (Evanston, Ill.: Northwestern Ph.D. Dissertation, 1966), p. 100.

25. Charlotte Johnson, "I Cover the Beachfront," *Atlantic City Press* (undated clipping, George Harding Jr. Collection).

26. HT to CT, June 16, 1918, NBMA; MP to EP, June 16, 20, and 21, 1918, MPBL, Letters from MP to EP, 16 June 1918 to 21 June 1918 Folder.

27. HT to CT, June 23, 1918.

28. Mead, p. 249; and www.firstworldwar.com/battles/belleau.htm, September 29, 2004.

29. Mead, p. 249.

30. Townsend Diary, July 30, 1918, p. 76.

## 7. The Desperate Peace Offensive

1. Townsend Diary, July 23–30, 1918, p. 67; Smith, p. 56.

2. Townsend Diary, July 23–30, 1918, pp. 67–69.

3. Ibid., July 30, 1918, p. 74.

4. Olson, p. 257. For Sargent's wartime experiences, see also Mount, pp. 352–365 and Chenoweth, pp. 94–95.

5. Olson, p. 254.

6. Ibid., pp. 257–258.

7. Ibid., p. 258.

8. Ibid.

9. Ibid.

10. Mount, p. 355.

11. Olson, p. 260.

12. Ibid.

13. EP to Chief, July Report, July 31, 1918, Folder 3; MP to EP, July 9, 1918, MPBL; and letters from MP to EP 9 July 1918 to 26 July 1918 Folder.

14. MP to EP, July 12, July 14, July 15, July 24, 1918, MPBL; and letters from MP to EP 9 July 1918 to 26 July 1918 Folder.

15. Townsend Diary, July 13–15, 1918, p. 45; and HT to CT, July 15, 1918, NBMA.

16. Townsend Diary, July 13–15, 1918, p. 46; and HT to CT, July 15, 1918, NBMA.

17. Townsend Diary, July 15–16, 1918, pp. 47–48.

18. George Harding, "The American Artist at the Front," *The American Magazine of Art* (Volume X, no. 12, October 1919).

19. Margaret C. Getchell, "In and Out of Germany with a Philadelphia Artist," Philadelphia *Public Ledger* (March 16, 1919).

20. Harding to Franklin Inn Club, July 11, 1918, quoted in Hood Dissertation, p. 81; and Harding Diary, undated, early July.

21. Harding Diary, July 14–15, 1918.

22. Harding, "The American Artist at the Front"; and Harding to Chief, August 1, 1918, July Report, Folder 6.

23. Peixotto, *American Front*, p. 80.

24. Ibid., p. 84; for the exact disposition of his troops, see "Historical Data—Thirty-Eighth Infantry," NARA, RG 120, Box 45, 38th Infantry—History Folder; and "Report of Operations of Company 'G'," 38th Infantry, July 15–21, 1918, NARA, RG 120, Box 45, Company G Operations July 1918 Folder.

25. "Historical Data—Thirty-Eighth Infantry," 38th Infantry—History Folder; and "Report of Operations of Company 'G'," 38th Infantry, July 15–21, 1918, NARA, RG 120, Box 45, Company G Operations July 1918 Folder.

26. See field messages dated July 15, 1918, NARA, RG 120, Box 43, Field Messages Folder.

27. Marshall, p. 398.

28. Mead, p. 398.

29. Smith, p. 63. He has more description of the battle on both pp. 63 and 64.

30. Peixotto, *American Front*, p. 83.

31. Ibid., p. 87.

32. Ibid.

33. Ibid., p. 88.

34. Ibid., p. 90.

## 8. Visiting the Wild Cowboy Spirits

1. Townsend Diary, July 16, 1918, p. 48.

2. HT to CT, July 16, 1918, NBMA.

3. www.rootsweb.com/~minewayg/WWIC.html, April 28, 2005; and Townsend Diary, July 17, 1918, p. 51.

4. Townsend Diary, July 17, 1918, p. 51.
5. For a history of the 1st Pursuit Group, see www.acepilots.com/wwi/us_1st_2.html, and www.1st fighter.org/history/1918.html.
6. Subjects of drawings submitted September 1, 1918, by Captain Harry E. Townsend. E.R.C., Folder 2.
7. www.acepilots.com/wwi/us_1st_2.html; and Townsend Diary, July 18–20, 1918, p. 54.
8. Townsend Diary, July 18–20, 1918, p. 55.
9. Ibid., pp. 56 and 52.
10. HT to CT, July 20, 1918, NBMA.
11. Ibid., July 18, 1918, NBMA.
12. Ibid.
13. Ibid.

## 9. Marshal Foch's Counteroffensive

1. Peixotto, *American Front,* p. 80.
2. Ibid., p. 96.
3. Ibid., p. 98.
4. Ibid., p. 94.
5. Stallings, p. 155.
6. Harding Diary, July 20–21, 1918.
7. Peixotto, *American Front,* pp. 91–93.
8. Report of First Lieutenant D. F. McGrew, commanding 37mm battery, 103rd Infantry, Operation period July 18–25, 1918, 2nd Battalion Reports of Operations July 18–25, 1918 Folder.
9. Report of Major J. W. Hanson, commanding 1st Battalion, 103rd U.S. Infantry, NARA, RG 120, Box 47, Operations of Period July 18–25, 1918 Folder.
10. Townsend Diary, July 22, 1918, p. 60.
11. Ibid., pp. 61–62; Frank R. Sibley, *With the Yankee Division in France* (Boston: Little, Brown, 1919), p. 221. According to www.worldwar1.com/dbc/2marne.htm, January 30, 2004, the 26th Division suffered fifty-three hundred casualties.
12. Townsend Diary, July 22, 1918, pp. 61–62.
13. Ibid., p. 64.
14. Ibid., p. 65.
15. U. G. McAlexander, Report of Battle, July 21–23, 1918, NARA, RG 120, Box 45, Operations July 1918 Folder; Robinson Murray, Report of Operations, 2nd Battalion, 38th Infantry, July 21–25, 1918, NARA, RG 120, Box 45, Operations July 1918 Folder; and Stallings, p. 162.
16. Hanon Fields Combs, "Report of Operations Company 'C'," 38th Infantry, July 22–27, 1918, NARA, RG 120, Box 45, Company C Operations Folder.
17. Harding Diary, July 20–22, 1918. Some of his reflections on this period may also be from early August but are not dated.
18. Harding, "The American Artist at the Front."
19. Harding to Chief, July report, August 1, 1918, Folder 6.
20. Townsend Diary, July 22, 1918, p. 66.
21. Smith, p. 53.
22. Townsend Diary, July 23–30, 1918, pp. 69–70.
23. Ibid., July 30, 1918, pp. 75–76.

24. Peixotto, *American Front*, p. 90.
25. Ibid., pp. 99–100.
26. Ibid., p. 91.
27. MP to EP, July 20 and 26, 1918, MPBL; and letters from MP to EP 9 July 1918 to 26 July 1918 Folder.
28. Mead, p. 265.
29. Stallings, p. 168.
30. Harding, "Drawing the War."
31. Peixotto, *American Front*, p. 100.
32. Ibid., p. 101.
33. Harding Diary, circa August 12–14.
34. Peixotto, *American Front*, pp. 103–104.
35. Ibid., pp. 105–106.
36. Mead, p. 266.
37. Peixotto, *American Front*, p. 106.
38. Colonel Ben W. Hough, Daily Operations Report, 6:00 A.M., August 1 to 6:00 A.M., August 2, 1918, and 6:00 A.M., August 2 to 6:00 A.M., August 3, 1918, NARA, RG 120, Box 29, Daily Operations Reports Folder; and Mead, p. 266.
39. Peixotto, *American Front*, p. 107.

## 10. The First Casualty of War Is Truth

1. Harding, "The American Artist at the Front."
2. Harold Evans, *War Stories* (Boston: Bunker Hill Publishing, 2003), p. 71.
3. HT to CT, July 18, 1918, NBMA.
4. Peixotto to Gibson, August 7, 1918, Folder 3.
5. HT to CT, July 18, 1918, NBMA.
6. E. R. W. McCabe, "General Policy Reference the Work of Official Artists," June 7, 1918, Folder 10.
7. Dennis E. Nolan Memoirs, typed manuscript, U.S. Army Military History Institute, Carlisle Barracks, Pennsylvania, Dennis E. Nolan Papers, Box 2, Dictations circa 1935 on World War I #1–21 Folder.
8. Peixotto Interview.
9. D. E. Nolan to the Chief of Staff, July 17, 1918, Folder 10; and Pershing to Chief of Staff, cable, July 18, 1918, Folder 10.
10. Banning to Smith, August 5; and Creel to Peixotto, September 9, 1918, EPBL.
11. Alfred Emile Cornebise, *Art from the Trenches* (College Station: Texas A&M University Press, 1991), p. 28.
12. Pershing noted that as of September 19 submission of art pieces were as follows: Aylward 19, Duncan 13, Dunn 17, Harding 19, Morgan 24, Peixotto 58, Smith 106, and Townsend 27. Pershing to Chief of Staff, September 19, 1918, Folder 10.
13. Holaday dissertation, p. 318.
14. Edgar M. Howell, "An Artist Goes to War: Harvey Dunn and the A.E.F. War Art Program," *Smithsonian Journal of History* (Winter 1967–1968).
15. Dunn to Chief, G.2.D., September 1, 1918, Folder 7.
16. Major Banning to Smith, August 13, 1918, Folder 10.
17. Mount, p. 360; and Olson, pp. 260–261.

18. Colonel J. R. M. Taylor of the General Staff, War College, Memorandum, August 19, 1918, Folder 3.
19. Smith to Banning, undated, Folder 4.
20. Major Robert M. Johnston to Lieutenant Colonel C. W. Weeks, September 6, 1918, "Banning Barrage," EPBL.
21. Major A. L. James to General Nolan, September 9, 1918, Folder 10.
22. Townsend Diary, September 8, 1918, p. 83.
23. Smith to James, October 21, 1918, Folder 4.
24. For example, the censors did suppress the fact that the soldiers suffered due to a lack of equipment, and the censors hid the mounting soldiers' death rate from pneumonia due, in part, to the dearth of military clothing and proper housing.
25. Karolevitz, *Where the Heart Is*, p. 53; and Cornebise, *Art from the Trenches*, p. 29.
26. Pershing to Chief of Staff, September 19, 1918, Folder 10.

## 11. Ramping Up in August

1. HT to CT, August 7, 1918, NBMA.
2. Marshall, p. 421.
3. HT to CT, August 10, 1918, NBMA.
4. Ibid., August 7, 10, and 11, 1918, NBMA.
5. Ibid., August 19, 1918, NBMA.
6. HT to Dwight Townsend, August 20, 1918, NBMA.
7. MP to EP, August 6, 1918; MP to EP, August undated, MPBL; and letters from MP to EP, 6 August 1918 to 16 August 1918 Folder.
8. Townsend Diary, September 4, 1918, pp. 79–80.
9. Ibid., September 5, 1918, p. 80.
10. Ibid., September 10, 1918, pp. 84–85.
11. Peixotto, *American Front*, p. 121.
12. Ibid., p. 114.
13. See www.wwiaviation.com/aces/ace_Fonck.shtml.
14. Townsend Diary, September 9, 1918, p. 84.
15. Ibid., September 7, 1918, p. 81.
16. John C. McCoy, "Evacuation Hospital #114," NARA, RG 120, Box 793, Evacuation Hospital 114 Historical Data Folder.
17. Peixotto, *American Front*, pp. 126–129.
18. Townsend Diary, September 11, 1918, p. 85.
19. Ibid., September 12, 1918, p. 90.
20. Ibid., September 12, 1918, p. 90.

## 12. The Saint-Mihiel Salient: A Bloodless Offensive

1. HT to CT, August 7, 1918, NBMA; and Townsend Diary, July 31, 1918, p. 77.
2. HT to CT, August 7, 1918 and September 12, 1918, NBMA.
3. Ibid., September 11, 1918, NBMA.
4. Harding, "The American Artist at the Front."
5. Harding Diary, September 12–16, 1918.
6. Harding to Chief, G.2.D., "September Report," October 2, 1918, Folder 6; Dunn to Chief, "September Report," October 1, 1918, Folder 7; and Karolevitz, *Where the Heart Is*, p. 11.

7. James J. Cooke, *The Rainbow Division in the Great War* (Westport, Conn.: Praeger, 1994), pp. 152–153.
8. Harding Diary, September 12–16, 1918.
9. Dunn to Chief, "September Report," October 1, 1918, Folder 7.
10. Peixotto, *American Front*, p. 129.
11. Ibid., p. 130.
12. John J. Pershing, *My Experiences in the World War*, vol. 2 (New York: Frederick A. Stokes, 1931), p. 261; Mead, p. 285; and www.worldwar1.com/dbc/stmihiel.htm, November 11, 1918.
13. Peixotto, *American Front*, pp. 130–132.
14. Townsend Diary, September 12, 1918, p. 90.
15. Mead, p. 295.
16. Harding Diary, September 13, 1918.
17. Townsend Diary, September 19, 1918, p. 101.
18. Ibid., September 13, 1918, p. 91, and September 14, 1918, pp. 94–95.
19. "A Yale Unit at the Front," *The Yale Alumni Weekly* (Vol. 28, no. 6, October 25, 1918); and Yale Hospital #39, NARA, RG 120, Entry 2129, Box 1324, Historical Data Folder.
20. Joseph M. Flint to Chief Surgeon, May 9, 1918, Yale Mobile Hospital #39 Historical Data Folder, Box 1324, RG 120.
21. Townsend Diary, September 13, 1918, pp. 91–92.
22. Ibid., September 14, 1918, p. 92.
23. Smith, p. 67; Townsend Diary, September 14, 1918, p. 93.
24. HT to Barbara Townsend, undated, 1918, NBMA.
25. Smith, p. 73.
26. Townsend Diary, September 14, 1918, p. 95; and Smith, p. 71.
27. Smith, p. 71.
28. www.yeoldwoburn.com/chronmem.PDF, November 16, 2004.
29. EP to MP, September 15, 1918, EPBL.
30. Peixotto, *American Front*, pp. 136–137.
31. Ibid., pp. 139–141.
32. Ibid., p. 142.
33. Pershing, p. 271.
34. Peixotto, *American Front*, p. 144.
35. Ibid., p. 147.
36. James H. Hallas, *Squandered Victory* (Westport, Conn.: Praeger, 1995), p. 139.
37. Peixotto, *American Front*, p. 150.
38. Ibid., pp. 151–152.
39. EP to MP, September 15, 1918, EPBL; MP to EP, September 15, 1918, MPBL; and letters from MP to EP, 15 September 1918 to 26 September 1918, Folder.
40. See www.worldwar1.com/dbc/stmihiel.htm, November 11, 1918; and Smith, p. 76.
41. Townsend Diary, September 16, 1918, pp. 98–99.
42. Townsend Diary, September 15, 1918, p. 97; and Mead, p. 297.

## 13. The Meuse Argonne and the Goddess of War

1. Townsend Diary, September 21, 1918, p. 102–103.
2. Ibid., p. 103.

3. Ibid., p. 102.

4. Ibid., September 22–24, 1918, p. 110.

5. Major A. L. James Jr. to GHQ, G.2.D., Officer in Charge, Photographic Sub-Section, Paris, September 25, 1918, Folder 10; Smith to Major A. L. Banning, October 21, 1918, Folder 4; and Townsend Diary, September 21, 1918, pp. 103–104.

6. Peixotto, *American Front*, p. 157; and Harding Diary, September 25, 1918.

7. Townsend Diary, September 25, 1918, p. 112.

8. HT to CT, September 25, 1918, NBMA.

9. Peixotto, *American Front*, pp. 158–160.

10. Harding Diary, September 25–26, 1918.

11. Peixotto, *American Front*, pp. 161–162.

12. Of the eight divisions, only the 77th, the 4th, and the 33rd had witnessed any combat; the relatively inexperienced troops hampered the Meuse-Argonne Offensive. See Thomas Fleming, "Goal with a Price to be Paid," *Military History Magazine* (October 1993); http://europeanhistory.about.com/library/prm/blpershingargonne2.htm, November 28, 2004. For numbers of troops as well as tanks and airplanes involved, see Mead, pp. 299–300.

13. Anonymous, "Memoirs & Diaries: Account of the German Attacks on Le Mort Homme, Verdun, 20–24 May 1916," www.firstworldwar.com/diaries/verdun_lemorthomme.htm, November 22, 2004.

14. Peixotto, *American Front*, pp. 163–164.

15. Ibid., pp. 164–165.

16. Harding Diary, September 26, 1918.

17. Getchell, "In and Out of Germany with a Philadelphia Artist."

18. Holaday, p. 320.

19. Ibid., p. 28.

20. Peixotto, *American Front*, pp. 165–167.

21. Ibid., pp. 167–168.

22. Ibid., pp. 168–169.

23. Stallings, p. 237.

24. Harry S. Howland to Commanding General, 35th Division, "Operations Report, September 25–26, 1918," EPBL.

25. "Veteran Officer Quits Army a Second Time," *New York Times* (November 14, 1920), EPBL. Peixotto kept a copy of this article until his death.

26. Stallings, 237; Mead p. 305; and http://usgennet.org/usa/mo/county/stlouis/35thdivision.htm, November 29, 2004.

27. Harry S. Howland to Lieutenant Clarence Sonnell, October 2, 1918, EPBL.

28. Harry S. Howland to EP, October 5, 1918, EPBL.

29. EP to Harry Howland, October 30, 1918; and Howland to EP November 27, 1918, EPBL.

30. Smith, p. 86.

31. Headquarters 308th Infantry, Report on Operations, September 26 to October 16, 1918, 77th Division, NARA, RG120, Box 28, 308th Infantry Report of Operations Folder.

32. Mead, p. 318; and www.longwood.k12.ny.us/history/upton/lost.htm, February 16, 2005.

33. Townsend Diary, September 28, 1918, pp. 116–117.
34. Ibid., September 26, 1918, p. 113.
35. Ibid., September 26, 1918, pp. 114–115.
36. Smith, p. 91.
37. Peixotto, *American Front*, p. 173.
38. Ibid., p. 174.
39. Ibid., p. 175.
40. Townsend Diary, September 28, 1918, p. 117.
41. Pershing, p. 298.

## 14. The Festival of the Dead

1. Peixotto, *American Front*, pp. 176–177.
2. Peixotto to Chief, October 30, 1918, Folder 3.
3. Peixotto, *American Front*, p. 170.
4. "Preliminary Patrol Report," September 28, 1918, NARA, RG 120, Box 27, Patrol Plan September 28–29, 1918, Folder.
5. Pershing, pp. 298, 323.
6. Peixotto, *American Front*, pp. 177–178.
7. Mead, p. 302; and Townsend, p. 119.
8. Smith, p. 80.
9. www.oryansroughnecks.org/history.html, November 20, 2005.
10. Mount, pp. 360–361.
11. Olson, p. 260.
12. Ibid.
13. William Howe Downes, *John S. Sargent: His Life and Work* (Boston: Little, Brown, 1925), p. 76.
14. HT to CT, October 3 and 6, 1918; and HT to BT, undated October 1918, NBMA.
15. HT to CT, October 6, 1918, NBMA.
16. Pershing, pp. 299, 330.
17. Peixotto, *American Front*, pp. 175–176.
18. Townsend, "Retrospect" from Diary, undated, p. 247.
19. Townsend Diary, October 10–15, p. 119.
20. Ibid., p. 121.
21. HT to CT, October 15, 1918, NBMA.
22. HT to BT, undated October, 1918, NBMA.
23. Townsend Diary, October 10–15, 1918, p. 120.
24. Ibid., October 10–15, 1918, p. 121.
25. Ibid., October 16–26, 1918, p. 122.
26. Mead, p. 307; and Stallings, p. 323.
27. Townsend Diary, October 16–26, 1918, p. 123.
28. Ibid., October 16–26, 1918, p. 124.
29. Mead, pp. 325–326.
30. Smith, p. 88.
31. 308th Infantry, 77th Division, Report on Operations, September 26 to October 16, 1918, NARA, RG 120, Box 28, 308th Infantry Report of Operations Folder.
32. Harding Diary, October 22–23, 1918.
33. Getchell, "In and Out of Germany with a Philadelphia Artist."
34. Pershing, p. 352; and Mead, p. 325.

35. Harding Diary, undated but circa early November 1918.
36. Smith, p. 89.
37. HT to Chief, October Report, November 4, 1918, Folder 6.
38. Townsend Diary, October 27, 1918, p. 125.
39. See www.worldwar1.com/dbc/bigshow.htm, November 24, 2004; and Mead, p.330.
40. Townsend Diary, October 27 and 29, 1918, pp. 125 and 127.
41. Ibid., October 31, 1918, p. 128.
42. Mead, p. 330.
43. HT to CT, October 18 and 27, 1918, NBMA; and Townsend, October 27, 1918, pp. 125–126.
44. Townsend Diary, October 29, 1918, pp. 126–127; and HT to CT, October 31, 1918.
45. Townsend Diary, October 30, 1918, p. 128; and HT to CT and BT, October 31, 1918.
46. Banning to Smith, September 30, 1918, Folder 4; Smith to James, October 22, 1918, Folder 4. The Committee on Public Information, along with the American Federation of Arts, was to manage the exhibitions.
47. Banning to Harding, October 25, 1918, Folder 6.
48. Townsend Diary, October 16–26, 1918, p. 125; and HT to CT, October 20, 1918.
49. "Banning Barrage," EPBL.
50. Townsend Diary, November 1, 1918, p. 128.
51. Smith, p. 90.
52. HT to BT, November 3, 1918.
53. Townsend Diary, November 4, 1918, p. 131; and C. W. Weeks to Acting Chief of Staff, G-2, GHQ, December 4, 1918, Folder 10.
54. Townsend Diary, November 5–7, 1918, p. 132.
55. Smith to Peixotto, November 7, 1918, EPBL.
56. Harding Diary, November 7–9, 1918.
57. Townsend Diary, November 12, 1918, pp. 139–140.

## 15. The Restoration of Light

1. For more on Peixotto's illness, see Peixotto, *American Front*, p. 179; A. L. James to EP, October 25, 1918; and EP to A. L. James, October 28, 1918, EPBL.
2. Peixotto, *American Front*, pp. 179–185.
3. Ibid., pp. 181–185.
4. EP to mother, November 23, 1918, EPBL.
5. Townsend Diary, November 11, 1918, p. 138.
6. Ibid., November 12, 1918, pp. 139–140.
7. Mead, p. 333.
8. Townsend Diary, November 12, 1918, pp. 139–140.
9. Smith, p. 93.

## 16. The Occupation and the Stories of Hardship

1. Townsend Diary, November 13, 1918, pp. 140–141.
2. Duncan was most likely with them, too, but his presence was not documented.

3. Peixotto, *American Front*, pp. 185–187, 188–189.
4. EP to mother, November 23, 1918, EPBL.
5. Peixotto, *American Front*, pp. 195–196.
6. A card titled "Logements Militaires" gave Peixotto permission to take rooms at the hotel in Sedan for November 16, 1918, EPBL.
7. Peixotto, *American Front*, p. 198.
8. Ibid., p. 199; and EP to mother, November 23, 1918, EPBL.
9. EP to mother, November 23, 1918, EPBL.
10. Townsend Diary, November 21, 1918, p. 159. He describes returning through the town on November 21 to discover that some of the shops had been looted by American soldiers.
11. Townsend Diary, November 17, 1918, pp. 144–145.
12. HT to CT, November 17, 1918, NBMA.
13. Townsend Diary, November 17, 1918, pp. 146–149
14. Ibid., November 17, 1918, pp. 149–150.
15. Ibid., November 18, 1918, p. 151.
16. Ibid., November 18, 1918, p. 152.
17. Ibid., November 19, 1918, p. 154; and HT to CT, November 21, 1918, NBMA.
18. Townsend Diary, November 21, 1918, p. 159.
19. James to Smith, November 19, 1918, Folder 4.
20. Townsend Diary, November 24, 1918, p. 164.
21. Ibid., November 25, 1918, p. 165.
22. Ibid., November 25, 1918, pp. 166–167.
23. Peixotto, *American Front*, p. 213.
24. Smith, p. 94.
25. Townsend Diary, November 28, 1918, p. 171.

## 17. Penetrating the Fatherland

1. Townsend Diary, December 10, 1918, pp. 173–174.
2. Peixotto, *American Front*, pp. 217–218.
3. Ibid., p. 218.
4. Townsend Diary, December 11, 1918, p. 177.
5. Peixotto, *American Front*, p. 226.
6. Smith, p. 100.
7. Ibid., p. 99.
8. Peixotto, *American Front*, p. 228.
9. Ibid., p. 224.
10. Getchell, "In and Out of Germany with a Philadelphia Artist."
11. Townsend Diary, December 12, 1918, pp. 182–183.
12. Ibid., December 12, 1918, pp. 182–83.
13. Ibid., December 15, 1918, pp. 186–187.
14. Ibid., December 16, 1918, p. 189.
15. Ibid., December 16, 1918, pp. 189–190.
16. Ibid., December 15, 1918, p. 189.
17. Peixotto, *American Front*, pp. 229–230.
18. Townsend Diary, December 18, 1918, pp. 192, 194.
19. Harding Diary, December 25, 1918.

# SELECTED BIBLIOGRAPHY

## Books

Asprey, Robert B. *At Belleau Wood.* New York: Putnam, 1965.

Chenoweth, Colonel H. Avery. *Art of War.* New York: Friedman/Fairfax, 2002.

Cooke, James J. *The Rainbow Division in the Great War.* Westport, Conn.: Praeger, 1994.

Cornebise, Alfred Emile. *Art from the Trenches.* College Station: Texas A&M University Press, 1991.

Creel, George. *How We Advertised America.* New York: Harper & Brothers, 1920.

D'Este, Carlos. *Patton: A Genius for War.* New York: Harper Perennial, 1995.

Duncan, Walter Jack. *First Aid to Pictorial Composition.* New York: Harper & Brothers, 1939.

Eisenhower, John S. D. *Yanks.* New York: The Free Press, 2001.

Ermoyan, Arpi. *Famous American Illustrators.* New York: Society of Illustrators, 1997.

Gallatin, Albert Eugene. *Art and the Great War.* New York: Dutton, 1919.

Hallas, James H. *Squandered Victory.* Westport, Conn.: Praeger, 1995.

Harding, George. *The American Expeditionary Forces in Action.* Self-published, limited edition, 1920.

Karolevitz, Robert F. *The Prairie Is My Garden: The Story of Harvey Dunn.* Aberdeen, S.D.: North Plains Press, 1969.

————. *Where Your Heart Is: The Story of Harvey Dunn, Artist.* Aberdeen, S.D.: North Plains Press, 1970.

Keegan, John. *The Face of Battle.* New York: Viking Press, 1976.

Luedemann, Judith M. H. *The Ancestry of Harvey Dunn.* Westport, Conn.: Pequot Press, 1973.

Marshall, S. L. A. *World War I.* Boston: Houghton Mifflin, 1964.

Mead, Gary. *The Doughboys: America and the First World War.* New York: Overlook Press, 2000.

Mount, Charles Merrill. *John Singer Sargent: A Biography*. New York: W. W. Norton, 1955.

Olson, Stanley, *John Singer Sargent: His Portrait*. New York: St. Martin's Press, 1986.

Peixotto, Ernest. *The American Front*. New York: Charles Scribner's Sons, 1919.

———. *Through the French Provinces*. London: T. Werner Laurie, 1914.

Pershing, John J. *My Experiences on the World War*, Volumes I and II. New York, Frederick A. Stokes, 1931.

Rickenbacker, Eddie. *Fighting the Flying Circus*. New York: Frederick A. Stokes, 1919.

Sherwood, Aubrey. *I Remember Harvey Dunn*. Privately printed, 1984.

Sibley, Frank P. *With the Yankee Division in France*. Boston: Little, Brown, 1919.

Smith, J. André. *In France with the American Expeditionary Forces*. New York: Arthur H. Halo, 1919.

Stallings, Laurence. *The Doughboys: The Story of the AEF*. New York: Harper & Row, 1963.

Taber, John H. *The Story of the 168th Infantry*. Iowa City: State Historical Society of Iowa, 1925.

Townsend, Harry Everett, and Alfred E. Cornebise, ed. *War Diary of a Combat Artist*. Niwot: University Press of Colorado, 1991.

U.S. Army Center of Military History. *The United States Army in World War I*, 3 CD-ROM Set. Washington, D.C.: U.S. Army Center of Military History, 2001.

Watson, Ernest W. *Forty Illustrators and How They Work*. New York: Watson-Guptill Publications, 1946.

## Articles

Adams, Adeline. "Ernest Peixotto's War Landscapes." *The American Magazine of Art*, June 1921.

Andres, Charles J. "Harvey Dunn: The Gift of Inspiration." *Step-by-Step Graphics*, March/April 1989.

Fleming, Thomas. "Goal with a Price to Be Paid." *Military History Magazine*, October 1993.

Harding, George. "American Artist at the Front." *The American Magazine of Art*, October 1919.

———. "Drawing the War." *The American Magazine of Art*, October 1939.

Howell, Edgar M. "An Artist Goes to War: Harvey Dunn and the A.E.F. War Art Program." *Smithsonian Journal of History*, Winter 1967–1968.

———. "Harvey Dunn: The Searching Artist Who Came Home to His First Horizon." *Montana Heritage Series*, Winter 1966.

Karolevitz, Robert F. "Harvey Dunn: Artist of the A.E.F." *Veterans of Foreign Wars*, November 1971.

Pitz, Henry C. "Four Disciples of Howard Pyle." *American Artist*, January 1969.

Schooping, Elaine. "The Restless Ghost of André Smith." *Orlando-Land*, March 1971.

Shively, Ruth. "One Man's Enduring Fantasy." *O! Arts Magazine*, January–March, 1998.

Watson, Ernest W. "Harvey Dunn." *American Artist*, June 1942.

Wilson, Edward. "Walter Jack Duncan: A Master Pen Draughtsman." *American Artist,* March 1957.

Wright, Helen. "J. André Smith—Etcher," *The American Magazine of Art,* October 1918.

## Web Sites

Note: Many Web sites have been created for divisions and regiments of the AEF, which I relied upon but are not listed below.

www.acepilots.com/wwi/us_1st_2.html

1st Pursuit Group History. Compilations courtesy of Staff Sergeant John DesHetler, 1st Fighter Wing History Office, Langley AFB, Virginia. Edited by Stephen Sherman, the webmaster of this Web site, AcePilots.com

www.archives.gov

The U.S. National Archives and Records Administration

www.army.mil/cmh-pg

U.S. Army Center of Military History

www.firstworldwar.com

An overview of the First World War, edited by Michael Duffy

www.loc.gov/folklife/vets

Veterans History Project. A Project of the American Folklife Center of the Library of Congress

www.scuttlebuttsmallchow.com

Scuttlebutt and Small Chow's History and Lore of the Old Corps. The Web sites of B. J. Omanson

www.usmm.org/ww1navy.html

U.S. Navy Ships Sunk or Damaged from Various Causes During World War I. Source: *American Ship Casualties of the World War, Including Naval Vessels, Merchant Ships, Sailing Vessels, and Fishing Craft,* Corrected to April 1, 1923

www.wfa-usa.org

Western Front Association, U.S. Branch

www.worldwar1.com/dbc

The Doughboy Center General Headquarters from The Great War Society. A Partnership with the Veterans History Program of the Library of Congress

www.wtj.com/wars/greatwar

The War Times Journal: The Great War Series

www.wwiaviation.com

A Pictorial History of World War I, in association with History Channel.com

# INDEX

Page numbers in italics refer to illustrations

on spectacle of war, 53, 270
studio space selected by, 26–27
war scenes as focus of work of, 55,
207, 209, *214, 282*
working conditions described by, 27
Smithsonian Institution, 305–6
snipers, 147, *147*, 161, *200*, 209, 280
soldiers in drawings
artillery, *180, 195, 199*
aeroplanes and aviators, *88, 106,
135, 136, 187, 272*
combat scenes, *30, 31, 66, 82, 89,
96, 98, 104, 106, 135, 142, 147,
151, 153, 180, 195, 200, 202, 208,
229, 230, 248, 257, 272*
daily life of, *29, 34, 56, 57, 95, 102,
142, 153, 159, 171, 202, 214,
235, 260, 261*
front lines and, *62, 82, 89, 104*
as preferred subjects, 175
wounded, *230, 231,* 249, *257*
Sonnell, Lieutenant Clarence, 236
Steese, Colonel James G., 170
Stevens, Lieutenant John H., 188
submarines, German, 16–17, 300
Summerall, Major General Charles P.,
279
Sweeney, Lieutenant Colonel Walter
C., 26–27, 28, 40, 54–55

tanks, *31*, 175, *197*, 199, 204, 213,
228–29, *229*, 230–31, 236,
238–39
Taylor, Colonel J. R. M., 175–76
Tonks, Henry, 118, 174
Torcy, France, 142, 144, 147
Toul, France, 66–67, 164, 185, 186,
187, 189–90
Tours, France, 24–25
Townsend, Barbara, 43, 44, 45, 103,
133, 138, 182, 208, 250, 264,
270–71, 302
Townsend, Cory, 43, 44, 45, 47, 48,
98–99, 103, 108, 121, 133, 138,
139, 167, 180, 181–82, 193–94,
194–95, 221–22, 250, 253, 264,
265, 267, 289, 302

Townsend, Dwight, 42, 44–45, 46,
182–83
Townsend, Harry Everett, *43*, 108,
305
aeroplanes and flying as interest of,
48, 55, 65, 66–67, 132, 134–38,
188, 190, 206, 216, 218–19, 221,
249
American victory viewed by, 301–2
approach to work by, 82–83, 84–85,
105–6, 114–16, 154–55, 170, 207,
265–66
armistice and, 278–80, 281
art training and earlier work of, 43,
50, 309
background of, 42–44, 309
Belleau Wood and, 94, 95–97,
98–105, 149
billet in private home, 54, 105–6,
185, 193, 218–19
career after the war, 309
Christmas after victory and, 302
on casualties of war, 83–84, 269
Château-Thierry and, 82–88, 89–90,
105, 110
combat scenes in work of, *30, 66,
82, 89, 104*
death of brother Hank and, 45–46,
47–48, 66, 87, 132, 138, 139,
182–83, 309
desire to fly, 121, 309
diary of, 65, 67, 83, 98, 114, 135,
148, 181, 185, 186, 191, 203, 215,
217, 219–20, 221, 231, 238,
254–55, 262, 263, 265, 278, 281,
288–89, 294
difficulty completing sketches by,
105–6
drawings by, *30, 66, 82, 85, 88, 89,
104, 136*
Dunn and, 50, 139, 194, 274
effect of war experiences on, 264
exhibits of work of, 271, 306
on fellow artists, 194, 219–20, 267,
274
Foch's counteroffensive and, 148–52,
154–55